The Secret History *of* French Cooking

ALSO BY LUKE BARR

Provence, 1970

Ritz & Escoffier

The Secret History *of* French Cooking

The Outlaw Chefs Who Made Food Modern

Luke Barr

DUTTON

DUTTON
An imprint of Penguin Random House LLC
1745 Broadway, New York, NY 10019
penguinrandomhouse.com

BOOK DESIGN BY ASHLEY TUCKER

Library of Congress Cataloging-in-Publication Data

Names: Barr, Luke author
Title: The secret history of French cooking / Luke Barr.
Description: New York, NY : Dutton, an imprint of Penguin Random House LLC, [2026] | Includes bibliographical references and index. | In English.
Identifiers: LCCN 2024060343 (print) | LCCN 2024060344 (ebook) | ISBN 9781524744731 hardcover | ISBN 9781524744755 ebook
Subjects: LCSH: Cooking, French—History—20th century | Cooks—France—Biography | Cooking—Experiments—History—20th century
Classification: LCC TX719 .B346 2026 (print) | LCC TX719 (ebook) | DDC 641.594409/04—dcundefined
LC record available at https://lccn.loc.gov/2024060343
LC ebook record available at https://lccn.loc.gov/2024060344

Printed in the United States of America
1st Printing

The authorized representative in the EU for product safety and compliance is Penguin Random House Ireland, Morrison Chambers, 32 Nassau Street, Dublin D02 YH68, Ireland, https://eu-contact.penguin.ie.

For Yumi

CONTENTS

Introduction

It was a moment of world-conquering triumph: Twelve chefs, pristine in their white toques, aprons, and jackets, standing on the tarmac at Orly airport in Paris in March 1974. Overnight rain had left the ground slick and reflective; just behind them, looming overhead, was the nose of an enormous Air France Boeing 747 jumbo jet; in the foreground were three antique cast-iron stoves. The men were posing for a photograph, lined up in a row, some of them brandishing copper saucepans, laughing. Here was the new generation of glamorous, modern French chefs, inventors of what the press was calling "nouvelle cuisine," cooking that was light, fresh, inventive, unencumbered by tradition. Their leader was Paul Bocuse, positioned in the center of the frame, and it was he who'd made the lucrative deal with Air France to oversee the in-flight meals and menus of the national airline.

The photograph was for a feature story ("A Grand Menu in the Sky") in *Le Nouveau Guide Gault-Millau*, a relatively new and hugely successful food magazine published by the two men whose names were on the cover, Henri Gault and Christian Millau, leading proselytizers of the nouvelle cuisine revolution. French restaurant cooking had become heavy, overly rich, and complacent—every menu, it seemed, listed the same Tournedos Rossini and all the other familiar classics. Haute cuisine was ossified, a cliché, they argued; the new guard was antiauthoritarian, liberated. Nouvelle cuisine chefs, in the pages of Gault and Millau's magazine, were auteurs of the French New Wave kitchen, a new kind of celebrity.

They called themselves the "Bande à Bocuse," a gang of renegades, rivals, old friends, and they were the talk of the town. And not just in Paris: Glowing accounts of nouvelle cuisine had appeared in the American press, hailing the rise of this rule-breaking culinary counterculture. Raymond Sokolov and Craig Claiborne in *The New York Times*, Gael Greene in *New York* magazine, feature stories in *Vogue* and *Esquire*—the Bande à Bocuse was everywhere. They'd even hired their own publicity agent (and since when had restaurant chefs ever had publicity agents? It was unheard of)—a young woman named Yanou Collart. She was intent on presenting the young chefs as cultural figures, on par with the movie stars and rock and roll musicians like Brigitte Bardot and Serge Gainsbourg who increasingly frequented their restaurants.

The Air France contract was a sign of their newfound status and global ambitions. Bocuse was already more famous than the others, an ambassador of French cooking, ubiquitous on television, imperious, quick-witted, and charismatic. His restaurant in Collonges-au-Mont-d'Or in Lyon, a city long considered the gastronomic capital of France, was topped with his name in giant, neon-lit capital letters. Gathered on the runway around Bocuse were the other key members of the nouvelle cuisine movement. There was Michel Guérard, who everyone agreed was the most brilliant of them all, and whose tiny restaurant on the outskirts of Paris, Le Pot-au-Feu, was always overbooked. There was Pierre Troisgros, who, with his brother, Jean, had introduced a dish of a thin escalope of salmon with sorrel sauce, cooked rare on a nonstick pan and served on oversize plates at their restaurant in Roanne, fifty miles west of Lyon. *Saumon à l'oseille* was already an icon of nouvelle cuisine. Roger Vergé's Moulin de Mougins in the South of France served Provençal-inspired dishes on a shady terrace in a converted olive oil mill, a favorite dinner destination during the Cannes film festival. And there was Gaston Lenôtre, master of desserts and patisserie, who brought a distinctly light touch to his fruit tarts and delicate mille-feuilles, and had opened a successful cooking school just west of Paris.

In the space of a few short years, nouvelle cuisine had upended the staid world of French cooking and, more than that, redefined the role and cultural importance of chefs and restaurants.

Far from the tarmac at Orly, far from the limelight, was another group of chefs, also trailblazers, young and ambitious, running their own restaurants. They generally received none of the sort of attention or accolades that Bocuse and his friends did. They were women.

Annie Desvignes had opened La Tour du Roy in Vervins, not far from the Belgian border, in 1971. She'd learned to cook at her mother's side at the family restaurant and struck out on her own after she got married, renovating an old manor house in rural northern France. The restaurant was a success, soon awarded a Michelin star, but when she applied to join the prestigious trade association for chefs, the Maîtres Cuisiniers de France, she'd been rejected. Rejected because she was a woman.

It wasn't just culinary trade groups that were men-only—so were restaurant kitchens. Stages, or apprenticeships, at the best restaurants were closed to women; it was nearly impossible for them to break in. Now, in 1974, Desvignes wanted to change that, banding together with other women to launch a new organization, to fight for their rights, respect, and recognition.

She was further galvanized when Paul Bocuse declared in a radio interview that "women have no imagination when it comes to cooking." Nouvelle cuisine was for men. He was being provocative, goading, always looking for attention, and his words stung.

Desvignes wrote to other well-regarded women chefs: Simone Lemaire in Normandy, whose restaurant, Le Tourne-Bride, served specialties of the region. Christiane Massia's L'Aquitaine, in Paris, highlighted vegetables and fish. So did Gisèle Berger's restaurant La Bonne Table in Clichy, just outside Paris—famous for its unusual seafood preparations, including lasagna and cassoulet. Élisabeth Bourgeois had opened a small restaurant in Avignon, and Olympe Nahmias and her husband, Albert, had renovated a former barbershop on the Left Bank in Paris and called it Olympe, drawing a chic, bohemian crowd and winning notices for Olympe's casual, original cooking.

All of these women were home- or self-taught, making their

way in a culinary world that relegated them to second-class status. But that was going to change. As Desvignes and her compatriots prepared to launch their organization for women chefs, they discovered they had a powerful ally—the most powerful man in French gastronomy. Robert Courtine was the restaurant critic for *Le Monde*, the largest newspaper in France; he was an old-fashioned conservative, defender of tradition, opposed to preservatives and food coloring and frozen fish, and deeply suspicious of anything newfangled. He hated Gault and Millau and all the overblown excitement in the press about nouvelle cuisine.

When Desvignes and Lemaire wrote to Courtine, he offered his unwavering support. He wrote glowing reviews of their restaurants, highlighting the women chefs' more traditional, home-style cooking, and offered to help get their new organization off the ground. Was there a certain irony in these feminist chefs forming an alliance with an archconservative? Yes. And there was something else, something that would only slowly reveal itself, a dark secret in Courtine's past that would cast a shadow over all that was to come.

At the airport in Paris, the photograph had been taken, and Henri Gault lit a cigarette and then spread his arms toward the chefs. *"Voilà la nouvelle cuisine française!"* he said. Behold the new French cuisine!—picture perfect. They all laughed. The revolution was underway, taking flight.

This 1974 moment—the newly minted Bande à Bocuse, the

breathless publicity, the women chefs preparing to stand up for themselves, the big-money Air France contract, the rival restaurant critics—all of it was emblematic of a new era. Post-1960s, everything was different; the world had shifted, opened up, full of possibility but also conflict and controversy. Between generations, between men and women, arguments about culinary invention versus tradition, about male chauvinism and women's rights, about art and commerce and good taste.

The currents of change and history were larger than anyone knew at the time, and for all these chefs, men and women, nothing would work out quite the way they thought or planned. But the story of nouvelle cuisine, with its drama, celebrity, money, and politics, its spectacular success and the inevitable, ferocious backlash, is very much the story of the birth of modern food and restaurant culture, the way we eat today. So much of the culinary present—from the scruffy-chic gourmet pizza joint to the decadent omakase hideaway, from frantic, televised cooking competitions to arguments about authenticity and ethics to the emergence of the celebrity chef (and the celebrity chef scandal)—can be traced to the events that began unspooling in 1970s France.

Nouvelle cuisine is where it all began.

PART ONE

Beginnings

1

1965

Crossing the Champs-Élysées in the late afternoon, dusk coming on, the night ahead of him, Michel Guérard could feel all the pent-up energy of a changing city. He was going to work. Le Lido, at number 78, just down the street from the iconic red awnings of Fouquet's brasserie, was a pillar of Paris nightlife, and Guérard was the pastry chef there. The club served six hundred dinner customers a night, but the food wasn't the reason people came. They came for the show—to see the Bluebell Girls.

The cabaret was a confection of titillating silliness—a chorus line of extravagantly costumed, high-kicking can-can dancers, innocent stripteases, and big band numbers interspersed with the occasional mime or topless snake handler. The tables were covered in white linen, set too close together, and filled with dark-suited men smoking cigarettes and bejeweled women in evening gowns. There were celebrities, socialites, and a lot of tourists. Americans and Brits. Le Lido was owned by the Clerico brothers, Joseph and Louis. They'd bought the club in 1946, and had more recently also purchased the Moulin Rouge in the seedier, red-light Pigalle neighborhood. The Clericos—former glass manufacturers made wealthy during the war—were now the princes of the Paris cabaret world. They'd installed vast kitchens and inaugurated elaborate dinner shows—guests eating and drinking and talking as they watched the performances.

The food was mostly unremarkable and always expensive, but it didn't matter. There was something magical—or was it just libidinal?—about the place, and Guérard loved it. The rush of the dinner crowd. The throngs of half-dressed women backstage, laughing. They towered over him in their heels. He was relatively short, and the dancers were required to be at least five foot eight. Many were former ballerinas deemed too tall for ballet; many were Russian or Australian.

Guérard was thirty-two and single. He'd grown up in the countryside of Normandy, the son of a butcher, and had been working in kitchens since he was seventeen. He'd trained at the Crillon Hotel and won the prestigious Meilleur Ouvrier de France (MOF) award in 1958 as a pastry chef. He'd also spent a few years working at top Paris restaurants, including Maxim's and Lucas Carton.

Now, at the Lido of all places, he'd had an epiphany. He had seen the future, and he had the old man, his boss Joseph Clerico, to thank.

Clerico was in his sixties and semiretired, having put his two sons in charge a few years earlier, in 1962—Jacki Clerico at the Moulin Rouge and Christian Clerico at the Lido. Joseph, meanwhile, hosted weekend dinner parties at the Château des Gondi in Villepreux, close to the palace of Versailles, a half hour west of

Paris. This was the Clerico family's grand estate, a formal, nineteenth-century castle with sprawling gardens, parkland, fountains, tennis courts, and horse stables. Joseph invited an eclectic group to his dinners, a cross section of Parisian high society and various creative types—artists, dancers, painters, and actors. And he'd recently asked Guérard to come to the château for the weekend and cook for his guests.

Guérard was an exceedingly charming man—maybe that's what had caught the elder Clerico's attention. He was, moreover, a perfectly trained chef, winner of the MOF award, and it was known to all that he aspired to be more than a pastry chef. Guérard said yes immediately.

There was no set menu, or any direction given at all about the food. Cook what you like, Clerico said to Guérard—anything at all. A glamorously casual, bohemian, modern, mid-'60s dinner party in a château outside Paris had no use for classical, old-fashioned cooking. Make something new, Clerico said. Guérard had free rein.

It was, for Guérard, a revelation, what he'd been craving: to break free of familiar haute cuisine formulas and rich sauces. To cook in a way that made sense of the present. This was the moment: the first inkling of the alchemy that would transform his cooking, and everything else.

He cooked quickly and simply—small chicken breasts, gently sautéed with slices of small cucumbers and sugar. A bit of cream, a bit of Noilly Prat vermouth. This was not a preparation found in any cookbook, or in Escoffier's teachings, or anywhere in the annals of French cuisine. The dish was light, unexpected, improvised, and that was the point.

The guests loved what he cooked. The energy of the city, of the time, had found its way onto their plates, it seemed. The food was intoxicating—not because it was outlandish or exotic but because it was original, and delicious. The sense of liberation Guérard felt went beyond the kitchen; it was connected to the experimentation all around, in art, in music, in film. There was a new energy in the air, formality and artifice giving way to something looser, sexier. You could see it in the films of the New Wave, in Godard's *Bande à Part* the previous year; you could hear it in "(I Can't Get No) Satisfaction" from the Rolling Stones, who'd just played three sold-out nights at the Olympia music hall in Paris. The Beatles had played twenty back-to-back shows at the Olympia in 1964, and Beatlemania had gone international. Teen starlet France Gall still dominated the radio with faux-innocent pop songs like "Sacré Charlemagne," but things were changing in fits and starts. In the middle of the 1960s, the world had turned from black and white to Technicolor. Or that's how it felt, anyway.

For the past few years Guérard had been living on a houseboat on the Seine, permanently docked near the Pont de la Concorde. The flat-bottomed barge—a *péniche*—belonged to a friend, a sculptor, and together they presided over a stream of friends and friends of friends who came to eat and drink and talk late into the night, records playing on the hi-fi.

Was there a disconnect between his life and his work? Between his classical training and his individuality, his creativity? Back at work in the kitchen at Le Lido the following week, Guérard, no doubt thinking of his dinner party triumph as well, came to the realization that he needed to open his own restaurant. Le Lido was fun, but it was a relic of the past—of late nineteenth-century cabaret entertainment, and of the Rat Pack 1950s too. (Indeed, Le Lido had exported its show to the Stardust casino when it opened in Las Vegas in 1958.) Guérard was full of ideas, and ambition. Here he was working in a cabaret kitchen, putting out spectacular, multitiered desserts for Elizabeth Taylor and other celebrity guests, but it was the simple, idiosyncratic chicken breasts sautéed with cucumbers and cream that inspired him.

Yes, one way or another—and despite the fact that he had almost no money at all—he was going to open a restaurant of his own.

Just a few blocks away from the Lido cabaret, Robert Courtine was eating dinner at Restaurant Lasserre, one of the best in the city, he thought. There were a handful of such places, lauded by both the Michelin and Kléber-Colombes guides, icons of French sophistication—the "grand tables" of Paris: Maxim's. Le Grand Véfour. La Tour d'Argent. Lapérouse. These were the city's historic three-star restaurants, most of them dating back to the eighteenth and nineteenth centuries, the palaces of French haute cuisine. Lasserre was a relative newcomer, opened in 1942. It occupied an elegant two-story building on Avenue Franklin Roosevelt, directly across the street from the imposing columns of the vast Grand Palais exhibition hall. The dining room was on the second floor, set under its famous retractable roof. During nice weather, one ate under the stars at Lasserre, all the cigarette and cigar smoke released into the night air every so often as the mechanical roof slid open.

Courtine looked around the room, his alert, intelligent gaze taking in the scene. The quiet murmuring of wealthy Parisians and the international beau monde at dinnertime, the calm, unhurried purposefulness of the waiters and captains. The decor was extravagant: off-white and gold fabrics on the walls with jewel-toned highlights; brocaded cut velvet lining the elevator; the ceiling painted by Louis Touchagues with dancing art deco–style women and winged horses; a profusion of white orchids everywhere; sparkling antique chandeliers, mirrors, candelabras, and Chinese porcelain—everything gilded, or crystal, or silver. It was almost too much.

Courtine loved it. On special occasions, the restaurant released caged white doves into the dining room. It was that kind of place.

He raised a finger to summon the waiter, who'd been lurking nearby obsequiously. Courtine was a VIP at Lasserre, and at every restaurant in France for that matter. He was the formidable, all-powerful, fiercely opinionated restaurant critic for *Le Monde*, the most important newspaper in the country. A word from Courtine could spell success or disaster for a restaurant, and he knew it. Lasserre was one of his long-time favorites; Courtine had been coming here since 1952, when he joined *Le Monde*, and he was treated as an old friend by René Lasserre, the proprietor. Courtine was never presented with a bill.

The waiter took his order for a glass of whisky—"un malt," he called it—his drink of choice.

The food at Lasserre was traditional and conspicuously "de luxe." Truffles, foie gras, oysters, and caviar; steak, lobster, duck, and quail. Noble ingredients, rich sauces, and classical preparations. Lasserre was perhaps the ultimate expression of postwar Parisian sophistication. For Courtine, the menu represented the glory of haute cuisine, the glory of France.

Courtine was a chauvinist. He believed in tradition. His views of restaurants and cooking were deeply intertwined with his view of France itself, and the primacy of French culture. The terroir. The land. The soil. Every ingredient was a reflection of its source.

He felt France in his bones. He was as passionate about an authentic *boeuf à la ficelle*—boiled beef and vegetables—at a loud workingman's bistro, served with a large pot of Dijon mustard and no other garnish at all, as he was about the delicately stuffed *poussin viroflay* he planned to order for dinner tonight at Lasserre.

He welcomed all styles and varieties of French cuisine. What he demanded was quality, and respect for history. What he abhorred was fast food in all its permutations. The "Americanization" of taste, the recent proliferation of vast *hypermarché* supermarkets, the ubiquity of frozen fish—even at gourmet restaurants. Courtine was steadfast in his contempt for all such trends, for shortcuts and "convenience," for all the cheap abundance of the postwar economic boom.

He waved for the waiter, ready to order.

Courtine was a slim man with a high, domed head, mostly bald, and extravagantly long sideburns; he was fifty-five years old. He wrote his weekly column in *Le Monde* under a pen name—La Reynière. He'd chosen the name in honor of the eighteenth-century aristocrat and gourmet Alexandre-Balthazar-Laurent

Grimod de la Reynière, famous in Napoleon's time for his lavish dinner parties and for writing the *Almanach des Gourmands*, a restaurant guide to Paris published between 1803 and 1812. Courtine liked the mystique the alias evoked—the power of the definite article and single name. It wasn't a question of anonymity, really; all the restaurateurs who mattered knew who he was and treated him royally. But the pen name was a cloak, obscuring his identity from the broader public. The single-name alias was also in the tradition of Curnonsky, the great food writer of the first half of twentieth-century France, whose real name had been Maurice Edmond Sailland. Curnonsky—widely referred to as the "Prince des Gastronomes"—had died nine years earlier, in 1956, and Courtine, a.k.a. La Reynière, had taken up the mantle.

For Courtine, the *poussin viroflay* epitomized the cooking at Lasserre: elegant, complicated, and opulent. A small spring chicken, deboned and stuffed with finely chopped spinach and flecks of ham, roasted and served with a truffle sauce. It was one of the restaurant's signature dishes, a version of Escoffier's classic poularde Princesse Hélène, a recipe dating back to the late nineteenth century. The plate arrived at Courtine's table with a garnish of an artichoke heart crowned with an array of tiny mushrooms. "The perfection of details" was the key, Courtine thought as he ate—the secret to great French cooking. At Lasserre, the plates were decorated as carefully as the room itself. His dessert was a similarly flawless confection, the timbale Élysée, a sweet, round cake served with ice cream and glazed fresh fruit and topped with a delicate spun sugar dome, an edible objet d'art.

It was the ideal meal. If he was forced to choose, Courtine would have to say that Lasserre deserved its three Michelin stars a bit more than any other restaurant in Paris. He admired most of all Lasserre's notably "few concessions to fashion," as he put it in his column later that week. Lasserre was of the old school, a classic. Of course, Courtine had his quibbles: the appearance of farmed quail on the menu, for example, which he considered "not worthy of the name." (Quail was increasingly popular, and customers apparently didn't care whether it was wild.) This was his job: to criticize even his favorite restaurants, to keep them in line. He would make disapproving note of the farmed quail in his column that week, too, even as he sang the restaurant's praises.

He smiled. Here was the defender of tradition at the height of his power, in his element in the glittering dining room at Lasserre, maintaining—singlehandedly, he sometimes felt—the unassailable grandeur of French haute cuisine.

Her sister had bought a castle.

It was like something out of a fairy tale: small and solid, stone walls rising three stories beneath a steep black roof, two towers rising higher still, one of them topped with a medieval, crenelated parapet, the other with an elegant conical spire. The Château du Mayet-d'École was in the countryside near Vichy—central France, west of Lyon—and dated back centuries. The previous owners had operated a small hotel and restaurant in the castle, and her sister would do the same. They called it the Hostellerie de la Reine Jeanne, and this was where Simone Lemaire was now working.

The château was set on a national highway—not the famous

"Nationale 7," memorialized in the Charles Trenet song from 1959, a celebration of driving south to the Mediterranean, vacation-bound. No, the Reine Jeanne was on the number 9, not far away, but there was still plenty of traffic on the two-way road through the countryside. The restaurant had been open a few weeks and was doing well.

Lemaire worked wherever she was needed—helping in the kitchen and the dining room. They had hired a chef to run the kitchen, and the sisters did everything else. Lemaire did all the shopping, keeping track of provisions and inventory, and it was she who first noticed the disappearance of various items: cuts of meat, boxes of truffles, and other ingredients. Who could it be but their newly hired chef? They decided to confront him.

The moment was both nerve-racking and strangely comical: The sisters locked all the doors except the main entrance, and waited. This was after lunch—midafternoon. When he saw them at the door, waiting with serious expressions on their faces, he laughed nervously.

"What do you have there?" the sisters asked.

They found an entire salmon and half a beef tenderloin hidden in his bag. They fired him on the spot. He was a thief, but they'd liked him, and so they agreed not to call the police. The chef in turn promised to spread the word about the Reine Jeanne, and to say only good things.

But now what? They had no chef, and dinner was in a few hours. They had two large reservations, one for fifteen people, the other for twelve. And these were important clients, groups of winemakers from the region. There was nothing prepared, no mise en place, their provisions plundered.

Lemaire would cook, they decided. She was good in the kitchen, if not professionally trained. She'd grown up watching her mother and grandmother cook in Normandy, in northern France, and learned from them. When she was twelve years old, she had single-handedly prepared lunch for twenty-five people, on the occasion of the first communion of one of the children of the household staff. The feat had entered into family lore.

Now she threw herself into the task at hand. She put on a white apron and tied back her hair. She found a good supply of crayfish and decided to use them for the appetizer, a simple sauté with carrots, shallots, parsley, and white wine—*écrevisse à la nage*. This required the careful cleaning and deveining of many dozens of the small freshwater shellfish but was otherwise a simple recipe. And for the entrée she would make a classic *poulet normande à la crème*, chicken with mushrooms in a cream sauce. The key was the Calvados apple brandy she would use to deglaze the pans, setting the liquor on fire as she did so, just as her grandmother always had. The quick flambé gave the dish an added depth of flavor.

Lemaire worked without stopping. Her sister dealt with the guests as they arrived, while Simone grated potatoes to make potato cakes, sliced apples for a simple dessert, and spooned the crayfish and broth into bowls. The work in the kitchen was an exhilarating sprint, until the moment it wasn't, and now Lemaire sneaked into the large garden behind the château, which the dining room overlooked. It was dark outside, lit up inside, and she watched, invisibly, as the men ate the first course, studying their body language and straining to hear snatches of conversation. They were nodding to each other, smiling. So far, so good.

She returned to the kitchen to finish the chicken—adding the cream, reducing the sauce over medium-low heat. Not long after she sent the chicken Normandy out to the dining room came word that the chef's presence was requested. The gathered winemakers wanted her to join them for a drink.

She walked into the dining room in her white apron and blond ponytail, and was met with confusion. Most of the men kept talking among themselves, ignoring her as they continued to eat.

"No, no, no," one of the men said, assuming the young woman standing before them was a kitchen assistant, a commis. "We want to see the chef! Where is the chef?"

"Well—I *am* the chef," Lemaire exclaimed. It was she who'd cooked their dinner, which she hoped was to their liking. She thanked them for their patronage.

The winemakers, now all silent, looked at her and began to smile.

Her heart was beating in her chest. Years later, that's what she would most remember about this moment in 1965: her heart beating in her chest. And the realization that she could do this. She could run this kitchen. She would cook for a living. As the winemakers raised their glasses boisterously and toasted her *poulet normande à la crème*, she saw a new possibility. A restaurant of her own, back in Normandy if at all possible . . .

Not far away, another young woman, Yanou Collart, was eating lunch.

Two hours east of the Reine Jeanne by car, just outside Lyon in Collonges-au-Mont-d'Or, on the right bank of the Saône River, was the restaurant owned by Paul Bocuse. It had just been awarded its third Michelin star, making it only the twelfth restaurant in France bestowed this highest honor. Robert Courtine—La Reynière—wrote approvingly of the promotion in his March 27, 1965, column in *Le Monde*:

> There will now be twelve "grand" restaurants. The twelfth three-star will not astonish anyone, because it is Paul Bocuse (L'Auberge du Pont de Collonges, near Lyon). This very great chef has the enthusiasm of youth at the same time as the mastery of experience, cooking for him is a friendship.

Yanou Collart's boss, Roger LaForest, had heard about the new three-star restaurant outside Lyon and determined that they would lunch there. The pair were on a business trip, en route from Spain, where they had been meeting with suppliers and clients of their employer, the Bic ballpoint pen company. LaForest was one of the top managers, brother-in-law to founder Marcel Bich. LaForest considered himself a gourmet and made a habit of eating at the best restaurants wherever he went. He drove a Rolls-Royce.

Collart, meanwhile, was his newly hired sales representative. She was twenty-seven years old and quite stunningly beautiful. Was that why he'd hired her? Perhaps. She didn't care. Collart had no trouble deploying her charm, her intelligence, and her drive to get what she wanted. And she knew exactly what she wanted: independence. She'd grown up in Belgium, worked as a fashion model briefly as a teenager, and taken the first opportunity to leave when offered a sales job at a pharmacy supply company. Soon enough, she was driving around southern France in a snazzy white Ford Consul 315, her clothes on hangers in the back seat and an enormous sample case in the trunk.

She loved being on the road in Provence, driving fast with the radio turned up and windows rolled down. She stopped at pharmacies and small-town doctors' offices, taking orders and collecting payments, sleeping in country inns and doing it all again the next day. She did not sell medicines, but rather everything else such places might need—bandages, creams, vitamins, you name it.

She'd met LaForest at a diet clinic in Grasse of all places—one of her regular stops. Grasse was just inland from Cannes and Antibes on the Côte d'Azur, and the center of the French perfume industry. The clinic belonged to Dr. George Pathé and catered to a glamorous, international clientele (as various as Cambodian King Norodom Sihanouk and American cookbook author James Beard) who submitted themselves for weeks at a time to the doctor's rigorous low-fat, no-sugar, no-salt diet in hopes of losing weight. As she concluded her business in the lobby of the large villa that housed the clinic and its guest rooms, Collart noticed a distinguished man smoking a large Montecristo cigar. She thought nothing of it. But ten minutes later she found the same man waiting for her at her car, pacing back and forth, still smoking.

His name was Roger LaForest, he explained. He'd been watching her work. Would she be interested, he said, in a job with the Bic ballpoint pen company? They needed someone with her energy as they expanded internationally. Did she speak English? Did she speak Spanish? Well, she could learn. Collart was intrigued and soon left the Belgian pharmacy supply company for the booming ballpoint pen business. Now here she was touring Europe with her new boss in a Rolls, listening to the actually quite interesting history of the ballpoint pen. Marcel Bich, born to an aristocratic family in Italy, had bought the patent for the new pen from Hungarian inventor László Biró, and proceeded to refine it, launching the iconic Bic Cristal in 1950, and now sold them by the millions and millions.

It was amusing to think that this lowly pen, made of hard clear plastic with a dark-blue cap—the mess-free, modern alternative to a fountain pen—was bankrolling their three-star lunch at Bocuse. And it was a lunch that would change everything—not because of the food but because of a case of mistaken identity.

They pulled up into the sloping driveway and parked in front of the restaurant. It was a large building painted in garish green, red, and gold, with an enormous green neon sign on the roof, in letters three feet high, announcing the name of the chef: PAUL BOCUSE. Inside were red carpets and patterned wallpaper, pictures everywhere—a happy, haphazard jumble of decoration. The service was formal and discreet; the food was traditional. LaForest ordered for the two of them:

Pâté Pantin Ferdinand Wernert
Poularde de Bresse en vessie

The pâté was en croute—made of veal and pork, baked in elaborately decorated pastry dough, and served in slices. The chicken was a Lyon specialty, the bird stuffed with foie gras and truffles, then poached in a pig's bladder. It was a dish for two, and came out of the kitchen looking like a pale balloon on a platter. This was carefully cut open, releasing the broth and revealing the tender chicken, which was then carved and served at the table. The food was magnificent, Collart and LaForest agreed.

After lunch, they ordered espressos, and now the waiter approached bearing a large book. Monsieur Paul, he explained solemnly—everyone on staff referred to Bocuse as "Monsieur Paul"—had requested that Collart sign the restaurant's guest book. Taken aback, she refused. If anyone should sign the book, she said, it should be her boss, Monsieur LaForest. The waiter retreated, and suddenly Bocuse himself was at their table.

"So, Marie Laforêt—you refuse to sign my guest book!" he said, in a tone that was somehow both confrontational and flirtatious. He was wearing his white chef's jacket, apron, and toque, all immaculate. He stood over them, awaiting a reply, his eyebrows raised.

Not at all, Collart explained, momentarily bewildered. Her name was Yanou Collart, not Marie Laforêt, and this was her boss, Monsieur LaForest—and now all became suddenly clear. She understood what had happened before either of the two men did: Bocuse had seen the name "LaForest" in the reservation book, and the Rolls-Royce parked out front, and jumped to the conclusion that she was Marie Laforêt, the actress and singer.

She ought to have been flattered, she supposed: Laforêt epitomized 1960s glamour and sex appeal, starring as the unnamed "girl" in *The Girl with the Golden Eyes* a few years earlier, and opposite Alain Delon in *Purple Noon*, the French adaptation of Patricia Highsmith's novel *The Talented Mr. Ripley*. She was also a pop star, a chanteuse, ubiquitous on the radio. Still, it was baffling to Collart that Bocuse had misidentified her. Apart from being the same age and a brunette, she bore little resemblance to the star, she thought.

Bocuse laughed as they sorted out the trivial misunderstanding, saying that they must nevertheless certainly sign the guest book—he insisted. Collart watched him, amused, as he charmed them effortlessly. Bocuse was magnetic, alert, rakishly self-confident. He was more striking than handsome, with a strong nose and heavy-lidded, deep-set eyes, a shock of black hair beneath the toque. He explained with a straight face that in order to prevent any such misunderstandings in the future, he would be adding small, identifying photographs to the guest book, and then he smiled. He wasn't serious, but it was a little hard to tell.

Collart and LaForest both signed the guest book as Bocuse looked on. It was a trivial moment, but a revealing one. The chef's intense interest in his VIP and celebrity guests made perfect sense. After all, his restaurant's newly earned three-star status had presumably attracted not only enormous press attention but also a new and glittering clientele—who in turn attracted yet more press attention. Celebrities were good for business. And more than that—all the attention had made Bocuse himself something of a star: the way he carried himself, commanded the room, seducing his guests both with his cooking and his persona.

Collart considered the power of celebrity, and the celebrity of the chef. She'd had a glimpse of the future at that moment, one that would change her life.

2

The Pot-au-Feu

In late 1965, Michel Guérard opened his own restaurant. It was called the Pot-au-Feu and was located on a rather grim side street near the harbor in Asnières-sur-Seine, a working-class suburb northwest of Paris—a good five miles from the center of town. Directly across the street was a factory that produced metal rivets of some kind. The place was tiny—thirty seats total, the tables crammed together in ways that made it nearly impossible to reach the bathroom.

He'd bought the café at an auction, sight unseen, for a paltry 20,000 francs, about the cost of a new car. (There'd been a murder on the second floor, he was told; maybe that was why it had been so cheap.) It was all the money he had—he'd scraped it together somehow, and without asking his parents for a single centime. This was important to him: He was a grown man, his own man, and wanted to make his way independently. And so here he was, an MOF award–winning chef, trained in the kitchens of

Paris's grandest establishments—Maxim's, the Crillon, Lucas Carton—running a decrepit bistro in seedy Asnières.

Before he bought it, the restaurant had served North African–inflected bistro dishes, tagines and the like. He'd renamed it Pot-au-Feu in honor of the long-simmering pot roasts he'd grown up eating every Saturday night as a kid, aiming for an unpretentious ambiance. He did his best to fix the place up; on the day he opened, he found three men napping on the front steps, factory workers from across the street on break. He welcomed them in.

But keeping the place afloat the first year proved to be a struggle. The clientele were mostly construction, factory, and dock workers from the neighborhood. He served sandwiches, rillettes, pastries, coffee—everything cheap. Still, the place was half empty most of the time. He tinkered with small, simple dishes but was hemmed in by fear of losing his already meager clientele. If the initial inspiration to open a restaurant had come during his freewheeling weekend dinner party cooking at the Clerico mansion in Versailles, he was now struggling to keep his head above water making lunchtime croque monsieurs.

What in the world was he doing? his old friend Jean Delaveyne asked him pointedly. Delaveyne was also a chef, owner of a restaurant called Camélia, in Bougival, just west of Paris. He was older than Guérard, in his mid-forties, and a mentor to the younger man. Delaveyne had also won the MOF award and, like Guérard, had come up initially as a pastry chef. He was an inventive cook—he loved discussing new recipe ideas with Guérard—and had come to visit Le Pot-au-Feu for the first time.

"Listen, Michel, you're a little prick." A "petit con," Delaveyne called him, affectionately, of course. "I see you here, and you're dying a slow death. But in the name of God, if you're going to die, at least die happy! Do what you truly want to do!"

He was talking about the food. Nothing wrong with a tiny, money-losing restaurant in a shabby neighborhood, as long as Guérard was cooking what he wanted to cook.

And Delaveyne was right. What did he have to lose? Guérard had opened Le Pot-au-Feu because he'd wanted to be independent, because he wanted to express himself. Not just to cook but to create. All around him he could feel it: Change was in the air. It was generational. Everyone was experimenting: in literature, in film, in theater, on campus. It was about more than politics, or sex, or drugs, or rock and roll, or any one particular thing. It was existential—a new thinking about how to live, a new disdain for authority. Guérard was still living with his friend the sculptor on a barge docked on the Seine, and he wanted to import some of the bohemian energy of the city to his restaurant. He just needed to figure out how to do it and also stay in business.

"No more sandwiches," Guérard declared. "I'm going to do what I want."

Guérard changed the menu that very week. He changed everything, aiming for a pared-down simplicity that was nevertheless exciting, new. His dishes had no heavy sauces or unnecessary ornamentation. He served his house-made foie gras totally plain: no aspic, no truffles, no parsley, nothing at all. It was a statement of purity—and of his own tastes and preferences. His vegetables were undercooked by the standard measure, brightly colored and with a bite to them. His chicken and duck were served in intensely flavored reductions with a hint of vinegar and no cream, just the sort of dishes he served his friends. He made a savory sabayon to serve with fish—an egg yolk whisked until thickened and frothy over low heat, with wine and herbs—rather than the usual fish stock reduction enriched with butter and cream.

He put a salad on the menu in the entrée section, with duck confit. And he invented what would become a trademark dish, his "salade gourmande"—also known as the "salade folle," or crazy salad. This was a composed salad, with lettuce, green beans, and asparagus, topped with thin slices of black truffle and foie gras. The combination of foie gras and a vinaigrette was considered a shocking breach of haute cuisine protocol. It wasn't done. But Guérard thought it made perfect sense. "For the first time, we dare to mix vinegar with foie gras!" he said, laughing. "This is a crime! This is liberation!"

Everything on the new Pot-au-Feu menu was light, fresh, and a bit provocative. The point was to break free of the past. He had every respect for the traditional preparations—handed down from Auguste Escoffier over the decades—but he wanted to simplify and purify his cooking; to focus in a radical way on the ingredients themselves; to find new and elegant combinations of flavors and textures, new interpretations of classic dishes. Classical cuisine could be "lifeless, inert, and apathetic," thought Guérard. He was determined "to be stubborn and to reject the traditional authority and whatever existed before." And without quite realizing it, he had opened a new avenue, a new path: that of the chef as an artist of sorts—an inventor, an auteur.

Within a month, lightning struck, in the form of a newspaper article by the venerable Francis Amunategui. He'd been writing a column called Dans Mon Assiette (On My Plate) for the weekly *Aux Écoutes* since the late 1940s, in which he highlighted his latest restaurant discoveries. Amunategui was one of the original postwar gastronomic writers, and notice from him invariably resulted in a crush of new customers. And so it was when he lauded the out-of-the-way restaurant in Asnières. That Friday—the day the paper came out—the Pot-au-Feu was full. And the next day too. There was a snowball effect: The restaurant was written up in one newspaper after another, and crowds of customers suddenly filled the small room, trekking out from Paris to a dingy suburb—a banlieue!—and finding their way through the side streets and then jostling their way to a table to taste Guérard's always-changing menu.

And indeed it was this sense of adventure and discovery that drew people: The exotically unglamorous location, the modest room, and the aggressively minimalist plating all stood in remarkable contrast to the grand formalities of the city's gourmet restaurants, just as the food itself stood apart. The style and ethos of the restaurant suited the cooking. Everyone could feel the energy and excitement of something new, of the moment.

The restaurant was a sensation.

Guérard was often sleeping only three hours a night, and they weren't even three continuous hours. Dinner service at the restaurant ended at around midnight, sometimes later, and after that he would head into central Paris to stop by the Lido nightclub, where he still kept an eye on the pastry department. Though he was no longer an employee, he still felt like a member of the family. And what better way to pass a late-night hour or two than backstage at the cabaret, in and out of the kitchen, enjoying a glass of champagne. Then at 3 a.m. it was off to Les Halles to shop for supplies for the next two days. Les Halles was the vast wholesale food market in the center of the city, thrillingly chaotic, jammed with traffic, open all night. This was the place Émile Zola had called "Le Ventre de Paris" (the belly of Paris) in the 1870s, and it hadn't changed much since. Guérard went three times a week.

Wandering among the acres of stalls in the dead of night, Guérard was looking for the ingredients he needed, but also for inspiration. What was fresh? What was in season? It helped that his parents ran a butcher shop and he'd grown up in the business (his older brother was now running the family boucherie in Mantes-la-Jolie, thirty miles west of Paris). Guérard knew his way around meat and would not be deceived or hoodwinked or sold inferior product—common enough at Les Halles. He started with beef: He needed the best prime rib and fillet, and he liked to see exactly what he was getting. Then it was on to the racks of lamb. The butcher said to him roughly: "You want lamb? Well then—there they are. Choose!"

It was a kind of game, a negotiation, sparring with the butchers of Les Halles, a test of bona fides. You had to prove you belonged.

Guérard kept an eye open for less expensive cuts and ingredients. He would take the pricey sea scallops, of course, if they looked good, but also whiting, mackerel, and cod, which were all cheap. Some of his best ideas were sparked by less "noble" ingredients: his whiting stuffed with julienned carrots, mushrooms, and celery root, for example, or his chicken wings with cucumbers—a dish that would become a trademark, one of his signatures. Chicken wings cost next to nothing, and he prepared them in an ingenious way, first poaching the pieces briefly, then removing the bones and sautéing them until golden. Combining these with cucumbers cut into small balls and cooked in butter with a little sugar was an idea he'd first had at the private dinner at the Clerico château. He refined the dish now, adding a light white wine sauce with shallots, mushrooms, tomatoes, and a bit of cream.

At moments like this, Guérard felt fully alive: alone in the teeming, predawn marketplace, surrounded by produce from hundreds of farms; the crates of fruits and vegetables; the purveyors of cheese, truffles, and foie gras; the butchers and fishmongers; all of it a delirious blur of sight, sound, and smell. Maybe it was sleep deprivation, or the overstimulation of Les Halles itself, but this was when he was struck by flashes of inspiration, ideas for new recipes, new juxtapositions of flavor, new possibilities. "What goes through my head!" he thought to himself. "Sensations caught in small haphazard moments, seemingly random, fortuitous." Cèpes with their fat, bulging stems; glistening pink-and-white veal sweetbreads; a vast pile of fresh oysters; the smell of strong coffee and fresh-cut flowers . . .

It was 6 a.m. by the time Guérard got home, where he slept for an hour or two before driving back to Asnières to begin preparing for the lunch service. (He would sneak in another nap after lunch.) He had four cooks working for him in the kitchen, and three waiters on the floor, all young men. The calm of the morning—peeling vegetables, making stock, boning fish—soon gave way to the trickle and then the rush of orders, all at once, the exhilarating madness of a kitchen operating at full throttle. Guérard stood at the hulking Molteni gas stove, calling out instructions, leading the charge.

The menu at Le Pot-au-Feu was handwritten and divided into three unlabeled sections: appetizers, entrées, and desserts. Listed at the top were the house aperitif, called the "Dalton," and an eight-year-old whisky "réserve du Savoy Hotel de Londres"—the famed London hotel produced a special reserve scotch under its own label, which Guérard imported. The dishes were described simply, with no hint of ostentation. There was the house-made foie gras (*foie gras frais de canard des landes, prepare à la maison*); the chicory salad with croutons, lardons, and Roquefort (*salade grande ferme, aux chapons, lardons et Roquefort*); and the escargots with mustard butter (*escargots de vigne en pots moutarde*). Among the entrées were the duck confit with salad (*la canard confit froid et la salade au vinaigrette*); grilled goose breast fillet (*filet d'aile d'oie fraiche grillé saignant*); and the roasted rack of lamb with parsley (*carre d'agneau persille rôti au four*).

Guérard's cooking was precise and subtle and, to his way of thinking, intuitive. Yes, the expected preparation for goose was a confit—the meat cooked slowly in fat—rather than grilled and served rare. But why not treat the dark goose breast like a steak? It was the sort of unusual dish that raised eyebrows but made perfect sense. It was delicious. Guérard also foregrounded vegetables and especially vegetable purees, delicate and mousse-like, that were for him much more than decorative garnishes. He made purees from celery root, watercress, green beans, beets, and leeks, all enriched with butter and crème fraîche.

Now, in the kitchen, Guérard was making the "crazy salad." It was the start of the dinner rush, but he himself was unrushed as he sliced black truffle into a sherry vinaigrette to macerate and meticulously arranged green beans and asparagus tips on a plate, while also directing the other cooks as they slid escargots into the oven and pureed vegetables. Guérard's wry, mischievous demeanor belied his total concentration in the kitchen. He never yelled, was in seemingly constant motion, and inspected every plate before it went out into the dining room.

The crowd at Le Pot-au-Feu was eclectic, more local at lunchtime, more Parisian at dinner. Guérard was proud that he'd held on to his neighborhood clientele even as he'd completely changed the menu. Factory workers came for lunch and late afternoon drinks. The small room was always crowded, cheerfully noisy, winter coats hung from hooks on the ceiling in the foyer to save space, the windows fogged up. There were young bohemian couples alongside buttoned-up businessmen—not to mention a certain criminal element. One of Guérard's first regular customers drove a conspicuous black Ferrari and soon announced to the chef: "Michel, I want you to teach me to eat." He was streetwise and charming, and Guérard was happy to oblige. He soon discovered the man was a member of the Gennevilliers mafia, based in the adjacent industrial port town. Who knew exactly what his business was, but he liked to eat, and so did his associates. At one point Guérard found a pistol stashed among the napkins in the restaurant's linen closet. He didn't ask any questions. Another night ended at two in the morning as a large group of men—some of them battle-scarred bruisers with "cauliflower ears," all of them from Gennevilliers—singing Berthe Sylva's sentimental 1920s chanson "Les Roses Blanches," about a poor Paris boy and his dying mother:

C'était un gamin, un gosse de Paris
Pour famille il n'avait que sa mère
Une pauvre fille aux grands yeux rougis
Par les chagrins et la misère . . .

(He was a kid, a kid from Paris
For family, he had only his mother
A poor girl with bright eyes, turned red
By the sorrow and misery . . .)

In March 1967, Le Pot-au-Feu was awarded a Michelin star. Guérard was surprised, delighted—shocked, even. It was a single star, but it meant everything: a badge of honor, recognition of his talent, manifestation of all the work, all the sleepless nights of the previous year. For his tiny restaurant in its unfashionable location to be listed in the red guide among the best in all of France was a rare achievement, and would undoubtedly bring new guests to Asnières.

The validation conferred by the Michelin guidebook listing soon led to a new burst of press attention. None other than *Le*

Monde's fearsome Robert Courtine, a.k.a. La Reynière, came to Le Pot-au-Feu to see what the "little pub on a sad street in Asnières" had to offer. His review offered grudging respect for the talent of the chef but bristled at any sign of what he considered faddishness. The popularity of the restaurant was, in itself, a strike against it. The sight of a roasted half tomato with garlic alongside the rack of lamb was met with scorn. The garnish had become a "mania" in restaurants lately, he felt, and did nothing for any dish, and never had. Nevertheless, Courtine wrote, "We ratify, certainly, the restaurant's rapid success."

This was his style: first person plural, the royal "we," his opinions dispensed with serene authority. He was also fond of metaphors, puns, and literary allusions. There was a wry, knowing humor in his pomposity. Courtine continued:

> Does this mean that we ratify without restriction? Maybe not. As it is, there is nothing to say, but we feel that the young chef is on the edge of the razor, that with success (that is to say, with the coming of a few more clients—of a certain breed of customers), he could easily switch to the side of distorting snobbery, the downfall of true cooking. There are not too many herbs yet, but we feel them coming, they hang on the wall, drying.

The herbs were a sign of the overly fussy, trendy cooking that Courtine despised—pandering to the crowd, the chic Parisians who always wanted something new. Still, the hanger steak with shallots he ordered was nothing less than "marvelous," he wrote. He also praised the leek tart, the pot-au-feu, the cheese and wine selections, the "exceptional" Calvados, the Bollinger champagne, and all the small details: "We must emphasize on the table two small pots of butter, one salted, one sweet, and two kinds of bread, including one from the countryside." The quality of such simple elements—the bread and butter—was all-important. "It is clear that Mr. Guérard (whose parents are butchers, and who knows how to serve a tasty meat) is committed to quality," he wrote.

On balance, the review was generally positive and admiring. It ended with detailed directions for how to find the out-of-the-way restaurant among the workshops, factories, and poorly lit side streets of Asnières, and a prediction of Guérard's continued success: "Let us reassure ourselves, and hope M. Guérard will keep up the good work."

To be a chef was to be a member of a brotherhood. The hard apprenticeship, the long hours and physical labor of the kitchen, the practical jokes and hazing that were de rigueur. Not all that dissimilar, Guérard thought, to the military. He'd served two-plus years in the French navy starting when he was twenty years old, in 1954, during the Algerian War. He'd been stationed at the naval base in Cherbourg, working as a cook. In the kitchen, as in the navy, the bonds were deep.

It was a small world, the restaurant business. Everyone knew everyone else. He and Delaveyne would visit each other's kitchens and talk about food and ideas for recipes, or stop by the Lido for late-night drinks. He owed his success to the man who'd urged him to take a chance on his own cooking. "Delaveyne saved me," he would say. "He gave me the right to be iconoclastic." To break the rules. To make up new ones. They knew another young chef, Alain Senderens, who was preparing to open a restaurant called L'Archestrate on a side street in the seventh arrondissement—just as small as Le Pot-au-Feu. Like Guérard, Senderens had trained at Lucas Carton and other top Paris restaurants and now wanted to strike out on his own. They met at Delaveyne's Camélia to discuss their plans over bottles of wine. "We'll meet in the evening for a snack between us and remake the world!" Guérard said with a laugh.

Then there were the Troisgros brothers, Jean and Pierre, also friends from their time working together at Lucas Carton, who now ran their family restaurant in Roanne, outside Lyon. Jean was the older brother, handsome and reserved; Pierre was cheerful and gregarious. They would stop by the Pot-au-Feu or the Lido when they were in town. Lyon was famous for its food, for its delicate quenelle dumplings and poached Bresse chicken, among other specialties. The Troisgros brothers were infusing their cooking with new and ambitious ideas gleaned from their travels and apprenticeships at other restaurants. They, in turn, had introduced Guérard to Paul Bocuse, whose restaurant in Lyon had won its third Michelin star just as Guérard was opening Le Pot-au-Feu in 1965.

Bocuse was a bit older than the others, and the first to be awarded Michelin's highest honor. He became, almost instantly, the unquestioned leader of their group. He was dashing, forceful, charismatic, always talking, joking, making connections. His cooking might have been classical, but more than any of the others, he perceived this new generation of chefs as distinct. They would not be relegated to the kitchen like their forebears; they would preside in the dining room as well. They would own their own restaurants and court press attention, instilling in French cuisine a new and looser sensibility, a sense of humor and irreverence.

They were a new generation, and they would be famous.

3

True French Cuisine

The way he saw it, Robert Courtine had been fighting for France—for the honor of France—his whole life. Before the war, during the war, and ever since, he'd put nation first. The history, grandeur, and, dare he say it, the superiority of his country was something he felt instinctively. Indeed, the ideal of France—*la belle France*—needed vigilant protection, even now. Especially now, in the current late-1960s moment of change and confusion. Courtine didn't care much for politics or politicians. He expressed his devotion and patriotism with a light touch—a wry and ironical attitude, weaving French cultural and literary history into his writing about food and cooking. Indeed, since the early 1950s he had devoted himself entirely to food, which was, in his mind, a singular repository of the very ideals he had always fought to defend. Yes, French civilization was most truly and essentially embodied in its recipes.

Courtine was prolific. Apart from his weekly Friday column

in *Le Monde*, he wrote for numerous other newspapers and magazines, including *Cuisine et Vins de France*, the country's preeminent food magazine. And he wrote books, one or two a year, meditations on cocktails, or Parisian restaurants, or asparagus, or cooking with flowers, and of course countless cookbooks. Not that he was much of a cook himself—he ate out every night of the week—but his taste and authority sold books. In 1963, he'd published *La Vraie Cuisine Française* (*Real French Cooking*), a comprehensive cookbook of the classics. In the introduction, he explained:

> Whenever in the civilized world men take their places at table with other aspirations than the mere satisfaction of hunger, the word "France" is synonymous with "perfection" in culinary matters. This universal respect for *la cuisine française* is respect for centuries of connoisseurship in cooking, eating and drinking.

The book was a celebration of French cuisine, high and low, everything from the preposterously elaborate eggshells ortolans ("With a very sharp knife cut off a piece of the rounder end of a new-laid or fresh egg. Empty it, line with butter, and slip inside it a larded and truffle-stuffed ortolan") to a straightforward Provençal daube ("Soak for a few hours in white wine with Cognac and olive oil. Season."). The recipes—many supplied by readers and friends—mostly lacked measurements or details; just how one went about larding and stuffing the tiny ortolan songbirds, for example, was left entirely unexplained, as was the seasoning of the Provençal stew. The book was illustrated with jaunty line drawings and caricatures, and interspersed with anecdotes, asides, literary quotations, poems, and jokes (*"Listen, waiter, is this stuff really pork?" "At which end of the fork, sir?"*). The consummately erudite yet also unpretentious narrator addressed himself to his reader, "the woman at home," the heart of the French family, intuitive cook, guardian of tradition, host of proper but never overly formal dinner parties: "Provided there is no successful politician present—provided you are in good company free of stupid snobbery and starchy formality—the hostess herself will indicate that this is a meal unspoiled by ridiculous taboos."

If *Real French Cooking* projected serene confidence in the immutable good sense and good taste of the prosperous French middle class—who, in Courtine's mind, knew how to cook without detailed recipes and whose manners were naturally impeccable—Courtine's true feelings were more complicated. France was besieged, he felt, authentic French cooking under attack on all sides.

First of all, and most fundamentally, was the degradation and pollution of the ingredients themselves. He'd been sounding the alarm about this for years: Additives, preservatives, hormones, antibiotics, herbicides, insecticides—all the modern tools of large-scale agriculture were ruinous for both good health and good flavor. He'd written a book more than ten years earlier, in 1956, called *L'Assassin Est à Votre Table* (*The Assassin Is at Your Table*), exposing the invisible dangers hidden in fruits, vegetables, meat, eggs, dairy, wine—everything was tainted, and the enemy was chemistry.

And it had only gotten worse in the years since; Courtine was now planning to release an updated version of the book, pointing out that in America, President John F. Kennedy had instituted consumer protections for agricultural products in the early 1960s, but what was France doing? Rachel Carson had published *Silent Spring*, her seminal and comprehensive indictment of the use of pesticides, in 1962. But France was woefully behind. "Will we keep our heads in the sand and eat ourselves to death?" he asked. They lived in an era of "supreme scientific vanity," he wrote. "Synthetic meat will soon be a reality. In the US, they have already developed a synthetic sausage."

But chemicals in the food supply and the specter of synthetic American sausages were the least of it, really. (It was the casings that were synthetic, made of processed collagen.) Courtine was adamant that the French government must step up and protect its citizens. Regulate the use of insecticides and hormones and all the rest. But what could the government—or anyone, for that matter—do about the Wimpy Burger?

Wimpy Burger was a sign of the times: Invented in Indiana in the 1930s and named for the Popeye comic strip character (catchphrase: "I'll gladly pay you Tuesday for a hamburger today"), the hamburger and milkshake chain had taken off in England in the 1950s and arrived in Paris in 1961. They were now proliferating, along with countless other so-called snack bars selling similar fare. The idea was fast, "atomic age" service. Paper napkins, drinks with straws, ketchup and mustard on every table, sugar dispensed in tiny paper packets, and no cutlery. American food was coming to Europe in a big way. The *New York Herald Tribune* reported from Paris: "Europe's Culture Falls to Hot Dog."

It was a lightly comic piece from Art Buchwald, who had fun with the contrast between the classic French nine-course meal and a ten-minute snack bar dinner, and who also put his finger on the *real* problem, which was the obvious popularity of these places:

> The tragedy is not that Paris snack bars have attempted to introduce the frankfurter, the hamburger and chili con carne, but that the French like the idea, and almost every one that has opened has been a success. . . . All signs in Paris point to bigger and bigger hot dogs and smaller and smaller chateaubriands.
>
> But we must warn our friends in Europe that there are just so many snack bars that Americans will stand for. We're a peaceful people in search of pleasure, but the sight of thick milkshakes in London, hot dogs *Americains* in Paris and tamales in Rome is enough to make any of us see red. You can go just so far with this American way-of-life gag and then we're ready to explode.

Sure, Buchwald could make light of the postwar Americanization of Europe, all the soft toasted buns and ketchup ruining the continent as a tourist attraction for pleasure-seeking Americans . . . But for Courtine, the insidious spread of bad food and bad manners was an affront. Food did not need to be fancy, or expensive, but it needed to be authentic, made with respect for tradition, and served with silverware.

The very idea of ketchup caused him to recoil. Ketchup was depressing.

A few years earlier, in 1965, Courtine had written a book called *Mangez-vous Français?* (*Do You Eat French?*). The book was a treatise, a cri de coeur. "We are in the days of snacks, only waiting for pills," he warned, imagining a dire future without any cooking at all. "Do young people no longer know how to eat?"

No, they didn't.

The snack bars were everywhere. It was, however, still possible to find a civilized, workingman's lunch in Paris—a plate of roasted chicken or veal kidneys and a glass of wine, say—for less than ten francs, pocket change. Courtine made a point of highlighting such places. "More and more, the noise and the crowds force us to submit to the despotic power of the sprawling city," he wrote in a column titled "Anti-Snacks." "Food is bought, cooked and served in chain restaurants, the famous round bread of the Wimpy, neon lights above empty boxes with jukebox and percolator soundtracks, and their 'fans' even get used to it all." But not Courtine. He refused to patronize what he scornfully called *"les mangeoires américanisées"*—the Americanized food troughs.

It was the spring of 1968, and in Paris the newspapers published dispatches from the war in Vietnam, the antiwar and civil rights protests in the US, and the percolating student sit-ins at the University of Paris Nanterre, where dormitories prohibited opposite-sex visitors at night. War and violence seemed distant, and the French students and their demands for sexual liberation quite trivial in comparison. In mid-March, *Le Monde* reported on the mood of the country: "The French are bored. They do not participate directly or indirectly in the great convulsions shaking the world; the Vietnam War moves them, of course, but it does not really affect them." President Charles de Gaulle was bored, the paper argued, attending agricultural fairs and not much else; the young were bored, too, only concerned about their sleeping arrangements.

Le Monde's assessment would turn out to be spectacularly wrong, as France would soon discover. The culture was shifting.

A new generation was coming of age, and even the seemingly minor question of who was allowed in whose dorm at night, for example, had taken on a sudden urgency. Who wrote such rules? What purpose did they serve? *"Il est interdit d'interdire!"* ("It is forbidden to forbid") and *"Soyez réalistes, demandez l'impossible"* ("Be realistic, demand the impossible") were among the slogans of the moment. The student protesters rejected the paternalistic authority of the university; indeed, they rejected authority of any kind, and their protests would soon expand to more political topics.

It was in this context that Courtine decided to launch a series of columns in *Le Monde* about the best restaurants in Paris. "Les Grands," he called them—the Greats. The establishment needed defending, he thought. Younger consumers and youth culture, broadly defined, were powering the success of "trendy" young chefs like Michel Guérard at the Pot-au-Feu as well as, paradoxically, the rise of snack bars and Wimpy burgers. It fell to Courtine to celebrate the sedate, burnished grandeur of French haute cuisine, as embodied by the iconic Paris restaurants Maxim's, Lasserre, La Tour d'Argent, Lapérouse, and Le Grand Véfour. All five had been awarded the maximum three stars by the Michelin guide year after year (the only restaurants in Paris with this designation); all five were world famous.

But it was not simply snobbery or prestige that drew Courtine to these five restaurants. They represented the continuation of tradition that went back centuries, and more immediately back to the seminal influence of the late-nineteenth and early-twentieth-century French chef Auguste Escoffier. It was Escoffier who had modernized, streamlined, and codified French restaurant cooking.

He had tamed the once-chaotic restaurant kitchen, imposing a division of labor among the various stations—the kitchen brigade—so that the chef at the grill, the chef responsible for fish, the chef in charge of vegetables and cold hors d'oeuvres, the saucier, and others all worked together smoothly, turning out dishes faster and more consistently than ever before. This innovation, which Escoffier had perfected at the Savoy Hotel in London in the 1890s, allowed for à la carte dining (as opposed to a set menu), and had also led him to simplify many of the recipes of classic French cooking—eliminating unnecessary garnishes, for example, so popular earlier in the nineteenth century. Marie-Antoine Carême, for example, the great chef of the early 1800s, was known for his elaborate "pièces montées," in which food for royal banquets was displayed in architectural fashion, grand spreads of meat and fish and desserts propped up on pedestals of inedible suet, marzipan, and spun sugar.

Escoffier decreed that everything on the plate was to be edible. "Surtout, fait simple" was his motto—"Above all, make it simple." In 1903, he'd published his opus, *Le Guide Culinaire*, a five-thousand-recipe cookbook that would become the definitive expression of modern French cooking for decades to come. The book was a systematic compendium of everything from the basics of stocks and sauces to all of the many subtle variations of classics like *blanquette de veau, cailles Lucullus,* and *mousselines de sole.*

Now, decades later, Escoffier remained the spiritual godfather of French cooking. Every chef in France had in effect been trained at the foot of Escoffier; his recipes were the standard model, and they were, by modern standards, not simple at all. And even as a new generation of chefs had begun to question the orthodoxies and complications of haute cuisine (for it was not only Guérard who was changing the formula—Courtine was well aware—there were others), the grand establishments like Maxim's and the Tour d'Argent kept the spirit of Escoffier alive.

And so, over the course of consecutive weeks in March and April 1968, Courtine turned his column to an assessment of the epitome of French cuisine at the highest level, the bedrock institutions of French culinary identity.

First stop: Maxim's, by the Place de la Concorde, with its iconic art nouveau dining room—mahogany paneling, stained glass, murals of nymphs and flowers. The restaurant dated back to 1893, had been a favorite of German officers during the occupation (Hermann Göring had been a regular), and more recently attracted celebrities and aristocrats including Aristotle Onassis, the Duke and Duchess of Windsor, and Brigitte Bardot.

Courtine arrived at 1 p.m. with a friend, a fellow gourmand who'd agreed to accompany him to each of the five restaurants. The menu was extensive and luxurious, with caviar and lobster appetizers, multiple soups and consommés, egg dishes, vegetable dishes, and entrées like coquilles Saint Jacques, medallions of sweetbreads with juniper berries, and pan-seared duck breast. Seasonal specials were listed at the top. They ordered simple appetizers—an egg in aspic for himself, scrambled eggs Magda for his companion, both classic preparations. These were to be followed by two of the daily specials, the coq au vin and the côte de boeuf. Courtine asked for a "pure malt" scotch as an aperitif—his usual—though seldom did anyone in France understand the difference between blended and single malt scotch. And now he asked the waiter casually, as if on a whim, if he might have a tomato salad to accompany his poached egg.

"But of course, monsieur!" came the reply.

Tomato salad was not on the menu, but his plan, he explained to his friend, was to "set a trap" of sorts for each of the restaurants—ordering this simple dish and observing how each establishment handled the request.

The scotch arrived at the table. It was a blended scotch, not the pure malt he'd ordered. None of the five great restaurants of Paris, it turned out, would manage to bring him a single malt scotch, not even Maxim's, which catered to an international clientele. Either the purveyors of scotch were doing a poor job promoting their wares, Courtine pointed out wryly to his friend, or the sommeliers were guilty of "a rather heartbreaking refusal to take an interest in their profession"—or both!

Courtine sipped his whisky and contemplated the appetizers as they arrived. They were solid, he decided—*honest.* This was a word he used frequently to describe a correctly executed dish made with fresh ingredients. The scrambled eggs Magda were soft, made with fine herbs and Gruyère cheese, just as Escoffier had instructed decades before, and the poached egg in aspic was simplicity itself.

As for the off-menu tomato salad: a disaster. It consisted of three tomatoes cut into wedges, unpeeled and unseeded. Courtine was not asked if he wanted any dressing for the tomatoes—olive or peanut oil, vinegar or lemon juice. No, the tomatoes were presented as if in a stable, he thought—fit for an animal. He was secretly pleased, of course, for his "trap" had worked. He had something to write about.

The entrées were perfectly acceptable—a chicken leg and wing in a red wine sauce, the beef presented with root vegetables. They drank a good burgundy with the meal, a 1961 Clos de la Roche, though it was served a little too warm. Courtine had ordered it "fresh," meaning at cellar temperature, but it was not. When it came to judging restaurants, the small details mattered—all of them. As he ate his lunch, and then the dessert and cheese and coffee that followed, Courtine cast an observant, critical eye on his surroundings. What were other customers ordering? How attentive was the hostess? And, for the purpose of the articles he was now working on, did this restaurant truly belong among "Les Grands"?

Maxim's, as ostentatiously luxurious as it was—the red-hatted, red-jacketed doormen with their gold brocades outside, the white-bow-tied waiters inside—was perhaps not quite up to snuff. Courtine would not soon forget the miserable tomatoes, or their price tag: He'd been charged an "indecent" ten francs for the dish.

The remaining four restaurants each rose to the challenge, more or less, of the Tomato Test. At the Tour d'Argent the following week, the tomatoes were well peeled, cut, and seeded, and seasoned with finely chopped herbs. He was not asked what sort of oil he wanted, but the salad was good anyway. He and his friend of course ordered the famous pressed duck—the restaurant's signature dish—each one presented with its number, tallying how many the restaurant had served since the late nineteenth century, by now in the hundreds of thousands. The room was spectacular, on the Left Bank of the Seine with views of Notre-Dame.

The same could not be said for Lapérouse, where the room struck Courtine as a bit "sad," a once great but now "abandoned temple." There were no flowers on the tables, or anywhere else, but the tomato salad was acceptable. At the Grand Véfour, there were spectacular flowers, and the tomatoes, properly seeded and peeled, came with olive oil and herbs. It was only at Lasserre, however, that the waiter responded to Courtine's request with the proper level of detailed interest. Did he want the tomatoes peeled? Cut in slices or rather quartered? Did he want olive oil or peanut oil, and what sort of vinegar did he prefer? The resulting salad was perfect.

Courtine's series of articles on the five "Grands" restaurants of Paris elicited great quantities of reader mail, many questioning his choice to limit himself to Michelin three-star establishments, others dubious about the purpose of the "Tomato Test," still others indignant at the relatively high prices he had carefully detailed. But that was exactly the point of the Tomato Test! You were paying, in these places, for the entire experience, not merely the tomatoes. A great restaurant gets all the details right: the atmosphere, the service, the flowers, the cooking. True, the prices were high, Courtine wrote, but on the other hand:

> How often have we found, by comparison, the much more excessive 30F of a supposedly gourmet lunch in such and such a fashionable tavern!
>
> Just like our couturiers, our craftsmen, these great restaurants are symbols of France. I did not want, in this investigation, to accuse them (one must, rather, defend them).

Great cooking needed to be defended. Courtine was no mindless proponent of the Michelin guide—it put too much emphasis on decor and luxury in his opinion—but they had eaten well at each of the three-stars, and as Courtine had exclaimed to his friend, "You pay a lot more in frightful trendy pubs."

Indeed, one of the reasons Courtine felt so strongly about "Les Grands," and tradition, was because of the attention recently being paid to "trendy" and "fashionable" restaurants, where the chefs felt free, it seemed, to discard Escoffier's *Guide Culinaire* and write their own recipes. It wasn't that he opposed such experimentation on principle, though he was suspicious of it, but rather that some members of the press were lauding such cooking beyond all reason.

Two critics, in particular, had caught Courtine's attention: Henri Gault and Christian Millau. They wrote jointly bylined articles for the weekly *Paris-Presse* newspaper and made a point of highlighting whatever was new and fashionable. They held the Michelin guide in disdain and, for the past few years, had been producing a guide to Paris restaurants, shops, and hotels called the Julliard.

They were newspaper hacks, thought Courtine, not true gastronomes. One of them had previously been a sportswriter, apparently. Gault and Millau were also much younger than Courtine—by about twenty years—coming of age after the war. He couldn't take them seriously.

And yet: The restaurants they championed were the talk of the town.

There was Guérard's Pot-au-Feu, the first of these new generation restaurants, which Gault and Millau described as "among the best small restaurants in Paris," highlighting its "young and beautiful clientele." "The music of Guérard is like the music of Mozart," Millau wrote rather hyperbolically; "the more you hear, the more you love it."

And now there was L'Archestrate, just opened in the early spring of 1968, where a twenty-eight-year-old chef named Alain Senderens was reviving and reinterpreting dishes from the sometimes ancient past, some of them rather unusual. The restaurant was minuscule—a single room, previously occupied by a coal merchant—on the rue de l'Exposition, not far from the Eiffel Tower. Senderens had trained at the Tour d'Argent, Lucas Carton, and the Berkeley, and had come to feel stifled by the unchanging rosters of dishes and sauces. "We did not have the right to change any recipe by one iota," he complained. "It was Escoffier, end of story. The tournedos? *À la Rossini.* The duck? *À orange.* Deer? *Sauce chasseur.* Inevitably, inexorably."

Courtine admired Senderens for his research and rigor. Archestrate served an escargot fricassee based on an eighteenth-century cookbook, stuffed turnips braised in cider, and a medieval-era-inspired eel dish, among other surprises. The menu was, overall, perhaps a "little too sophisticated for its own good," Courtine thought, but Senderens possessed a subtle imagination.

Still, Gault and Millau's celebration of Senderens stuck in Courtine's craw. "The *palme* for originality this season, in Paris, belongs without a doubt to the young Alain Senderens," they declared, calling Archestrate "astonishing."

Gault and Millau prized novelty above all.

Courtine had a different agenda. To uphold the standards of French cooking. To resist novelty, and insist on quality: *la vraie cuisine française.*

Every morning, Courtine squeezed himself a lemon for breakfast; that was all. He was a thin man with an ascetic streak. Despite all the extravagant restaurant meals he consumed, his weight hadn't changed in twenty years—a fact he viewed with some pride. He avoided bread, sugar, and sweet desserts whenever possible. He drank at least a liter of mineral water every day: This was, he believed, the secret to good health.

Courtine did not work at *Le Monde*'s offices on the rue des Italiens—he just dropped off his column there once a week. His days were filled with social events—he was invited to everything: awards ceremonies, restaurant openings, gala dinners. He served on various juries and panels; he attended wine tastings. As *Le Monde*'s restaurant critic, his authority was unquestioned, but he wore that authority lightly. Always witty and sarcastic, he was at the center of the French culinary scene, a small world in which everyone knew everyone else. Still: Courtine maintained an air of mystery about him. He was a man of many secrets and contradictions.

No one, for example, seemed to have ever visited him at home, or met his wife, Elise, who guarded her privacy. She was ill, he explained—convalescent. They had no children. He hated children, he would say, only half joking.

His past, too, was hazy. He'd been raised by his grandmother in the Ardèche region, south of Lyon. She was a great cook. "She never ate with the men; she served them standing up and ate in the kitchen. That's how it should be," he would say, laughing. The simultaneous chauvinism, sentimentality, and humor of that statement was typical. Did he mean it, exactly? Was it true? When asked how he'd got his start as a restaurant critic, he told amusing stories about how he'd once been a political writer, but descriptions of food kept finding their way into his stories. He'd interviewed a prominent official, he said, and spent more time describing the bouride fish soup they'd had for lunch than the man's political positions. This was more myth than truth, as it happened.

But the mystery and mythology of Courtine only added to his power. He was a brilliant writer and raconteur, and his passionate devotion to French cooking would soon lead him into battle with the new generation of chefs and their "trendy" cooking. He would prove to be a powerful foe, and the conflict far-reaching and consequential for all involved. For Courtine, the very soul of French cooking, and identity, was at stake.

4

"The Dinner of the Century"

In May 1968, the student protests at the University of Paris—now against discrimination, consumerism, imperialism, and the police state—ignited a broader strike. The streets were filled with demonstrators and tear gas, the French political establishment shaken. Yanou Collart watched from the balcony of her small apartment and soon joined the workers and students at the barricades, alongside her boyfriend, Alexandre Baloud, who was a reporter for Europe 1 Radio. She carried his bulky Nagra tape recorder as he conducted interviews and typed up his notes for the book he said he was working on about the momentous events of that spring. Her apartment, over the following weeks, was increasingly filled with papers, magazines, and research materials. Baloud had moved in.

Collart, meanwhile, continued to work for Bic, attending corporate meetings and long lunches with Roger LaForest and their associates at the best restaurants in Paris. But more importantly, as it turned out, she'd also taken on a sideline, working with a new hair salon on its public relations.

This had happened quite by accident: Collart was a regular client, and the proprietor, Claude Maxime, had noticed both Collart's charm and the fact she seemed to know everyone in Paris—socialites, businessmen, restaurateurs, journalists, politicians. Of course, this wasn't exactly true; yes, she'd been immersed in Parisian society by dint of working for the well-known LaForest. But she still saw herself as an outsider, and her role as ornamental, at least in part—she was the vivacious beauty among the dark-suited businessmen.

On the other hand, she was fearless, and, more than that, she wanted to escape the staid corporate world of ballpoint pens. And so she leaped at the opportunity, part-time and provisional as it was. Maxime's salon was on Avenue Kléber, and like Collart, Maxime was in her late twenties, just establishing herself. For Collart, the salon represented glamour, fashion, and luxury, everything she wanted. She knew nothing about press relations or the fashion business, but she made sure not to mention this to Maxime.

The first thing she did after taking the job was to stop at Le Drugstore, at the top of the Champs-Élysées, a few blocks from the hair salon. Le Drugstore was a trendy retail space, open at all hours and seven days a week, with a bookstore and newsstand, pharmacy, record shop, and delicatessen. Collart perused copies of the *Herald Tribune*, *Le Figaro*, *Elle*, and *Marie Claire*, looking for the names of journalists who wrote about beauty and fashion. She decided to call the doyenne of fashion reporters, *Figaro*'s Hélène de Turckheim, right then and there, from the phone booth at Le Drugstore.

Improbably, Turckheim answered, and listened, bemused, as Collart made her pitch: She was a client of the Claude Maxime salon, she explained, helping with promotion, and unfortunately did not know the first thing about how to go about it! She admitted she'd simply looked up Turckheim's byline and would be grateful to know what it would take to get her client into the paper?

Turckheim just laughed. Collart's guileless audacity was disarming.

Well, Turckheim said, she was working on a story about 1940s-style femme-fatale glamour—the Veronica Lake / Lauren Bacall look. And if Collart could wrangle a celebrity willing to pose for photos and if Maxime could reproduce the look—the voluptuous waves of hair, the distinctive part—well then, they might have something.

"Elga Andersen would be perfect," Turckheim said.

Collart had her assignment. But how would she ever find Elga Andersen, let alone convince her to appear in an article about her hairstyle? Andersen was a well-known young German actress who'd starred in a number of comedies and comic thrillers—movies like *The Eye of the Monocle* and Bob Hope's *A Global Affair.*

Two days later, Collart was still pondering the problem when fortune struck. She was in a newly opened nightclub called Saint-Hilaire, near the Jardin du Luxembourg on the Left Bank, out for dinner with a friend. The impresario of the club stopped by the table to welcome them, and in passing introduced the architect who'd designed the club. "Meet Christian Girard," he said, "the happiest man on earth. He designed this magical place from scratch, and he's married to one of the prettiest women in the world, Elga Andersen!"

Collart jumped out of her seat, momentarily speechless.

"Elga Andersen!" she exclaimed. "I must meet her!" Stammering and overexcited, she described the possible story in *Le Figaro* and how urgent it was that she speak with Elga, immediately, and what a remarkable coincidence it was that she and Girard happened to meet just days after her conversation with Hélène de Turckheim—and did he know Turckheim? She was the premiere fashion writer at *Le Figaro*—

The architect interrupted her gently, attempting to calm her down, and then said he would not give out his wife's number, but if Collart wanted to write Elga a note, he would be sure to deliver it. "It's up to her to decide if she's interested," Girard said, patting her on the cheek like a child.

And so Collart wrote a brief, impassioned note to Elga, gave it to Girard, and spent the night worrying whether she'd said the right things, what Girard would say to his wife, whether Elga would indeed call her . . . She could barely sleep.

At 3 p.m. the next day, her phone rang.

"Hello, this is Elga Andersen. I'm looking for Yanou," came the lightly German-accented voice, speaking French.

"Yes, this is—this is—this is me. I'm Yanou!" she said. They agreed to meet that afternoon—in two hours' time—for a drink at Fouquet's, the brasserie on the Champs-Élysées.

This was the beginning of Collart's new career, the very first moment that counted: She was sitting in a booth at Fouquet's, and here came the stunning Elga Andersen, dressed in an all-white pantsuit, her blond hair in a ponytail, glamour personified. The room fell briefly silent, all eyes on the two women as Collart rose to greet her and Elga kissed her on each cheek and they sat down.

Collart was ecstatic. She had found her way into the rarefied world of celebrity, at least for a moment, not by attaining fame but rather by facilitating unseen connections in the culture—between the hair salon, the fashion journalist, the nightclub impresario, the architect, and of course the actress. That she and Andersen were now sitting face to face in a chic Parisian restaurant seemed inevitable. And it had all happened by accident, or at least through lucky coincidences.

The story in *Le Figaro* was a smashing success, and Collart soon found herself more involved with Maxime's salon—arranging photo shoots and press for fashion shows (couturier Louis Féraud had commissioned Maxime to style his models, for example), and introducing herself whenever possible to new contacts in the industry. She was bold—shameless even. She showed up outside the RTL Express radio show studio and managed to present Philippe Bouvard, the well-known host, with a pair of new silk shirts.

"Monsieur Bouvard, I love everything you do, but I hate the oversized collars of your shirts!" she said.

Still wearing his headphones, Bouvard was dumbfounded. "Do you sell shirts, mademoiselle?" he asked. Not at all, she answered. Like everyone else, it seemed, he was soon charmed, and agreed to meet her for dinner the next day.

Margret Dünser was another new friend—one of the Continent's preeminent society reporters, known for her celebrity interviews and regular TV specials. Collart had convinced her to profile Maxime, and somewhere along the line Dünser had begun asking Collart for help tracking down and booking guests for her show—race car drivers, pop stars, actors, socialites . . .

One thing always seemed to lead to another for Collart. When Dünser explained that her holy grail interview subject was the iconic singer and actor Maurice Chevalier, who had turned her down repeatedly for years, it just so happened that Bouvard, the radio host, was willing to put in a call on her behalf. When Chevalier agreed to the interview—the very next day!—Dünser was practically in tears.

By the summer of 1968, Collart had quit her job at Bic and gone into business for herself. She'd also split with her boyfriend, Alexandre, and asked him to move out. He'd been working out of her apartment all year when she discovered, talking to a friend, that he'd apparently abandoned the book project months earlier, and never said a word. She felt betrayed at some level—she'd been encouraging his work on the spring protest movement, and all the while he'd been tending to his tan and his tennis game. On the other hand, she now had room in the apartment to set up a small office for herself.

Collart was off and running. Independent. She'd found a job for herself that had no name, really—technically she was a "press agent," but she was nothing like the buttoned-up men who came before her. A new space in the Parisian beau monde of the late '60s had opened up, more international, more freewheeling, and faster. Collart embodied the moment. Indeed, her own glamour was her currency; she gave the impression of knowing everyone, and of being known herself, but this was an illusion borne of her ambition and relentless, seductive charm.

In the fall of 1969, she traveled to London, hired by Dünser to help set up TV interviews for her next special, with Peter Sellers; Alfred Hitchcock; the new James Bond, George Lazenby; Formula 1 champion Graham Hill; pop starlet Sandie Shaw; and maybe, just possibly, one of the Beatles. Collart managed to corral all the interview subjects, calling friends who knew friends who were music and film producers and the like. John Lennon and Yoko Ono canceled at the last minute, sadly, but she did befriend Anthony Fawcett, the couple's assistant, who toured her through Swinging London, showing her the scene.

She was building her client list, organizing events, handling press. A dinner party on the Côte d'Azur, a press trip to Moscow, an American music producer who needed her help navigating the Midem recording industry trade fair in Cannes. There were trips to New York City and Los Angeles, introductions (via that American music producer) to José Feliciano, Peter Falk, Clint Eastwood, Gregory Peck, and countless other boldface names.

Collart basked in celebrity, always eager to pose for a photograph with Brigitte Bardot, or Billy Wilder, or Jack Nicholson, or Gérard Depardieu. Many of these photographs were taken in restaurants. Indeed, much of her job—when she wasn't on the phone—seemed to take place over lunch and dinner. She made a point of booking her meetings at the best restaurants, both new and au courant as well as iconic spots. She brought a client to the up-and-coming chef Roger Vergé's restaurant Moulin de Mougins in the hills above Cannes. She was a regular at the Tour d'Argent in Paris, which was beloved by Courtine and known for its international clientele. And so it was no surprise when Claude Terrail, the proprietor of the Tour d'Argent, asked her to publicize his annual Bastille Day holiday dinner in July 1970. Yes, of course, she said.

This was another new beginning for Collart. Restaurants were a rising nexus of celebrity, luxury, taste, and glamour; when Paul McCartney ate at your restaurant, the press noticed. When she'd visited Hollywood the previous year, Collart was asked about Michel Guérard's Pot-au-Feu (his Michelin star had earned him notice even overseas) and could she help with a reservation? The chefs and their restaurants, she realized, were the subjects of increasing interest and fascination—and Collart was perfectly placed to help them capitalize on it.

There was another person who had reached the very same conclusion: Paul Bocuse.

The late 1960s had seen ever more attention for chefs and restaurants: articles in newspapers and magazines, the rise of new guidebooks and publications. "Paul Bocuse is something of a phenomenon even in France, where great chefs are to be expected," reported *Vogue* magazine in a profile of the chef from 1968, describing the "solemn gastronomes from America and Britain who book tables and order meals six months in advance" as well as the dowdy Lyon locals who filled the restaurant, "the women often of unbelievably exuberant build, plainly of the opinion that the rewards of having brought up a healthy family lie in being able to set aside any obligation to maintain slenderous charms." *Vogue*'s snide descriptions of the overweight bourgeoisie aside, the article celebrated Bocuse and his restaurant, as many others did.

There was, indeed, a growing cadre of journalists devoted to food and travel and "lifestyle," as it was called. None more so than Henri Gault and Christian Millau, who had moved on from the Julliard guidebooks and in 1969 launched a magazine called *Le Nouveau Guide*. The premiere issue carried the cover headline "Michelin: Don't Ignore These 48 Stars!" and highlighted the many young chefs they considered rising talents—all overlooked by the powerful Michelin guide. The voice of the magazine was witty and opinionated, with news of restaurant openings and advice about the best dishes to order at Le Pot-au-Feu or Archestrate or Bocuse.

Bocuse welcomed the attention, of course, but was determined to take a more active role in promoting French cuisine. And so he decided to form a group, L'Association de la Grande Cuisine Française, a kind of trade organization for the top restaurants in France. Why should they let Gault and Millau take the lead when they could do it themselves?

"What can we do?" he asked his compatriots in the spring of 1971. "Because the way things are going, soon, it will not be us who talk into the microphone."

He invited Michel Guérard, Jean and Pierre Troisgros, Roger Vergé, Louis Outhier, Jean-Pierre and Marc Haeberlin, Pierre Laporte, Charles Barrier, Raymond Oliver, and René Lasserre to join him. The group—all men, needless to say—included the most exciting chefs of the moment, as well as some of their mentors, stalwarts of haute cuisine like Barrier, Lasserre, and Oliver, who'd hosted a popular TV cooking show in the 1950s and owned Paris's iconic Le Grand Véfour. The idea was to promote themselves as a group, define themselves as the best of France, and—crucially—enter into sponsorship and promotional arrangements with interested parties.

Bocuse called Collart and told her about his plans for the new association. He wanted her to handle press relations, he said. Their paths had crossed many times over the years since they'd met at his restaurant in 1965, when he mistook her for a pop star. Now she was running her own public relations firm, and they would go into business together.

They launched L'Association de la Grande Cuisine Française at a press conference in Paris, in the wood-paneled dining room at Le Grand Véfour. Collart invited the press; Bocuse and the other chefs posed for photos with an enormous, five-meter-long sausage made by his favorite Lyonnais charcuterie, Bobosse. This was just the sort of theatrical gag Bocuse loved.

The chefs also announced their first joint event: It would be called "The Dinner of the Century," to be held at Pierre Laporte's Café de Paris in Biarritz in September, a resort destination suitable for a celebration. They would all be cooking the dinner, together—this would be a culinary extravaganza like no other—the greatest chefs in the world creating the greatest dinner ever conceived, and tickets were on sale now!

"The Dinner of the Century" sold out immediately, within hours. Tickets were 300 francs—rather more than the cost of a meal at any of the chefs' restaurants—but it made no difference. The dinner promised to be much more than a meal; it would be a festival of modern, state-of-the-art French cuisine, the epitome of taste and luxury.

Collart made the most of the interest in the event, and managed to book Bocuse and Guérard on the TV talk show *L'Invité du Dimanche* (*The Sunday Guest*). The show featured roundtable interviews with celebrities and intellectuals discussing the topics of the day in serious tones. Shows like this were a mainstay of French television; there was usually someone smoking a pipe. In this case the topic was the new popularity of gourmet cooking, and the other guests included food critics and historians who discussed the invention of the fork and the importance of wine as Bocuse and Guérard cooked a meal live on set. The program concluded with everyone enjoying the salmon they'd prepared, and fresh strawberries glacées for dessert.

In the first week of September 1971, the chefs of the Grande Cuisine Française descended on Biarritz. Laporte's restaurant was on the Place Bellevue, overlooking the beach. Biarritz was a resort town on the Atlantic in southwest France, Basque country, long a favorite of royalty and newly popular with young, long-haired surfers. The weather was beautiful. The chefs were all staying at the grand Hôtel du Palais, as were many of the guests who'd flown in for the dinner, set to take place the following evening.

Now, Collart gathered Bocuse and the other chefs at the hotel pool for press interviews and photographs. The pool was on a terrace, and the beach below was crowded with sunbathers under umbrellas and kids running in the waves. The mood was festive, but Collart was already nervous about seating arrangements and all the other logistics of "The Dinner of the Century." She'd done her job well: The press was in full attendance, magazine and newspaper writers from all over France, food and restaurant critics, including the influential Robert Courtine of *Le Monde*, as well as the international press, including the Paris correspondent of *The New York Times*.

Collart had brought a prop for the photographs, a giant frying pan—another silly gag, much like the outsize sausage Bocuse had brought to their first press conference in Paris. They gathered around it, laughing in their bathing suits, pushing each other into the pool. Soon they were all in the water—along with the frying pan—even Charles Barrier, who did not know how to swim. He had to be helped out of the pool by two of the others after the photos were taken.

It was all good fun, and good press. There was Bocuse, the leader, always the center of attention; Roger Vergé, dashing, mustachioed, his hair already graying at forty; Jean Troisgros, the older of the Troisgros brothers; Jean-Pierre Haeberlin, who, with his brother, Paul, ran the much-admired Auberge de l'Ill in the Alsace; and Guérard, the youngest of the group, mischievous and wry—everyone called him the boy genius. Then there were the older, more established restaurateurs: Laporte, whose Café de Paris kitchen they'd all be cooking in tomorrow; Raymond Oliver of the Grand Véfour; Barrier, whose namesake restaurant was in Tours, in the Loire Valley; and René Lasserre, proprietor (though not chef) at the famous Lasserre.

It was an impressive group, that much was certain. They had eighteen Michelin stars among them. And such a gathering of forces—banding together, cooking as a group—had never been done. Could they possibly live up to the sky-high expectations they'd set for "The Dinner of the Century"? Of course not. But they would try.

The next day, as Collart worried that the men seemed a bit cavalier in their preparations for the dinner, and after a skirmish broke out in Laporte's kitchen—the cooks on the line objecting to being given orders by the self-important Michelin-starred chefs—the guests began arriving for dinner. It was 7:30 p.m.; there were about a hundred of them, the social elite of Biarritz and Paris, dressed in black tie and gowns. The police had set up barricades on the plaza, holding back the crowds of curious onlookers, who spotted minor French celebrities like comedians and TV personalities Thierry Le Luron and Jacques Martin and various other singers, dancers, and socialites—and a skiing champion. But it was the chefs who were the real stars, resplendent in their immaculate white jackets and toques. They had prepared a suitably elaborate menu for the occasion:

Consommé moscovite

Louvine braised in red Graves

Crayfish-tail timbale

Wild duck in a white Haut-Brion

Ragout of truffles

Puree of corn with foie gras

Cheeses

Fruit basket "des Dix"

THE WINES

Dom Pérignon rosé 1959

Moët et Chandon 1964 (in magnum)

Chateau Haut-Brion (Graves) 1962 (in magnum)

Moët et Chandon 1914

Armagnac Laberdolive 1904

Izarra verte

The dishes were a mix of classic preparations, inventive interpretations, and luxurious ingredients, a modern update of an Escoffier-style menu. The cold consommé was a traditional first dish, served with an unusual spoonful of caviar; "louvine," the Basque term for sea bass, was served filleted with mushrooms and pearl onions in a rich red wine sauce. The crayfish timbale was a favored dish at the Troisgros restaurant—cooked in a court bouillon and sprinkled with chopped chervil and tarragon. The duck, meanwhile, came in a white wine sauce and was surrounded with stewed truffles, cut into quarters. Perhaps the most surprising dish was the puree of corn with foie gras. Corn was relatively unknown in France, and to serve it with foie gras was unheard of—a lowly grain usually reserved for feeding chickens, now paired with the ultimate luxury, goose liver?

All the food was well received, the crowd babbling in happy excitement as an orchestra played and bottles of champagne were opened.

At the critics' table, however, there was some grumbling. Why was the sea bass in red wine sauce served with pink champagne? The dish itself was excellent, they agreed, the fish standing up to the sauce. But it called for a red wine, despite the popular belief that fish did not pair with red. They knew better, and asked for the Bordeaux that was set to be served with the duck. When that arrived, they complained that the wine was too warm, and would the waiter please provide an ice bucket?

Collart observed all this with some trepidation.

It got worse: The crayfish were "bland and over rich," the critics decreed. The wild duck hadn't been hung long enough—the hunting season having only just begun—and the truffles were surely not fresh. "Don't these gentlemen, these great chefs, know that in this particular season one can only get canned truffles?" asked Courtine. Of course they knew. "But they believe in all their naiveté that truffles are indispensable to great cuisine, even when they are not first-rate. Whereas great cuisine must be just that—first-rate."

And as for the corn puree with foie gras—the novelty elicited among the critics a decidedly mixed reaction. Many were charmed, but not Courtine.

"In 1971, to create a puree of corn mixed with foie gras is more than a crime or a sin," he announced dramatically. "It is depravity!" They all laughed. Foie gras should not be debased in this way, he said, shaking his head, smiling ruefully. The critics poured themselves more wine. They were enjoying themselves.

The next day, the chefs said their goodbyes and wondered at the success of the spectacle they'd just pulled off, the grand debut of the Grande Cuisine Française. Sure, there'd been hitches and bumps along the way—the menu and the cooking hadn't been perfect—but the event had been electrifying. The eyes of the world had been on them. The *New York Times* headline read: "7 Chefs Cook 'Dinner of Century'—Were There 6 Too Many?"

Bocuse took the criticism in stride. Let the bitter John Hess of the *Times* complain that the dinner was too expensive; let Courtine of *Le Monde* call the dinner "a show rather than a meal" and "ridiculous." This was the price of fame. Of course the critics would disapprove. For a purist like Courtine, success itself was cause for suspicion. He wrote:

> Coming back on the plane, I kept repeating the phrase to myself: the Dinner of the Century? So be it. Every century has the dinner it deserves . . . As I considered the caricature called *le Tout Paris*—with everybody who "is" anybody now in Paris—with all its bogus glory, its wailing stars, its hustling painters, its simpering dancers, and its dashing swells—as I considered them all, I told myself that that dinner was *their* dinner!

A new generation of chefs had found a new audience—the "dashing swells" Courtine despised. Led by Bocuse (and with Collart's help), they would exit the confines of the kitchen and find their place on a larger, more public stage. They would conquer the world.

"You've got to beat the drum in life," said Bocuse of his unabashed talent for self-promotion. "God is already famous, but that doesn't stop the preacher from ringing the church bells every morning."

And as for Courtine, well, the battle lines had been drawn.

5

Bande à Bocuse

They were a gang, a posse, a club, a *bande à part*—a band of outsiders, to borrow the title of Jean-Luc Godard's 1964 New Wave film. The core group of young chefs congregated around Paul Bocuse had known each other since they were young, training in many of the same restaurants, overlapping stints of apprenticeship, crossing paths as they came up. They were friends, rivals, compatriots. They were the new generation; they were the "Bande à Bocuse."

The brothers Jean and Pierre Troisgros had met Bocuse in 1950, in Paris, when the three of them worked at Lucas Carton, a revered restaurant on the Place de la Madeleine on the Right Bank. Jean and Bocuse were both twenty-four years old; Pierre was twenty-two. They were already well trained—Bocuse had been working for Fernand Point at the three-star La Pyramide in Vienne; the Troisgros brothers for their family restaurant in Roanne. But now they were in the big city, here to soak up the speed, polish, and sophistication of a Parisian restaurant kitchen.

They were country boys, a little wide-eyed in the midst of the postwar boomtown that was the capital. They loved it.

Jean and Pierre were inseparable. They lived in a pair of tiny rooms in a fifth-floor walk-up near the Porte Maillot metro station on the outskirts of Paris. The rooms were barely one hundred square feet, but they were cheap. Bocuse lived in suburban Courbevoie, even farther out, in a furnished room he drove to on his motorbike every night after his shift. They were all at work by 9 a.m. every day: Jean was the chef grillardin, working the grill; Pierre was the chef entremetier, in charge of vegetables and soups; and Bocuse was the chef garde manger, overseeing the pantry and the cold hors d'oeuvres. They formed the brigade, along with the chef saucier, considered the most important position—making the sauces—who was older and had been there for years. The chef—their boss—was Gaston Richard, who'd been working at Lucas Carton since the late 1920s.

Richard was of the old school: a strict disciple of grand French cuisine, of Auguste Escoffier and other early-twentieth-century masters like Theodore Gringoire and Louis Saulnier. The menu at Lucas Carton changed every day, but the dishes were all classics: escargots de Bourgogne, truite meunière, noisette d'agneau, all turned out perfectly. The brigade worked like clockwork.

Still: There was downtime. The days were long but the afternoons were slow. Indeed, Chef Richard made a habit of taking a long late lunch at a brasserie across the street called Le Colibri, where he met with friends from other restaurants and inevitably returned half drunk a few hours later.

And so the chefs of the brigade found ways to keep themselves occupied and entertained. There were jokes, pranks, wagers, and gossip. Bocuse was a master of these pursuits, as it turned out. One day, for example, he managed to nail Pierre's espadrilles to the floor of the cloakroom. They all laughed uproariously at Pierre's puzzled consternation at the unmoving shoes. Soon Pierre was laughing too—and plotting his revenge.

On their days off, they roamed Paris together in the afternoons, sneaking into theaters and shows, stopping for beers along the way. They found a café with a pinball machine and jammed the mechanism in a way that gave them endless free games. Jean had procured a slingshot, and they walked through the nearby Jardin des Tuileries shooting at sparrows. Bocuse managed to knock one to the ground, stunned, and he quickly captured the bird and brought it back to the restaurant, where he released it into the kitchen as they prepared for the dinner service.

Richard shouted in confusion as the befuddled sparrow flitted around the room and someone grabbed a broom. Bocuse and the Troisgros brothers stifled laughter behind their hands like overgrown schoolboys.

Another day, Pierre was cleaning some pheasants and set aside the lungs and other viscera. Just before he and his friends left for their break, he wedged it into his cheeks. This was the pleasure of a good prank: the anticipation, the preparation, the *reveal.* As they walked through the prosperous neighborhood, heading somewhere or another, aimlessly, passing by the Place Vendôme, the Ritz hotel, Pierre began to cough.

He coughed and coughed, retching violently, and then convulsed, suddenly ejecting a disgusting, bloody mass of tissue onto an adjacent shop window. Splat.

Jean and Bocuse looked on in horror.

"Ah, that's better," Pierre exclaimed, wiping his mouth as he continued walking.

It was well worth the full twenty minutes of concealing bird innards in his mouth just to see the expressions on their faces at that moment. He burst out laughing.

They were just idiots, living "la vie bohème," as Pierre would say ironically, bound by their lack of money and a palpable sense of postwar liberation. They'd all done their time in the army; they'd survived the privations of war and occupation. And, indeed, their wartime experiences as teens—foraging for food, making do with shortages and rations—had instilled both a deep appreciation for the pleasures of good cooking and a skill for improvisation that would serve them well in the future.

Over the course of the 1950s and '60s, Bocuse and the Troisgros brothers stayed close, and the Bande à Bocuse would expand as other young chefs came into its orbit—Roger Vergé, the Haeberlin brothers, Louis Outhier, Alain Chapel, Michel Guérard—a brotherhood of the kitchen.

Bocuse set the tone. He had taken charge of his parents' restaurant and earned three Michelin stars before any of the others. He took food and tradition seriously but maintained an air of devil-may-care machismo that was the key to his charisma. He loved hunting, and scuba diving, and stories about the war: He'd joined the Resistance as a teenager and had been shot fighting the Germans in 1945 outside Strasbourg, where he was treated by American medics. They'd given him transfusions of "liters and liters of American blood," which, as Bocuse explained it, made him partly American himself—all brash ambition and optimism. An American GI had also inked a tattoo of a rooster—le coq gaulois, proud symbol of France—on his left upper arm. (He would later sometimes describe it as a Bresse chicken, one of the mainstays of his menu.)

After their time with Bocuse in Paris, the Troisgros brothers had parted ways for a bit, Pierre going to work at La Pyramide with Fernand Point (where Bocuse had worked before going to Lucas Carton), and Jean at the Hôtel de Crillon in Paris. By the mid-1950s, their father, Jean-Baptiste Troisgros, had convinced them to return home, and, somewhat reluctantly at first, they took over the restaurant.

It didn't happen all at once. Pierre, for his part, had no desire to return to sleepy, provincial Roanne after having seen more of the world beyond it. But one of the chefs in his father's kitchen was ill, and so he agreed. Just temporarily, he said, until Jean could replace him—they would take turns helping out when necessary.

But Jean and Pierre's father wanted them both back. He had seen the future: Even in working-class Roanne, center of the French textile industry, tastes were changing. A new, postwar prosperity had dawned, bringing with it new mobility, more travel and tourism, a new openness. And, most important to a restaurateur, a new interest in sophisticated cooking. Jean-Baptiste was not a chef; he was an *"homme de la salle"*—a "man of the room"—welcoming guests, making them comfortable, pouring the wine. He was the gregarious owner and face of the restaurant, and had an intuitive sense of what his clientele wanted. They were arriving in new Citroëns, and they wanted more than rustic stews and grilled fish; they wanted dishes that were a bit showier, a bit more inventive, with some foie gras and truffles perhaps . . . just the sort of haute cuisine, as it happened, his sons were now able to produce.

And so they did. The restaurant was transformed—renamed Les Frères Troisgros—and began accumulating Michelin stars and other accolades. In the press, over the course of the 1960s, the brothers' impeccable training at the best restaurants in France was always noted, as was their friendship with Bocuse.

For all his star power and success, Bocuse was a notably generous advocate for his fellow chefs. Yes, he maintained, even twenty years later, the attitude of a renegade schoolboy. His pranks had only gotten more elaborate: He had, for example, gone through the trouble of relabeling a tin of foie gras as dog food, and then opening it blithely for friends at a picnic as they watched, speechless. "It's all I could find—I'm sure it'll do fine," he said, taking a bite. He was a joker, but he always looked out for his friends.

When the food critic Christian Millau came to Lyon for a story about Bocuse and his restaurant in 1965, he was given the royal treatment. But Bocuse also insisted he visit the Troisgros brothers in Roanne, an hour's drive away. This was no casual mention of another good restaurant in the area: Bocuse was animated and forceful—Millau hadn't yet eaten at Troisgros? He must absolutely make the trip. He must.

Millau made the trip, and he was floored. Just across from the train station in Roanne, he found a small, modest restaurant with "an absolutely fabulous atmosphere of friendly complicity," he wrote. "One has the impression that, under father Troisgros' merciless gaze, himself gifted with a talented palate, the two brothers are reinventing the cooking twice a day." Millau's review of Les

Frères Troisgros was heralded in the *Paris-Presse* newspaper with the headline "I Have Discovered the Best Restaurant in the World!"

Every morning, Bocuse got on the phone for a round of calls with his fellow chefs, checking in, trading news and gossip, scouting for talented young cooks, recommending various suppliers and tradesmen. He was the center of the network. And on the day the *Paris-Press* came out the first thing he did was call the Troisgros restaurant to offer his congratulations. He was genuinely pleased to have helped bring his friends into the limelight. They were the Bande à Bocuse, after all. They were in this together.

Bocuse also made a point of roping his friends into his promotional and business dealings. "We're stronger together than alone!" he would say.

When he was invited by *Holiday* magazine and an English wine dealer to cook a dinner at the Rainbow Room in New York City in 1966, he invited his friends along. When he was later invited to Japan and China, he did the same. Guérard, Vergé, the Troisgros brothers, and the rest of the Bande à Bocuse all traveled with him frequently, as did noted winemaker Georges Duboeuf and foie gras producer Jean Rougié. Bocuse was fast becoming a kind of culinary ambassador, bringing French cooking to the world, packing truffles into his carry-on and dispensing savoir faire and charisma wherever he went. He liked being the center of attention, and he traveled with an entourage of friends.

If there was a seamier side to Bocuse's charm, drive, and celebrity, it was his relentless womanizing. This was something everyone knew and no one talked about, not openly. His wife, Raymonde, helped run his restaurant, and they had a grown daughter, Françoise. But he pursued extramarital affairs everywhere he went and had indeed recently fathered a child, a son named Jérôme, with his mistress of many years in Lyon, Raymone Carlut. He had another, younger mistress, it was whispered, also in Lyon, named Patricia Zizza. And a girlfriend in Tokyo, too, apparently. He was insatiable. "I adore women, and we live too long these days to spend a whole life with only one," he would say.

Still, business always came first.

The first commercial contract Bocuse arranged for his newly created Association de la Grande Cuisine Française in the early 1970s was with Air France—they would be designing the onboard meals for the airline's glamorous new 747s. The work took many months, developing recipes in the vast Air France kitchens at Orly, learning the ins and outs of preparing dishes to be served at high altitude. The first-class menu included caviar, mussels and scallops pie, veal pot-au-feu with foie gras and julienned vegetables, and opera cake. Economy-class meals were less elaborate but similarly ambitious, with entrées like spring chicken with lime, pork with prunes, and salmon with green peppercorns. Air France announced the new menus created by the "Grande Cuisine Française" in an international advertising campaign, and the chefs famously celebrated their high-profile success on the tarmac at Orly, posing for photographs for Gault and Millau's *Nouveau Guide* magazine.

"Voilà la nouvelle cuisine française!" declared Henri Gault definitively. The chefs had created a movement, maybe even a revolution.

Just as the dashing young chefs of the Bande à Bocuse were becoming ever more famous, Simone Lemaire was opening her own restaurant in Le Pin-au-Haras, in Normandy—called Le Tourne-Bride. She was back home in northwest France, where she'd grown up, and where her mother and grandmother had taught her to cook. Lemaire's experience running the Reine Jeanne with her sister, doing all the cooking more or less by herself, had given her the confidence to take on a restaurant of her own.

And now here she was. She hired a small staff—cooks, assistants, waiters. She did not have the full kitchen brigade found in larger restaurants, but she made do. The setting was magnificent: This was horse country, and the Tourne-Bride was on the grounds of a vast equestrian complex built at the direction of King Louis XIV in the eighteenth century. There were stables, saddle makers, and horse-drawn carriages, all surrounding an elegant château and drawing a steady stream of visitors and tourists. She'd won the concession to run the restaurant on the state-owned property because of her family's roots in the area.

Le Tourne-Bride itself was housed in a two-story stone building with a steep gabled roof and multiple chimneys. There were tables on the terrace in front under umbrellas and an enormous vegetable garden in the back, where Lemaire had also planted a variety of herbs and where a freshwater pond, fed by running water, allowed her to keep a supply of trout, shrimp, and frogs.

The menu reflected the region. Poulet à la normande (chicken with mushrooms in cream sauce), of course; frog's legs and pearl onions in an apple cider reduction; flounder with tomatoes and cream; quail with juniper berries. Well-made classics, and always popular.

When Robert Courtine passed through while writing a review of the restaurants of Normandy, he remembered Lemaire's cooking from the Reine Jeanne and told her so. He noted the traditional normande dishes on the menu, but also that she excelled at recipes from other regions as well—the duckling à la Duchambais, for example, in a sauce made with red wine and brandy and enriched with pureed duck livers and cream, a Bourbonnais specialty. Courtine made particular note of her fresh ingredients. "The menu usefully specifies that it does not use frozen products," he wrote in *Le Monde*, "and the wine selection is beautiful."

Still, Lemaire was well aware of the difference in how her restaurant was received compared to the all-out excitement surrounding the young men of the Bande à Bocuse. She had seen the notices about the new Air France menu, she had seen the articles about Bocuse's Association de la Grande Cuisine Française and the extravagant "Dinner of the Century," and she had not failed to notice that all the chefs in these photographs and news stories were men. It went without saying—it was indeed entirely unremarkable—that the future of French cuisine was in the hands of the men who had trained at the great restaurants of France.

Such preparation had not been an option for her, or any other woman. The system of formal training for cooks in France, dating back to the nineteenth century, consisted of a series of "stages," or apprenticeships, open only to men. And so was admission into the Association des Maîtres Cuisiniers de France, an honor reserved for top chefs in France—all men. The work of the chef was considered too grueling and physically demanding for a woman.

There was of course a long history of women-run restaurants in France—Mère Brazier and Mère Fillioux and the other "mères" of Lyon and beyond, the "mothers" of French cooking, celebrated for their traditional, regional dishes. They were respected as cooks, practitioners of great craft but not of haute cuisine. This was reserved for the men, the "maîtres cuisiniers," the masters of cooking.

And so Lemaire was entirely home- and self-taught, opening Le Tourne-Bride in the shadow of her far more prominent male counterparts. Coming of age in the postwar 1950s, sensing the liberation and possibility of the 1960s, honing her talent and then launching a restaurant of her own—all this she shared with Bocuse, Guérard, the Troisgros brothers, and the others. But as a woman she was on a different path.

And she was not the only one. Indeed, all over France, a new generation of women chefs was emerging. In 1971, in the small town of Vervins in northern France, not far from the Belgian border, Annie Desvignes opened a restaurant called La Tour du Roy. She had apprenticed briefly at age fifteen at Raymond Oliver's Grand Véfour in Paris and later learned patisserie with Gaston Lenôtre, and then found herself shut out—the professional track was not open to her—and so she went to work with her mother. Together they operated a restaurant in Sars-Poterie for a few years, also in the north, and now Desvignes was married and striking out on her own. She'd found a beautiful but decrepit manor house with turrets and conical spires, and undertaken extensive renovations to turn it into a restaurant and inn.

In southern France that same year, Élisabeth Bourgeois opened a restaurant called La Férigoulo on rue Joseph Vernet in Avignon. She was twenty-two. Bourgeois had been working in kitchens since she was fourteen, first at her parents' restaurant in the Luberon, and then, after getting married and having a child, as a cook for hire. Wandering the narrow streets of Avignon one day with a friend—they were shopping—she'd seen a small storefront for sale and blurted out: "What if I set up a restaurant of my own?" And so it came to be. She'd never had a day of formal training as a cook; now she was a chef and restaurateur.

In Paris, meanwhile, Dominique Nahmias and her husband, Albert, were preparing to open a tiny restaurant in bohemian Montparnasse, on the Left Bank. They'd just had a baby, and Dominique—known to all by her nickname, Olympe—was unhappily studying law. Albert had finished his degree in sociology from the University of Paris Nanterre, where the May 1968 movement had begun (and where protest leader Daniel Cohn-Bendit had also studied sociology), but he was now unable to find work. Olympe's talent as a cook—she would often prepare much-admired dishes for family and friends—led the two of them to contemplate an escape from the world of school. They would sit at the café Le Select in Montparnasse, cigarette smoke and jazz and conversations about metaphysics in the air all around, and talk about a place of their own. Just around the corner on the rue du Montparnasse, in fact, was an old barbershop run by a man from Alsace, and he apparently wanted to retire. Would he sell them the space? Was the barbershop big enough to accommodate a small restaurant? Yes, they would soon discover—it was. They would call the restaurant Olympe.

Lemaire, Desvignes, Bourgeois, and Nahmias were at the forefront of a new French women's movement in food—under the radar but very much of the moment.

None of these women knew each other—not yet.

One of the keys to success, Bocuse and the other chefs discovered, was the defining, trademark dish. Something special, available only at your restaurant—something new. It might be a new twist or interpretation, a simplification, an unusual presentation, a foreign ingredient, something for the press to write about, in any case. This was the dish you presented when posing for a magazine photographer in your chef's whites and toque, the dish first-time customers simply *had* to order.

It was good business to stray from the precepts Escoffier had laid down at the turn of the century. It was also a sign of the times. The chef, in his new, modern incarnation (and, in the press, it was always a he) was more than a technician, more than a well-trained practitioner of French culinary tradition. The modern chef was an artist, an auteur.

And hadn't Escoffier himself invented new dishes and techniques? He'd named countless dishes after royal figures and opera stars (pêches Melba, for example, for the Australian opera singer Nellie Melba) and had simplified French cooking for the late-nineteenth-century restaurant kitchen. He had codified tradition in his seminal *Guide Culinaire* but also—with some exasperation—embraced the idea of the chef as creator: "Novelty is the universal cry—novelty by hook or by crook!" He'd written in the preface to the 1907 edition of his cookbook:

> It is an exceedingly common mania among people of inordinate wealth to exact incessantly new or so-called new dishes. Sometimes the demand comes from a host whose luxurious table had exhausted all the resources of the modern cook's repertory, and who, having partaken of every delicacy, and often had too much of good things, anxiously seeks new sensations for his blasé palate. . . . Personally, I have ceased counting the nights spent in the attempt to discover new combinations.

Now, in the 1970s, the Bande à Bocuse was once again discovering new combinations. Unlike Escoffier, however, they did not see themselves as toiling away to invent dishes for wealthy, blasé clients. No, they saw cooking not merely as a service but as a form of self-expression. Bocuse, Guérard, Vergé, Senderens, Lenôtre, the Troisgros brothers—they had all been trained in the classic tradition but had found their own style. This was a new idea, born in this moment, that cooking might reflect a chef's personal taste, desire, and instincts.

Guérard may have been the first to realize this when he remade the menu at Le Pot-au-Feu in 1966, to much acclaim. He put dishes on the menu no one had ever quite seen before. He served foie gras with turnips glazed in brown sugar, for example, instead of the expected apples or grapes. And he discovered something most important. "People are not against these small audacities," Guérard told his friends—just the opposite. His customers welcomed novelty.

The dish that broke through and became famous was the "salade gourmande," as it was called on the menu—lettuce with perfectly cooked crisp green beans and asparagus in a light vinaigrette with slices of foie gras. It was not Guérard but his friends and fellow chefs who began calling it the "crazy salad"—"la salade folle"—and the name stuck. The idea was for the salad to derive its richness as much as possible from foie gras instead of from olive oil. Perfectly logical, thought Guérard. In any case, the salad was a hit.

Bocuse's signature dish was more traditional. In fact, Bocuse's cooking wasn't innovative at all, except in his emphasis on using only the freshest ingredients. He had learned a great lesson all those years ago working for Fernand Point at La Pyramide: to focus on ingredients, on craftsmanship. Like Point, he served his green beans al dente, not overcooked, dressed with chopped shallots and olive oil. (When he served the beans to the food critics Henri Gault and Christian Millau, they nearly fainted. The best they'd ever had, they said.) He also had the traditional Lyonnais chicken poached in a pig's bladder on his menu, but the showstopper, the pièce de résistance, was Bocuse's loup de la Méditerranée en croute—Mediterranean sea bass wrapped in pastry.

It was a work of art: a flaky, golden, egg-washed crust in the shape of the fish enclosed inside, complete with detailed fins, gills, scales, and a single eye. The dish was presented on a large platter and then divided and served tableside. (Like the dish itself, this was an old-fashioned gesture; the modern style was generally for dishes to come straight from the kitchen to the table.) The fish was stuffed with a delicate lobster mousse made with ground pistachios, truffles, and cream.

Bocuse's stuffed, pastry-wrapped confection was an ingenious, theatrical updating of a dish that went back to Escoffier, the saumon Nesselrode, stuffed salmon baked in dough. "Do not break the crust except at the dining table," warned Escoffier in his *Guide Culinaire*, and the same went for Bocuse's version. The presentation was all-important. There was indeed something inherently delightful about a fish wrapped in pastry and elaborately decorated as a fish . . . it made people smile. Soon, every newspaper and magazine article about Bocuse was inevitably accompanied by a photograph of the loup en croute.

But no dish was more groundbreaking or influential than the Troisgros brothers' *escalope de saumon à l'oseille* (escalope of salmon with sorrel sauce), which they invented together, experimenting in the kitchen in the early 1960s, long before their Michelin stars and many accolades. The radical idea was to slice the salmon not into steaks, as was usual, but rather across the length of the fish to yield large, thin slices, which were gently flattened with a mallet. The method was taken from Italian cooking, in which veal was often cut this way, for veal piccata, for example. Indeed, the phrase "escalope de saumon" was entirely new and audacious—never seen on a menu before—taking a culinary term used to describe a cut of meat and applying it to fish.

Instead of lemons, as was traditional, Jean and Pierre Troisgros used fresh sorrel to give the sauce its necessary acidity, adding the torn leaves to a reduction of fish stock, shallots, white Sancerre, and dry vermouth, then adding butter and crème fraîche. They cooked the salmon in a newfangled nonstick Tefal pan, with no added oil and for only twenty-five seconds on one side, fifteen seconds on the other. The fish was served over a pool of the sorrel sauce on a very large plate. (The standard dinner plate was too small for the large slices of fish, so they used decorative chargers from Limoges. Eventually they had custom plates made with a circumference of thirty-two centimeters.) As the dish became more popular, the brothers also commissioned a local silversmith to make a sauce spoon perfectly suited to the salmon, with a flat edge to cut the fish and indented to collect the sorrel sauce as well.

The dish was considered shocking because it was served still visibly undercooked at the center, rushed directly from the kitchen on its dramatically enormous plate. It was also tender and delicious. Everyone had to try it. *Escalope de saumon à l'oseille* was instantly famous, a sensation.

"Finally, an intelligent salmon," said *Le Monde*'s Robert Courtine, a critic not generally disposed to appreciate culinary innovation. Even *The New York Times,* a continent away, had noted the dish, described as "a filet of Loire salmon in a sourgrass sauce," and as "one of the most brilliant achievements of Troisgros."

Indeed, the Troisgros' salmon was an emblem of the moment, a sign of the times. It wasn't any one thing; it was the combination of all of them: the unusual cut of the fish, the quickness of the cooking, the inventive sauce, the dramatic plating and presentation, the excitement in the press.

Jean and Pierre Troisgros, Bocuse, Guérard, Vergé—all of the Bande à Bocuse were good friends, but they were also highly competitive. Each of them paid close attention to the others, noting who was cooking what, who had developed a new recipe or approach. They inspired each other but would never steal an idea. This was the absolute and unspoken code of honor among them: no plagiarism.

"We share a respectful creativity," said Guérard.

"Matisse and Picasso are not copied, they have their styles," said Senderens. "There is this same respect among us chefs."

Still—inspiration and homage were common enough. When Guérard saw the large plates the Troisgros brothers were using to serve their salmon with sorrel sauce, he wanted to use the idea for his own specialties. The style and drama of the large-format presentation was brilliant. And so he traveled to Roanne to visit the brothers in person. After lunch (of *escalope de saumon à l'oseille,* naturally), he asked: Would they mind if he also began using the thirty-two centimeter plates at Le Pot-au-Feu?

It was a matter of respect. Yes, of course, the brothers answered without hesitation. And a moment later they returned from the kitchen with a heavy wooden crate: twenty-four of the large plates, a gift from Troisgros to the Pot-au-Feu.

PART TWO

Fame

6

The Ten Commandments

The offices of *Le Nouveau Guide* were a spectacular mess: piles of books, magazines, and newspapers everywhere, empty wineglasses teetering on top; photographs, headline ideas, and page layouts stuck to the walls; telephones, typewriters, notebooks, and overflowing ashtrays on the desks. The rooms were in a rear apartment on a narrow street in the Latin Quarter—rue Maître Albert near the Place Maubert. Henri Gault and Christian Millau had launched their food and restaurant magazine in March 1969 with a tiny staff, all crammed in the small space. There weren't enough chairs, so they used old Bordeaux wine crates for extra seating.

Right from the start, the *Nouveau Guide* positioned itself in opposition to Michelin, pointing out great, lesser-known restaurants and needling overpraised favorites. "The Stars That Michelin Ignores" and "A Few Small Disagreeable Things About Paris Restaurants" were typical headlines. The writing was breezy, literary, and never self-serious, the magazine full of color photographs, line drawings, and opinionated capsule reviews and roundups—"Our 200 Favorite Bistros in France for Less Than 20f" and the like. A cover story on Paris nightlife was illustrated with a topless dancer and psychedelic starbursts; another explained how to mail order specialty food items. The magazine published letters from readers, along with pointed replies from the editors—long discussions about what was in fact the best bistro in Lyon, about restaurant price markups on wine and bottled mineral water, about the safety of vacuum-packed smoked salmon.

Gault and Millau were determined to take on the sclerotic, Olympian hegemony of the annual Michelin guide, in which anonymous "inspectors" awarded (and sometimes removed) the all-important stars with no explanation. Indeed, there was no writing in the Michelin guide at all, only stars, addresses, phone numbers, and prices. No photographs, only maps. In rare cases, a list of specialties.

"Michelin is mute," Millau declared, "while we are talkative."

The *Nouveau Guide* was modern, of the moment, and full of color. "We don't belong to the same France as Michelin," the editors said. "We're responding to a new need. The restaurant is an element of modern leisure and culture, as much as weekends and holidays at Club Med." Gastronomy was a pleasure to be discussed—like love and romance—not a dogma to be upheld. The hierarchy of Michelin stars did not reflect "real France" but rather "official France, conventional and fixed in its mayonnaise," wrote Millau.

> Michelin pretends to give stars only to the cooking, but in reality, it is the decor, the comfort, the style, and the clientele's degree of opulence that are determinative. Having an infinitely less "proper"

> idea of France and of the French, we think that culinary talent has nothing to do with the quality of a tablecloth or the presence of a parking valet. Why is a saddle of rabbit any less good served on oilcloth than on fine linen? Why shouldn't there be as much talent in a small restaurant as in a big one?

Gault and Millau were not alone in their criticism of the Michelin guide—many restaurateurs agreed, and even the traditionalist defender of the "Glories of French Cooking" (that was the title of his newest book, published in 1971), Robert Courtine, had recently said in *Le Monde*: "The truth is that, little by little, Michelin has let itself go judging not only the food on the table but the setting, the comfort, the luxury, becoming unfaithful to itself and to its own definition of the stars." A running joke in the *Nouveau Guide* was Michelin's obsession with the decor of restaurant toilets and washrooms. (It was common knowledge among restaurateurs that a three-star Michelin rating required maintaining deluxe bathrooms.)

The *Nouveau Guide* was generally unimpressed with the trappings of luxury and bourgeois propriety, the Christofle silverware and Baccarat crystal, and instead put chefs and their cooking at the center of the picture. The editors also put *themselves* at the center of the picture: Gault and Millau were the opposite of anonymous. They printed their names on the cover of the magazine in all capital letters, right under the title. They made themselves a brand: "Gault-Millau," a duo, inseparable. Soon they were receiving mail addressed to "M. Gohetmillo."

The story of French cooking was an ongoing drama in the pages of the magazine, chefs rising and falling, new dishes and ingredients coming in and out of fashion, the dining rooms of various restaurants serving as glamorous backdrops for the grand ambitions of young chefs and for the literary flights and amusing quips of the *Nouveau Guide*'s critics. And readers loved it.

Gault and Millau had been working together since 1961, first at the afternoon newspaper *Paris-Presse,* and now on their own. Neither had started out writing about food—they covered news and politics, sports and culture. But a weekly column about restaurants, written by Gault and edited by Millau, had taken off. One thing led to another.

They were the same age—both had just turned forty—and they made for an odd couple. Millau was small, nervous, full of ideas, talkative, and relentless. He arrived at the office early in the morning, and if he said he'd have a story written by 4 p.m., it was done at 4 p.m. Gault, on the other hand, was tall, self-confident, reserved, and a bit professorial. He was possibly the more elegant writer, but if he said he'd have a story written by 4 p.m., it was never done at 4 p.m. He strolled into the office in the late morning, unhurried, an apologetic smile on his face.

In any case, the magazine was an instant success. Gault and Millau released a new issue of the *Nouveau Guide* on the first Friday of every month, and copies sold out fast. The print run was expanded; advertising poured in. André Gayot, who'd also worked at *Paris-Presse,* took on the role of publisher, managing business affairs and leaving Gault and Millau to write about epic lunches and dinners at the restaurants of Paul Bocuse, Michel Guérard, the Troisgros brothers, and all the other rising stars of French cooking, capturing the spirit and energy—and personalities—of the new generation.

Gaston Lenôtre, the pâtissier, was described in an October 1969 profile in the magazine as the "Caesar of Chocolate Ganache." Ensconced alone in his test kitchen, he was reinventing his already successful pastry shop business and exploring a systematic rationalization and modernization of his techniques. "Innovations must be tested in the laboratory," Lenôtre explained, "not in front of the clientele. Cooking is math." Lenôtre was a proponent of using only the freshest ingredients—never frozen—and sourcing the best-quality butter (from Normandy and Charente), Avola almonds (from Sicily), and hazelnuts (from Piemonte) for his desserts. Lenôtre's signature was delicacy and lightness—his mousses and meringues were ethereal, his buttercreams and ganaches glossy and dense with flavor. It was all achieved, according to the article in the *Nouveau Guide*, with technical prowess and experimentation, although in the end, Lenôtre said, "I trust only my taste."

In the South of France, on the Côte d'Azur, Gault and Millau highlighted the glamorous cooking of Louis Outhier and Roger Vergé, whose restaurants stood out among the many mediocre, overpriced, resort-town tourist traps of the Riviera. Outhier's L'Oasis was in the village of La Napoule, on the outskirts of Cannes, on a road just opposite the harbor. The vast, shaded terrace encompassed palm trees and a fountain and was full of flowers, lush and exotic. Outhier, meanwhile, was rather austere, a slim, meticulous man who wore striped dress shirts and ties beneath his chef's jacket, and no toque. He smoked cigarettes, a rarity among chefs. Like Bocuse, he'd trained with Fernand Point. The *Nouveau Guide* described his cooking as "eliminating the slightest fault in taste, the slightest concessions to the clichés which, on the coast, so often serve as principles." Outhier's dishes were "uncompromising . . . made with products selected with maniacal care—*le loup en croute*, light, perfumed, topped with tarragon sauce and a puree of fresh tomatoes; duck pâté; turbot with truffle cream; langoustine with brandy and cream," all magnificent.

A fifteen-minute drive across town was Vergé's Moulin de Mougins, also on the outskirts of Cannes (in Mougins) but inland, in the hills. It was located in an old inn he'd recently bought and renovated, in 1969, "transforming within a few months what had been a mediocre restaurant into one of the best on the Côte d'Azur," explained the *Nouveau Guide*. Vergé was as gregarious as Outhier was reserved, dashing and handsome, with a large mustache and "velvet eyes and silver temples" reminiscent of the classic film actor Robert Le Vigan. His cooking was southern French, Provençal, and casual. "How can one resist the duck filets with foie gras, the chicken with green peppercorns, the stuffed artichokes *à la barigoule*, the admirable cheese, the exquisite pastries," the magazine asked. Julia Child was a frequent guest—she and her husband, Paul, had built a small vacation house in a village nearby and came to dinner when they were in France.

There was the thrill of great cooking and eating in the pages of the *Nouveau Guide*, and that thrill always connected to the essential character and personality of the chef—Lenôtre scientific and mathematical, Vergé seductive and charming, Outhier rigorous and intense. Of course, this sort of shorthand was reductive, but it made sense. The chefs of this new generation were no longer simply reproducing traditional, canonical dishes; they were putting a new spin on French cuisine, making it their own, making it exciting again. Their idiosyncrasies and obsessions were changing how France ate.

For Millau, it was Guérard who was the genius, the boy wonder of the Pot-au-Feu in Asnières. Guérard was always good humored, playful, and intelligent, and so was his cooking. When Millau asked the chef to describe his greatest ambition, Guérard had replied, "To cook like the bird sings!" Exactly, thought Millau, who wrote: "Have you ever heard a nightingale sing a false note? There you have the cooking of Michel Guérard. The clarity, the harmony, the tone always just right, the impression that everything goes without saying, and that it is all really that easy." Guérard's cooking was "astonishing, inventive, always changing, always delicate," the magazine reported, singling out his green bean salad with foie gras, the chicken breast with cucumbers, the ham roasted in hay, the pear tart, and, of course, the pot-au-feu. A large photograph of an impish, grinning Guérard accompanied the review, and the caption read: "M. Guérard, the greatest suburban chef in the world"—a small joke about his restaurant's out-of-the-way location.

Bocuse, unofficial leader of the rising generation of French chefs, was of course all over the pages of the *Nouveau Guide*, described as a "chef among chefs" and "an extraordinary natural talent," a man "dominating his métier and imposing his style," and the "new *monstre sacré* of Lyon." He was larger than life, already a legend. An article in 1970 celebrated his many famous pranks—sending an extravagant bouquet of flowers to the wife of a local judge, with a card signed with the name of a prominent local attorney. Or the time he sent a magnificent porcelain vase to a local politician, luxuriously packaged but smashed to pieces, with a card signed with the name of the man's fiercest rival. The idea was always to perplex the recipient completely, at least for a while. All would be revealed the next time he came to Bocuse's restaurant, amid shouts of laughter.

Bocuse's cooking was confident and charismatic, infused with reverence for the freshest ingredients. One of the great lessons he had learned from Fernand Point those many years ago at La Pyramide was not to overcook his vegetables, which sometimes confused his guests. A letter to the *Nouveau Guide* complained:

> I ate very recently at Bocuse and had marvelous *tournadoes à la moelle.* But they were accompanied by green beans "painted" far too green in my opinion for them to be natural. I believe you should draw M. Bocuse's attention to this, because it is disagreeable to see, and certainly wrong.
>
> M. Mouchet, Paris (9e)

To which the editors replied:

> You are going to give Paul Bocuse a heart attack. "Painted" green beans, good lord. If they are too green, dear Monsieur (and so good), it is because they are cooked very little. Please don't make us believe that the French have forgotten the true taste of vegetables.

The voice of the magazine was authoritative but always conversational. Indeed, just as they turned the chefs they wrote about into characters—personalities—so Gault and Millau did the same to themselves. This was the style of the 1960s New Journalism, to write yourself into the stories you were telling, to bring literary craft to reportage. (An old friend of Millau's, Antoine Blondin, wrote brilliant, minutely observed stories for the sports newspaper *L'Équipe* about the Tour de France, for example, turning the annual bicycle race into a grand epic.) Gault was overweight, he noted wryly, unlike his mysteriously svelte coeditor Millau, and so he signed himself into a weight-loss clinic in Crans-sur-Sierre, Switzerland, in the fall of 1972. "Ten Days, Seven Kilos Lighter" was the headline above the lightly comic reportage, in which Gault wandered the halls of the clinic, bewildered, contemplating the many, many decadent restaurant meals in his past and his current abject deprivation. "I ask of you only one effort," the young doctor said to Gault, "that of making none. Let yourself be carried away by the wave. In a few days, you will pass through a period of depression."

The doctor turned out not to be a medical doctor at all, but a former journalist turned diet expert named Christian Cambuzat. He took great interest in Gault's recommendations for the best bistros of Lyon, writing down names and addresses even as he gently enforced Gault's strict daily regimen of very tiny meals and great quantities of mineral water and tea with honey. In any case, Gault left the clinic fifteen pounds lighter and turned it all into an entertaining story for his readers.

Millau, meanwhile, apprenticed himself in the kitchen at the

Troisgros brothers' restaurant in Roanne, marveling at the apparent chaos and total precision of the operation:

> Everything seems to be done at the same time, and according to silent laws that escape me. While he slices the thrush terrine, Pierre has one eye on the other end of the room, on the grilled bread, and, when a moment later he cuts the two escalopes from a piece of salmon and passes them to Jean for sautéing, finds a way to observe at the same time that George has cut his strips of truffles poorly, that Christian has dredged too much flour on the frog legs, and that we have forgotten to feed the dog.

Pierre was the voluble, cheerful leader of the kitchen, Jean the serene and talented older brother, and Millau had joined the cheerful gang of commis—assistant cooks—and struggled to keep up, peeling potatoes far too slowly as he watched the astounding orchestration of each element of multiple dishes as the orders came in, all coming together at the last moment on the plate.

After four days in the kitchen, Millau was exhausted. "Grand cuisine is fascinating, but it's also as tiring as a marathon," he wrote. "Well now," the brothers said, "you're leaving already? Too bad—we were just starting to get used to you!"

Gault and Millau had become friends with their subjects, cheerleaders for their favorite chefs and restaurants, and the premier chroniclers of the French culinary scene. They rose in stature as critics and commentators just as their friends gained fame in their kitchens. And they were the first to realize that all the food they ate, and all the restaurant news they reported, and all the quirks of personality that drove chefs to create their signature dishes, that all this was part of a larger story. Gault and Millau had connected chefs and restaurants to the new and changing France, the popular culture.

At the Cannes film festival in May 1973, Ingrid Bergman handed out awards from a bare stage in front of a raucous crowd, accompanied by Diana Ross (whose film *Lady Sings the Blues* had opened at the festival) and other members of the jury. The mood was countercultural: The druggy surrealism of Alejandro Jodorowsky's *The Holy Mountain* was the talk of the festival; the jury prize went to Jean Eustache's *The Mother and the Whore*, in which young Parisian lovers smoked cigarettes and discussed post-1968 politics at Les Deux Magots café and found themselves embroiled in a love triangle. And then there was Marco Ferreri's *La Grande Bouffe*, a satire of bourgeois consumerism in which four friends spent a weekend preparing very extravagant meals and eating themselves to death. The film was overloaded with food, comical quantities of wild boar, venison, lamb, guinea fowls, sides of beef, and many dozens of chickens.

"My friends and I have gathered for a gastronomic seminar," Philippe Noiret explains to one of the women (most of them prostitutes) the men have invited to dinner, gesturing to his friends Marcello Mastroianni, Ugo Tognazzi, and Michel Piccoli. Soon enough, the film descends into grotesqueries—an unrelenting indictment of curdled gourmet decadence. By the end of the film, they're all dead.

Audiences and critics were shocked. The Cannes crowd jeered

and booed loudly. "I am ashamed to be French!" shouted one woman repeatedly after the screening.

"I hardly dare to talk to you about the *Grande Bouffe*, a filthy and scatological film," wrote the critic for *Télé 7 Jours*. *Paris Match* declared: "Shame on the producers of this film, shame on its director, shame on the actors who have agreed to wallow in snooping snouts and growling with pleasure in such mud that will never stop sticking to their skin." "What Makes 'The Grande Bouffe' Different from a Porno Movie?" asked *The New York Times* in a headline.

And yet, for all its titillation, *La Grande Bouffe* resonated. The film was a frontal attack on the sanctity of the French haute bourgeoisie, on snobbery and self-satisfaction. It was a rambunctious satire, and the venerable edifice of French cuisine—French gastronomic tradition—was the butt of all the jokes. In a way, the film made the same point as the new generation of chefs shaking up the culinary establishment, rejecting snobbery and unthinking tradition.

At least, that's how Yanou Collart saw it. She watched the film at its Cannes premiere in the theater on the Boulevard de la Croisette, just opposite the beach, and felt it spoke to the current moment. Food and cooking had become part of the cultural-political conversation, as much as movies, clothing, and rock and roll. In her mind, Michel Guérard and the Troisgros brothers were as "countercultural" as the film directors Jean Eustache and Marco Ferreri.

In the theater, Collart sat between the French sculptor César and the singer and actor Yves Montand. She was working the festival, as she often did, hired to manage the publicity for various producers, arranging dinners, parties, and events. Her public relations business was booming, encompassing film, music, fashion, theater, and, of course, restaurants. Her clients included Jean Castel, whose private club Castel on rue Princesse was a mainstay of glamorous Paris nightlife; the first French "rock opera," *La Révolution Française*, from Alain Boublil and Claude-Michel Schönberg, who would go on to write *Les Misérables*; and American fashion designer Vicky Tiel, whose skintight jumpsuits were featured in the 1965 comedy *What's New Pussycat?* and whose latest collection Collart planned to present as the "New Tango in Paris," borrowing her theme from Bernardo Bertolucci's controversial and erotic 1972 film, *Last Tango in Paris*.

Collart had recently begun a love affair with Lino Ventura, a bona fide movie star who played gangsters, toughs, and detectives—and who was also married. They were reasonably discreet, meeting in hotels and restaurants (long lunches at Roger Vergé's Moulin de Mougins, for example), but the press did not cover the personal lives of celebrities as a rule, so they were safe. They were in love! She visited Ventura on set (he was always filming), and his connections in the European film world would prove useful to Collart.

She was on the move, living the life. From Cannes to Marrakech to Paris to Berlin. In her home office in Paris on rue François Premier, the phone was always ringing. (It was exceedingly difficult, because of typical French phone company intransigence, to add another telephone line, so, for the time being, she made do with one. Her clients were frequently confronted with a busy signal.) She bought an old Rolls-Royce Silver Cloud (practically an antique, it was the 1956 model but ran well enough) and drove herself around town, a young woman flamboyantly on the make.

When Ventura saw the car for the first time, he was amazed. "But who drives this thing?" he asked, wondering if she had a chauffeur. The Rolls was enormous.

"I do," she replied, laughing, sliding behind the wheel.

She was making a name for herself. And restaurants and chefs were a key to her public relations business, even as it expanded. Everyone wanted to eat in the best restaurants. Everyone wanted to meet the chef.

She'd recently been introduced to Dena Kaye, for example, daughter of Danny Kaye, the comic actor and singer. "Yanou, you must meet my father," she'd said forcefully—he loved food and cooking, apparently. "He will adore you!"

Kaye was a star of the 1940s and '50s—playing the lead in *The Secret Life of Walter Mitty* in 1947, *Hans Christian Andersen* in 1952, and opposite Bing Crosby in 1954's *White Christmas*, among many other films, not to mention countless Broadway, radio, and television productions. He was an icon in Hollywood, and well known enough even in France that fans stopped him in the street. He had a mop of red hair, a big nose, and an easy smile. And it turned out his interest in food was real: When he called on Collart after arriving in Paris on a trip in 1972, he asked for a personal tour of a farmers' market.

It was a Saturday, and she drove them west out of the city, to the market in Vaucresson, Kaye criticizing her driving and joking the whole way. He was a flirt, but Collart was used to that. When they got to the market, Kaye stopped at every stand and vendor, tasting samples, asking detailed questions about vegetables and cheeses and local specialties, with Collart translating nonstop. He was insatiable, and soon followed by a crowd of onlookers and autograph seekers.

Kaye quizzed her about the latest restaurant news: Was Maxim's still the place to go? Who were her favorite chefs? What were her favorite dishes? Did she like to cook herself? He loved to cook, he said—especially Chinese food. And how about lunch? He was hungry, and proposed they eat at Le Coq Hardi, in Bougival. This was a classic, old-school place, founded in the nineteenth century and popular ever since, with multiple dining rooms and magnificent terraced gardens on the Seine.

Well, said Collart, how about something entirely different? A tiny, unassuming restaurant in Asnières, surrounded by factories—but très chic? Michel Guérard's Pot-au-Feu, she said, was one of her favorites.

They arrived at Le Pot-au-Feu at 2 p.m. and stayed all afternoon. The two witty men hit it off immediately, Guérard cooking, Kaye eating, Collart eating and translating, all of them discussing the dishes in great detail. Guérard's puff pastry was a revelation, and Kaye wanted to know exactly how to make it. The key was the meticulous incorporation of cold butter into the dough, folding it into thirds and rolling it out a total of six times, creating the delicate layers of crisp pastry. Guérard used the pastry in many of his appetizers, accompanying asparagus, scallops, and crayfish.

They ate a simple lunch of duck breast with turnips, which were small and sweet, sautéed in butter and a pinch of sugar. Dessert was honey ice cream with raspberry coulis. So much better than vanilla ice cream, they all agreed, and the raspberry sauce was a vivid counterpoint.

The meal was, for Kaye, a new kind of restaurant experience, absent all formality but rigorously precise. The youthful, energetic, casual glamour of both the restaurant and the chef was compelling. It made perfect sense that a Hollywood celebrity should be found here in Asnières rather than at Maxim's or any other such place.

He vowed to come back soon. He wanted Guérard to teach him to make the puff pastry dough himself.

In October 1973, Gault and Millau threw down the gauntlet.

The cover story in that month's edition of the *Nouveau Guide* was illustrated with a drawing of a chick bursting out of an egg; it wore a small chef's toque and was crowing the words "Vive la Nouvelle Cuisine Française" ("Long Live the New French Cuisine"), while a large hen, also wearing a toque, looked on with a dismayed, worried expression in its bloodshot eyes.

The illustration was comical, but the intent of the article was perfectly serious—to lay down a marker, to announce a new era, to define its terms, to announce its importance. And also: to give a name to the new style and philosophy of the kitchen. "Nouvelle cuisine" was born in this moment—it had been happening in restaurants since the late 1960s, it had defined itself among the Bande à Bocuse, but now, to the public, it had a name and true definition.

Inside the magazine, the same artist, the venerable Roland Sabatier, had fashioned a more explicit version of the quasi-revolutionary, new-generation message, an image of a fat chef lying on his back, dead or dying, while a young, slim chef stood above him with a triumphant foot on the old man's enormous belly, a smirk on his face, holding a sign stabbed into the dead chef's heart, announcing, once again, the title of the magazine's cover story: "Vive la Nouvelle Cuisine Française."

Out with the old, in with the new. Gault and Millau would be the proselytizers of the revolution in cooking. Just as the nouvelle vague—the French New Wave—had freed François Truffaut, Jean-Luc Godard, and Éric Rohmer a decade earlier to experiment with form and narrative convention, to shoot in a looser, improvisational style, to take cameras off tripods and use natural light, to engage the politics of the moment . . . so, too, Gault and Millau believed, nouvelle cuisine stood for the future of cooking. The *Nouveau Guide* would be the *Cahiers du Cinéma* of the French food world. French New Wave directors were auteurs and so, too, were restaurant chefs; nouvelle cuisine would stand alongside nouvelle vague cinema and nouveau roman books.

It was Gault who'd come up with the idea of a grand statement—a manifesto. He'd come into the magazine offices one morning with a single page of handwritten notes. "Here are our ten commandments!" he said, a wry smile on his face. He wanted to express the larger idea, the philosophy, of the new generation of French chefs. Just the previous month, in its September issue, the magazine had published a story headlined "The Bande à Bocuse Awakens Great French Cuisine," with a group photograph of the men in question posed in a wine cellar, a "mafia of good taste and a lust for life," all in their chef's whites and tall toques: Bocuse, Guérard, the Troisgros brothers, Vergé, Lasserre, Chapel, Outhier, Lenôtre, and other members of Bocuse's Grande Cuisine

Française. But for Gault and Millau, nouvelle cuisine went beyond the personalities of these newly famous chefs. It was a challenge to the establishment.

"We are not iconoclasts," wrote Gault and Millau. "We defend, with even some bad faith, certain glorious old restaurants whose downfall would be far too painful." Nouvelle cuisine was not an attempt to discard history, or insult the great gourmands of the past, like the bon vivant Curnonsky, the iconic food columnist so influential in the first half of the twentieth century. The editors wrote:

> But it is precisely this image of the bon vivant, fat and corpulent, a napkin tied around his neck, dripping with veal gravy, béchamel, and vol au vent, honored and decorated by professional food and wine associations, Bacchic and an oenophile, the loud, drunken singer and enthusiastic groper of waitresses that we would like to erase from memory. They are repugnant and we are not afraid to say that these people do not know how to eat.

Gault and Millau might well have been describing the overstuffed characters in *La Grande Bouffe*; the editors scorned the rich, heavy sauces and overcooked "papier-mâché-like fish" and "jellied meats" still found in respectable restaurants and prescribed in cookbooks. The Bande à Bocuse was remaking French cooking, and Millau's ironically grandiose "Ten Commandments" would codify the disparate elements of the culinary moment:

FIRST COMMANDMENT:

Shorter Cooking Times—for most fish, all crustaceans and shellfish, for red meat, and certain green vegetables.

SECOND COMMANDMENT:

Utilize New Ingredients—shop at the market and cook what is fresh and in season; seek out fresh and high-quality products from around the world.

THIRD COMMANDMENT:

A Shorter Menu—fewer choices, all fresh and cooked to order. The happy elimination of the bain-marie and its day-old, lukewarm sauces.

FOURTH COMMANDMENT:

Do Not Be Dogmatically Modern—embrace technology and refrigeration, but be aware of the danger of frozen seafood, for example, which ruins flavor.

FIFTH COMMANDMENT:

Embrace Avant-Garde Techniques—precision stoves and ovens, blenders, mixers, nonstick pans, all the tools of the modern kitchen.

SIXTH COMMANDMENT:

Abandon the Hanging and Marinating of Meat—these are sad methods of food preservation.

SEVENTH COMMANDMENT:

Avoid the Terrible Rich Brown and White Sauces—they are inane and mediocre. Better to use reductions, fumets, butter and cream.

EIGHTH COMMANDMENT:

Don't Ignore Diet and Health—lightness and freshness are paramount.

NINTH COMMANDMENT:

Avoid Overdecoration and Overcomplication—food should look and taste like what it is.

TENTH COMMANDMENT:

Pursue Constant Invention—use your imagination. There is no sacrilege. Nothing is forbidden.

The style of cooking prescribed in these commandments, they hastened to explain, was nothing they had invented, but rather a description of the cooking of the new school of French chefs. The magazine was merely outlining a new ethic, a new aesthetic.

Dishes should be both simple and original, the ingredients fresh and cooked quickly. Menus should be short, and always changing, based on what was fresh, and the chef's inspiration. Food should be healthy. Stews and braises were out; poaching and steaming were in. Heavy, flour-thickened sauces were banished. Fish was seared quickly—like the Troisgros brothers' famous salmon—and served with vegetables pureed in a newfangled Robot-Coupe machine. The food was lighter.

More than anything else, though, what animated nouvelle cuisine was a sense of freedom, the license to invent, to discover, to experiment. New combinations sprang up, like crab with pineapple or baked fish with apples, for example, served at Jean and Paul Minchelli's Le Duc, in Paris, a seafood restaurant much admired by Gault and Millau. Le Duc also served various raw and marinated fish dishes, sushi and ceviche-inspired scallops, herring, sea bass, and sardines. Troisgros also served raw fish—salmon cured with coriander seeds—and so did Bocuse. Guérard made a pot-au-feu with duck instead of beef. New (or at least rediscovered) ingredients were all the rage, from green peppercorns to ginger to star anise and seaweed. Fruit was put in salads alongside foie gras and shellfish. At Moulin de Mougins, Roger Vergé served warm spiny lobster with his green salad and chervil sauce, mixing warm and cold ingredients in the same dish.

Yes, in recent years, and especially post-1968, young French chefs had liberated themselves from classic haute cuisine, from the drudgery of the tournedos Rossini and the duck à l'orange. Indeed, the very terminology of French cooking was being altered—pâtés, terrines, sausages, and rillettes were now suddenly being made of fish and vegetables. There was of course the Troisgros "escalope" of salmon. Jacques Pic, meanwhile, served a "boudin" sausage made of pike at Maison Pic in Valence; the Troisgros brothers were also turning out vegetable "terrines" of all kinds, as well as a lobster "navarin," the term for lamb stew; and at his namesake restaurant outside Lausanne, Frédy Girardet served a "fricassee" of scallops with endives, limes, and ginger.

The inventive, auteurist art of nouvelle cuisine extended to its presentation, with chefs paying close attention to the arrangement of the food on the plate. Jean and Pierre Troisgros had led the way with their salmon on its enormous plate. They had poured the sorrel sauce beneath the salmon rather than over it, creating a pool of color and contrast. This approach (as well as the large plates) was spreading everywhere.

Gault and Millau had touched a nerve. The ideas of nouvelle cuisine, percolating in the kitchens of young chefs and in the pages of the *Nouveau Guide* for a few years already, now crystallized with the publication of Gault and Millau's ten commandments. "Vive la Nouvelle Cuisine Française" was a story everyone could understand, and everyone had an opinion about.

"Nouvelle cuisine" had inserted cooking into the cultural conversation and made chefs (or some of them, anyway) into a new kind of celebrity. The face of the movement would be Paul Bocuse. He embraced the moment, describing his dishes in typically rakish fashion as being like a "slender young girl in a see-through blouse" compared to the "heavily corseted 1900s beauties" of Escoffier's classic French cuisine.

The French loved to talk about their food, and so did the rest of the world. French haute cuisine was the pinnacle, the standard, and it was undergoing a transformation. Nouvelle cuisine had arrived in the spotlight, and was ready to go international. But there were still some barriers that no one was willing to break.

7

Cuisine de Femme

The restaurant on rue Montparnasse was tiny, crowded, smoky, and loud. There were only twenty-eight seats in the place—music blaring, waiters rushing around, the sidewalk outside crowded with people hoping to enter. This was Olympe, a new Paris hot spot, on a fall night in 1973. The Rolling Stones' latest single, "Angie," number one on the French charts, was playing on the radio; the restaurant was open later than most in the city, until 1:30 a.m., and cultivated an atmosphere of chaotic, bohemian intimacy. In the kitchen in the back of the narrow room stood Olympe herself, the chef for whom the restaurant was named, the star of the show. She wasn't dressed like a chef, however—she wore a short skirt and chic Maud Frizon high-heeled shoes, her dark hair in a short bob, and needless to say, no toque on her head. She was twenty-three, and beautiful, and her cooking was the talk of the town.

It had all happened so fast: from idle, late-night conjecture,

Olympe and her husband, Albert Nahmias, dreaming of their escape from the doldrums of student life and academia, to this improbable, thriving success, a locus of food and pleasure on the Left Bank. The restaurant felt like freedom. Her legal, married name was Dominique Nahmias, but now she was the glamorous and single-named Olympe, reborn as a chef and restaurateur.

The Alsatian barber who'd sold them the storefront had lived alone in small quarters in the back of the shop, which was outfitted with a rudimentary kitchen. This was where Olympe now cooked; Nahmias had done the entire renovation himself—DIY bricolage, everything slightly crooked but straight enough—installing partitions and repainting walls. They found a console from the 1920s, which they set up as a bar, and secondhand tables and chairs. They had no money, but the retired barber was understanding. "No problem, just pay me when you can," he'd said, to their great relief.

Olympe cooked what she wanted. She had no formal training (she'd been in law school until a few months ago, after all), but she'd learned from her father, growing up in the small inn her parents opened after the war in the town of Méounes-lès-Montrieux, not far from Toulon in Provence. Her father had been a lawyer but loved to cook; for her thirteenth birthday, he'd given her a copy of Ali-Bab's *Gastronomie Pratique*, the early-twentieth-century culinary encyclopedia and cookbook—one of the founding texts of modern French cuisine, alongside Escoffier.

But Olympe didn't cook from that cookbook, or any other. She improvised dishes half remembered from childhood, and experimented with whatever ingredients she found in the early-morning market stalls at Les Halles. She cooked everything to order—there were no long-simmering stews on the menu. She avoided elaborate sauces (which she'd never learned to make anyway) in favor of minimalist reductions. She highlighted vegetables, in a terrine of zucchini and eggplant with fennel, tomatoes, apple, and mint, for example. Was it "nouvelle cuisine" she was cooking? She didn't care what it was called. It was hers—her style, her taste, her attitude.

Her *ecrevisse*—crayfish—were instantly popular, and soon became her trademark. She prepared them in different ways: poached in a court bouillon and served with crème fraîche and cayenne pepper; sautéed with curry and cream; roasted with tomato sauce and chopped herbs. She bought the shellfish in crates and cooked them alive to ensure maximum freshness.

Everything was presented as simply as possible. She loved exotic spices and new flavors, and sought out new ingredients and provisions at Le Monde des Épices, the only shop in Paris that sold Middle Eastern and Indian staples like coriander, cumin, preserved lemons, and Tellicherry peppercorns. She befriended one of the proprietors, Mme Izrael, and learned to make her own spice mix with curry and ginger and rubbed it over legs of lamb before roasting them. She made a spring salad of poached turnips, artichokes, carrots, and peas served with a lemon vinaigrette and a dash of paprika.

Olympe's freewheeling, improvisational cooking suited the moment and milieu—Paris Left Bank bohemian cool. The restaurant was soon filled with theater and movie people, artists, musicians, intellectuals, and students. Her youthful glamour announced a new kind of restaurant chef—self-taught, rebellious, liberated.

The image of the female chef in France had long been dominated by the so-called Mères Lyonnaises—the mothers of Lyonnais cooking: Mère Fillioux, Mère Guy, Mère Lea, Mère Bizolon, Mère Castaing, and most of all Mère Bourgeois and Mère Brazier. They were icons of traditional French cooking, dating back to the 1920s and '30s, when Brazier and Bourgeois had been the first women to be awarded three stars by the Michelin guide. (The term *mère* to describe a woman restaurateur dated back even further, to the late eighteenth century.) These women were by definition matronly, even grandmotherly. They wore long aprons and exuded formidable, well-fed traditionalism.

Olympe was the opposite of matronly. She represented a new generation, liberated from the old mores. She'd never been particularly political, but certainly the post–May 1968 atmosphere fostered a new sense of possibility. The women's liberation movement had gained momentum and notice; doors were beginning to open.

Olympe ran the kitchen with the help of two assistants. Nahmias, meanwhile, ran the front of the house, welcoming guests, and also handled the restaurant's suppliers. He had bread delivered every day by car from the South of France—better than anything to be found in Paris, he was convinced. He sought out underappreciated and less expensive wines from small producers. He found himself happily immersed in the day-to-day rush of running a small business—it was as if a huge weight had been lifted from his shoulders. He'd been unable to find an academic position as a sociologist, and his disconsolate search for work had now given way to frenetic action, the thrill of the restaurant.

Nahmias had been born into a large Jewish family in Morocco, and they'd moved to the South of France when he and his siblings were children. (His parents had grown up in British-occupied Palestine and Egypt before settling in Morocco; the family eventually left Morocco during the postwar exodus from Arab North Africa, driven in part by antisemitic violence.) They were immigrants in France—outsiders. And even though Nahmias was soon perfectly assimilated, he remained aware of subterranean currents of prejudice. It was unspoken for the most part, hidden: a sense of not quite belonging, particularly when it came to elite institutions and academia.

But he and Olympe were making their own way now, unburdened by history or tradition, refugees from bourgeois propriety, from the world of schooling and credentials. Olympe was cooking what she wanted, and so what if she'd never done a "stage" or trained in any formal way. And for Nahmias, the politics and prejudices and insularity of the university were now in the past. They were restaurateurs, embracing the late-night energy of the city.

And yet: Even amid the din of laughter, music, and the clatter of dishes in the one-room restaurant, Nahmias heard the whispers. Beware, he was told. Was it a fellow restaurateur, or a supplier, or a journalist who told him? The fact that he was Jewish was no secret, and there were some, he was told, who might hold that against him. Look down on him in some way.

He couldn't care less, he said. Why should he? He'd been around long enough to know how some French people thought of Jews, and to hell with them.

But there was more to the story. Yes, of course, antisemitism existed; that was not the point. No—the rumors, the whispers, were about a specific group of people, a cadre of powerful figures in the culinary world who held antisemitic beliefs. They were former collaborators, supporters of the Vichy regime during World War II, and now members of the gastronomic establishment. One of them, indeed, was the most powerful restaurant critic in France: Robert Courtine of *Le Monde*.

Could this be true? Nahmias wondered. After all, *Le Monde* was the apotheosis of the postwar French liberal establishment, founded in 1944 in the wake of the liberation of Paris from the Nazis, and edited from then until his retirement in 1969 by Hubert Beuve-Méry, who'd been a prominent member of the French Resistance. Why would he hire a onetime collaborator? Courtine had been at the newspaper since the early 1950s, and Beuve-Méry would have known, surely, about Courtine's wartime history.

Ah, but here was the murky reality of France in 1973. The war and its aftermath had long been subject to a kind of willful, uneasy forgetting, a conspiracy of silence and amnesia. Amid the postwar economic boom and Gaullist national unity, the sins of collaboration had receded into the fog of the past. Soon enough, it seemed that every Frenchman recalled being a member of the Resistance thirty years earlier.

Still, the information circulated, true or not. Beware Courtine.

Nahmias kept his head down. He and Olympe had found success, and no critic, former Vichy collaborator or not, could change that. Or so he hoped.

And in any case, Nahmias and Olympe would soon have a chance to meet the man and see for themselves. Courtine was coming to Olympe. The *Le Monde* critic had made a dinner reservation for the following week.

They were under the radar, ignored by the press. The new generation of women-run restaurants springing up around France got none of the breathless attention the men of the Bande à Bocuse did. It wasn't that the press was hostile, but rather that the conversation about haute cuisine and gourmet restaurants was inevitably and unquestionably centered on men—the inheritors of Escoffier's legacy, all in their tall white chef's toques. But while there were no front-page articles, the reviews—and the Michelin stars—were coming.

In Vervins, in the north of France, Annie Desvignes had spent the previous two years renovating the ramshackle manor house she and her husband had bought near the center of the small town. The Tour du Roy was an imposing structure, with turrets and spires, dating back to the twelfth century. There were twenty-two guest rooms and a large dining room with views of the green landscape and rolling hills in the distance. It was the perfect setting for a small hotel and restaurant—at least once they managed to get heat and electricity installed. The work was arduous, expensive, and never seemed to end.

Annie's husband, Claude, had attended hotel school, and he ran the front of the house, while Annie ran the kitchen. Her cooking, learned mostly from working with her mother at the family restaurant, was easygoing, and for the most part, she cooked to order: turbot poached in milk with a sorrel sauce, dorade fillets with tomato sauce, sautéed sweetbreads. She was known for her terrines and pâtés, all house made, and also for her desserts, including the tarte à la Duflot, an apple tart named for the local man, M. Duflot, who sold Annie the Boskoop apples he grew in his nearby orchard.

The Michelin guide awarded her a star, and listed her terrines, her rabbit in cider, and her sorbet as specialties. She was thrilled to be recognized: A single star signified "a good restaurant in its class."

In Normandy, at the Tourne-Bride, Simone Lemaire also received a "good restaurant in its class" star from the thick, red, all-knowing guide, and she, too, was glad to be acknowledged. Her cooking relied on fresh ingredients—from her garden, from her freshwater pond. She did all her own shopping at local farmers' markets and purveyors, examining each cut of meat and fish, demanding the best.

Lemaire was self-confident and direct, and knew what she wanted. She roasted quail and poached turbot and improvised sauces. Her pan-seared filet mignon came with an orange reduction and pommes Darphin—fried grated potatoes, similar to Swiss rösti.

In Avignon, Élisabeth Bourgeois and her restaurant, La Férigoulo, received no stars from the Michelin guide but did earn warm reviews in the local press.

"*Je suis completement autodidacte!*" she would say proudly—she was completely self-taught. She wished she'd had real training in a restaurant kitchen, but that had never been an option. "It's not allowed," she marveled. "Women are not allowed to enter the kitchen." So she did things her own way, in the kitchen and in the dining room. The decor was haphazard, the dishware rustic, hand-painted. She could not afford Christofle silver or crystal glasses. The restaurant was in a former antiques shop, and succeeded in spite of her youth and inexperience.

"That will never work—you're crazy!" her husband said. "You only know how to cook your mother's gougnasse!" Well, we'll see about that, she replied. They'd married at eighteen and now had an infant daughter, but she was determined to make it work somehow.

She took what her mother had taught her (how to make terrines, sauces, all the basics of French cooking) and added her own ideas. Her Provençal bourride, a fish stew served with aioli, was made with scallops instead of the traditional monkfish or other white fish. The dish was astonishingly popular, as were her ever-changing daily specials.

Lemaire, Desvignes, Bourgeois, and other women like them were opening restaurants to respectful notice, managing small staffs rather than full kitchen brigades, serving happy customers, cooking creative dishes. But they found themselves relegated to what seemed a second tier of cooking. Theirs was not haute cuisine; it was "cuisine de femme," women's cooking. Venerable, to be sure—beloved even. But not the same category as the restaurants heralded in Gault and Millau's *Nouveau Guide* or awarded three stars in the Michelin guidebooks.

They were not professionally trained, after all—they were not members of the club, the fraternity. They were women.

The irony was all too plain. As women, they'd been excluded from apprenticeships and training "stages" at the best restaurants and had struck out on their own, taking risks, defying expectations. And yet it was the young, supremely well-trained men of the Bande à Bocuse who were lauded as renegades, the daring rule-breakers.

Annie Desvignes decided to take action. She was no radical or revolutionary, and she wasn't interested in politics. But it was a matter of fairness: Why was she as a female chef treated so differently than her male counterparts? She had opened her restaurant, the Tour du Roy, and made it a success. She had earned a Michelin star. Her cooking was widely admired. And yet the insular world of the French culinary establishment was off-limits to her.

She'd trained for a time with Raymond Oliver a decade earlier, but formal schooling and accreditation had been closed to her—an impossibility. The same was true for awards and prizes. Every four years Desvignes would see another handful of young chefs celebrated after winning the Meilleur Ouvrier de France competition, wearing the honorary blue, white, and red–striped collar with their chef's whites, photographed at the Élysée Palace with the president. They were always men—always.

It was a waste of time to dream of becoming an MOF, as the winners were called. The awards highlighted the most refined and detailed haute cuisine methods; Desvignes's rustic, ingredient-focused dishes would surely be scorned as unsophisticated. But what about membership in the trade organization Maîtres Cuisiniers de France? This was an organization founded in 1951 to promote French cuisine and heritage, to uphold tradition.

As Armand Froissand, the founder of the group, explained:

> The Master Chefs are above all established commercial cooks, who have set themselves the following goals: the maintenance and dissemination of the culinary art of our country, universally recognized as preeminent; encouraging young people to learn to cook, ensuring the continuity of the profession; the improvement of our craft, so essential to life. Our members are therefore above all tradesmen who wish to do better each day than the day before and whose ambition is satisfied when the client, on the basis of his judgment, appreciates the results of their skill and practice.

Annie Desvignes sent a letter to the Maîtres Cuisiniers, introducing herself and applying for membership. She received an immediate and rather pompous rejection letter: Women were not eligible for membership, it said, describing the organization as a "closed academy where the spirit breathes." The manly spirit, apparently.

Desvignes was angry but not surprised. What had she expected, really? Still, the contemptuous superiority of these men galled her. She upheld the tradition of French cooking as well as anyone. Why should she not be accepted as a member of the profession?

In this moment of frustration and indignation, an idea was born. If women chefs were to be summarily excluded from the "closed academy" of French gastronomy, Desvignes surmised, then what they had to do was form their own association. But how, exactly? She began writing letters to other restaurateurs she knew, even distantly, including Simone Lemaire in Normandy, outlining her plan and asking for advice.

She also sent a letter to Robert Courtine at *Le Monde*, describing her unfair rejection by the Maîtres Cuisiniers de France, and more generally the hostility of the French culinary establishment toward women. Courtine had previously written favorably about her restaurant, as well as others run by women chefs, and she hoped he might be sympathetic. She described her idea of forming an association of women chefs and asked for his help.

To her surprise, Courtine wrote back. She hadn't expected much. After all, Courtine was the most important food critic in France, and she was a little-known chef from Vervins with a complaint about the powers that be and a seemingly futile plan to launch a new, women-run restaurant organization. But Courtine offered his full-throated support. He had no patience or sympathy, it turned out, for the small-minded guardians of tradition at the Maîtres Cuisiniers de France. Courtine viewed women's cooking as a bedrock of the French culinary heritage.

He would gladly introduce Desvignes and her proposed organization to other women chefs. She should also write to Odette Kahn, the editor of *Cuisine et Vins de France*, the leading gastronomic publication. Kahn would surely be sympathetic—perhaps she could even help run the new association. And of course, once the group was officially launched, Courtine would certainly write about it in his columns in *Le Monde*.

When Robert Courtine arrived at Olympe on rue Montparnasse, he sat quietly at a corner table, ordered a single malt scotch, and looked around the room. He was trim, wearing a blazer and tie, and alert, observant, and polite. He was inconspicuous. He sat alone, and drew no attention to himself.

Olympe was in the kitchen, and Albert Nahmias was apprehensive. Here was Courtine, the all-powerful "Reynière" of *Le Monde*, rumored antisemite, about to order dinner, about to pass judgment.

The small restaurant was busy, as always, waiters rushing plates to tables, Nahmias pouring wine, clearing tables, and seating customers. He introduced himself to Courtine and received a polite smile in return, and suddenly Courtine stood up.

"All this food," he asked, still smiling, gesturing at the dishes on surrounding tables, "all this food is really being cooked by your wife, Olympe?"

"Yes, of course," Nahmias replied.

Courtine pretended to be skeptical. "No," he declared, half in jest. "It's you, isn't it? You are the chef!"

"I can't even cook an egg!" Nahmias protested, but now Courtine strode toward the back of the restaurant and opened the door to the kitchen.

Olympe was at the small stove, in the midst of the dinner rush. Courtine burst out laughing, introducing himself to Olympe with a stream of flirtatious compliments and jokes about her "kitchen boudoir," a reference to the restaurant's dim-lit intimacy.

It was clear he'd known perfectly well that Olympe was the chef; his questions about who was cooking were just a game, an amusement.

Back at his table, Courtine ordered Olympe's famous crayfish, served with an artichoke salad; the vegetable terrine; and the leg of lamb with caramelized onions. He ordered a bottle of wine. He seemed to be enjoying himself.

Nahmias watched from across the room, stopping at the table every so often. Courtine's sly, half-hidden smirk, his wry, arched eyebrow, his amused, knowing glances, the twinkle of superiority in his eyes—it was all enormously charming and intimidating at the same time. Was it his position as *Le Monde*'s powerful critic that infused his persona with a certain menace? Or was it his erudition and irony that softened his implicit threatening authority? Or was it both?

And knowing, as Nahmias did, the rumors about Courtine's collaborationist history only heightened this sense of danger. And yet: Nahmias liked him anyway.

And Courtine evidently liked Olympe too. In his column, he would soon describe her as the "youngest and prettiest of Parisian chefs," lauding her various crayfish preparations, her leg of lamb, her duck with fried zucchini, and her desserts as possessing "clarity and perfection, a rare and subtle wisdom. It would take nothing for me to dare to register Olympe on my list of *les grande* restaurants of Paris."

Olympe and Nahmias were over the moon. Their little Left Bank restaurant had been anointed. They were on their way.

8

The Slimming Diet

Two things happened in 1974 that would change Michel Guérard's life. The first was a seemingly mundane decision, made by an anonymous bureaucrat somewhere in the depths of the city planning office, that the rue des Bas in suburban Asnières needed to be widened. So dramatically widened, in fact, that Guérard's restaurant, the Pot-au-Feu, along with every other adjacent building on the block, was to be demolished.

By order of the government, then, the Pot-au-Feu would close its doors in June. The property had been expropriated. This was unwelcome news, to say the least: Business was strong, the dining room always full, and Guérard established as one of the most exciting young chefs in France. He'd been awarded his second Michelin star in 1972, he'd been lauded by Gault and Millau and other critics, and now what?

The second seismic event of 1974 for Guérard was that he had fallen in love. Her name was Christine Barthélémy, and she was thirty years old, beautiful, and highly accomplished. They'd met two years earlier at a nightclub, Regineskaia, where Guérard was overseeing the kitchen and menu. Ever since opening the Pot-au-Feu, Guérard had kept a hand in the nightlife business. He still stopped by the Lido, the cabaret where he'd gotten his start, and he'd befriended Régine Zylberberg, the singer and impresario of the iconic Chez Régine in the Latin Quarter.

Régine—known to all by her first name—was a regular at the Pot-au-Feu, and she'd convinced Guérard to help launch her Russian-themed cabaret on the Champs-Élysées, Regineskaia, attracting socialites, actors, and pop stars, the sort of place where you'd see Sammy Davis Jr. and Odile Rodin eating dinner together.

Guérard had never felt any inclination to settle down and get married—despite the inevitable and persistent urging of his parents. He liked his single, sleep-deprived, bohemian life; he still lived on the houseboat on the Seine by the Pont de la Concorde. But Christine had changed all that.

He'd received a telephone call out of the blue: "My name is Christine Barthélémy, and you were kind enough to welcome my young chef for a stint in your kitchen, and he was very happy with everything he learned." She wanted to thank him in person, she said, and so he invited her for drinks one night at the newly opened Regineskaia.

They hit it off immediately. Her long, slightly unkempt dark brown hair was parted in the middle; her eyes were serious. She was managing a small spa resort in Eugénie-les-Bains, in southwest France, she said—this was where the chef she'd sent to train at the Pot-au-Feu now worked. Barthélémy had attended HEC Paris, one of the best business schools in France, and worked for a bank in Mexico before joining her family business, which turned out to be thermal spas.

It didn't take long for Guérard to realize that Christine was unimaginably wealthy. How could she possibly be interested in him, a mere chef? She was the youngest daughter of Adrien Barthélémy, who owned five spa resorts in the South of France, and who had, more consequentially, founded a cosmetics and skin-care company called Biotherm, which made products originally derived from the plankton growing on the surface of the water at his first spa, in the French Pyrenees.

Biotherm had grown rapidly in the years since its founding in 1952, and Barthélémy and his partners had recently sold the company to cosmetics giant L'Oréal. He was now intent on expanding his spa resort business; Christine had taken charge of the smallest of them, welcoming guests for restorative baths in the Aquitaine countryside west of Toulouse.

Eugénie-les-Bain was in the middle of nowhere, Christine said, laughing—Guérard would have to visit sometime, to experience the calm of country life.

Two years after that first date, the unexpected had happened: He was thirty-nine years old, and for the first time in his life, he was serious about a woman—he was settling down.

Now, in the spring of 1974, with his restaurant slated for demolition, Guérard was at a crossroads. He was a rising star and suddenly, unexpectedly untethered. It was liberating, in a way—anything was possible.

His first instinct was to move from suburban Asnières to the center of Paris, and to take on a high-profile restaurant. This was the logical next step; he'd made a name for himself in the city, established a devoted clientele, and was at the forefront of a new generation and "nouvelle cuisine"—his stock was high. And indeed there were a number of grand old Parisian restaurants in dire need of culinary renovation. The rumors and speculation were immediate. What about Lapérouse, on Quai des Grands Augustins overlooking the Seine? Or Laurent, in its cream-colored nineteenth-century mansion by the Élysée Palace? Or even Maxim's, just off the Place de la Concorde?

All three were undeniably iconic, prestigious, dowdy, and threadbare. All three could, in other words, sorely use an infusion of Guérard's creative energy and cachet. But there were complications, financial and otherwise. Lapérouse, for example, he just didn't like at all. Guérard found the restaurant suffocating, with its low-ceilinged salons and old-fashioned, poorly placed kitchen. He wasn't interested.

The food and kitchen at Laurent, meanwhile, seemed fine when Guérard visited, but the service in the dining room was dismal. "You almost feel like you're in a school cafeteria," he said to Christine. This was a problem, as he would be contractually obligated to retain the entire staff were he to buy the place. Still, he thought he could make it work, particularly when his friend and fellow member of the Bande à Bocuse, René Lasserre, offered to send customers his way. Restaurant Lasserre was only a few short blocks away and was perennially overbooked. Another friend, the pâtissier Gaston Lenôtre, also offered to join Guérard in the bid for Laurent.

In the end, though, Guérard was outspent. The swaggering

French-English financier Jimmy Goldsmith bought Laurent, more or less on a whim, for four times what Guérard had offered. So much for that.

The Maxim's deal also fell through. After the proprietor of the landmark art nouveau property, Louis Vaudable, agreed to sell, negotiations stalled opaquely. There were endless discussions about the ownership structure and various shareholders and the value of the restaurant's vast wine cellar. Finally, according to Vaudable, there had been objections from some of the restaurant staff—they would refuse to work for "a *petit cuistot* like Guérard." True, he was short, but "little cook" was an insult. Who knew what the actual reasons were, but Maxim's would not be the site of his next chapter.

As Guérard's high-profile Parisian prospects crumbled, though, a new idea was germinating, courtesy of Christine. Why not come to Eugénie-les-Bains? He could join her in the ramshackle château turned spa hotel and take over the kitchen. Leave Paris and not look back.

The middle of nowhere. Escape from the politics, preening, and false promises of the city. The beauty of the lush, fertile landscape of southwest France. He immediately thought of other restaurants far afield from Paris. "Paul Bocuse has succeeded in Collonges-au-Mont-d'Or, and the Troisgros brothers in Roanne. . . . Why not Eugénie-les-Bains?" he said. "It may be my destiny."

This was not defeat, he told himself, but a new beginning.

Michel and Christine weren't married yet, but now they were partners. The hotel occupied a large estate in the center of

Eugénie-les-Bains, named for Empress Eugénie, wife of Napoleon III, who stayed there on her way to Biarritz in the 1860s. The four-story building was surrounded by gardens; the famous thermal baths were also on the property. The couple moved into a small château a few miles away, in a neighboring village. Château de Bachen, it was called—beautiful but dilapidated, and renovations would last for years, it seemed.

In the blink of an eye, in the summer of 1974, Guérard had moved from a houseboat on the Seine to a château in Gascony; from an overcrowded, celebrated one-room restaurant to a sedate and little-known resort hotel; from a kitchen the size of a closet to a kitchen so large it contained a fireplace taller than he was; from bachelorhood to cohabitation and imminent marriage. Everything had changed.

It took a while for Guérard to adjust. He felt as if he were "floating," he told Christine, and he reacted by working as hard as ever. Christine ran the resort with HEC-trained business acumen, and he focused his attention on cooking.

Here he was, in a "lost corner in the middle of nowhere," starting over. He found inspiration, first of all, in the local markets, among the suppliers and purveyors of fresh fruits and vegetables, meat and fish. Just as he had previously wandered around Les Halles in Paris in the early mornings, planning a menu based on what was in season, he now did the same in southwest France.

He added dishes to the menu designed to highlight what he found: a small plate of three delicate pastries, each filled with different and ever-changing seasonal ingredients; "les feuilletés légers de saison," he called them. A plate with three small salads garnished the same way—"les trois salades impromptue"—

mushrooms, chervil, green beans, foie gras, truffles, smoked fish, whatever struck his fancy.

As he'd always done at Le Pot-au-Feu, he amended and experimented with classic French dishes, finding ways to surprise his guests. He made scallop quenelles—a traditional preparation, gently poached mousseline dumplings—but hidden inside them was a light confit of lobster and carrots. He put the fireplace in the kitchen to use, roasting whole lobsters, infusing the tender meat with unusual smokiness. He planted an herb and vegetable garden behind the restaurant and served "small stuffed vegetables fresh from the garden."

Guérard had left his Paris clientele behind and now had to make a name for himself all over again. He was wary, most of all, of being seen as an arrogant, leather jacket–wearing big-city interloper, someone who didn't belong, cooking food people didn't want. Instead, he found diners open to his innovations and ideas, which they'd read about in the Paris press. His charm was undeniable; his food was delicious.

But there was a problem, he realized, a crucial adjustment he would need to make.

The clientele at Eugénie-les-Bains came to take the waters, for the curative benefits of the natural hot spring. They came for their health—and a good number of them suffered from rheumatism, or diabetes, or heart problems, or were overweight. They had been admonished by their doctors to eat healthy food, to lose weight. Not that Guérard's cooking was especially rich or heavy to begin with; his nouvelle cuisine was light and fresh compared to traditional French restaurant cooking.

Still: He watched with dismay as the orders came into the

kitchen with special requests for grated carrots and celery slices and other punitively minimalistic preparations. He decided to attack this circumstance head-on. At Les Prés d'Eugénie, as the restaurant was now called, guests would be offered something better than grated carrots. He would create a new, separate, dietetic menu.

Dieting spa-goers were his immediate inspiration, but the truth was Guérard had long been interested in diet and health. He'd read French biologist Lucie Randoin's studies of vitamins and nutrition, and followed recent debates about food additives and preservatives, topics of increasing interest in recent years. More directly, he had quite accidentally, purely as a lark, developed a "dietetic menu" a few years earlier in Paris, an experience that would now prove highly valuable.

One of his regular customers at Le Pot-au-Feu ran a hair salon on Avenue Montaigne for the celebrity coiffeur Antonio, known for his chic luxury. Antonio owned a Rolls-Royce, for example, which he sent to chauffeur favored clients from their homes to the salon. In 1968, he'd asked Guérard to design a menu of light snacks to be served at the shop—emphasis on *light*.

Guérard had sprung at the challenge in his hyperkinetic way. He was fully committed at Pot-au-Feu but always open to side projects, checking in at the Lido, talking with Régine about her nightclubs—why not a lunch menu for Antonio's glamorous, weight-conscious clientele?

He called the café-within-the-salon La Ligne—the Line—and devised a menu of small snacks, salads, sandwiches, lunch plates, and desserts. Except for the desserts, every item was listed with its calorie count—an unusual innovation: clear oxtail soup with sherry, hot or cold, 250 calories; tomato salad, 165 calories; grilled salmon with herbs, 285 calories; fresh Iranian caviar with toast, 250 calories, and so on. The menu was illustrated in mod 1960s style with the slim silhouette of a nude woman lounging at the top of the page, holding a glass of wine and taking a bite of what looked like a cracker, her hair in a perfect bouffant bob.

La Ligne had been an experiment. He'd learned that diet food could be luxurious and playful; he'd kept foie gras on the menu, for example (one serving, 1,200 calories), as a gesture of defiance and insistence on pleasure.

Now, at Les Prés d'Eugénie, Guérard set about redefining the genre, forging what he thought of as a "parallel cuisine," reducing sugar and fat without sacrificing taste. He called it "cuisine minceur"—slimming cuisine—and began developing recipes that were as refined and delicate as the haute cuisine preparations on the menu.

It was an interesting puzzle: to remove cream or butter or olive oil from a béarnaise sauce or mayonnaise or salad dressing, for example, and then attempt various substitutions. Fromage blanc turned out to be surprisingly useful in many cases—a mild, fresh cheese similar to crème fraîche or ricotta, and low in fat—and he used it to make mayonnaise and the perfect low-calorie salad dressing, whisked together with white wine vinegar, soy sauce, Dijon mustard, and fresh herbs.

Another area of exploration was in the realm of pureed vegetables, which Guérard used to add intense flavor and color to various sauces. He added small amounts of pureed carrots and onions to one of his fromage blanc mayonnaises, for example, and pureed mushrooms into both béarnaise and lobster sauces.

The vegetables could replace the traditional egg yolks, butter, cream, or flour in "binding" sauces and would be a mainstay in his cuisine minceur.

Guérard took to steaming and poaching chicken and veal—cooking "à la vapeur," as it was called, preparing delicate meat in a way that added flavor but no fat. He poached chicken drumsticks (bones removed and stuffed with morel and other mushrooms) over a marjoram-infused stock and served them with thinly sliced vegetables and a sauce made with pureed watercress, mushrooms, and fromage blanc. He baked sea bass covered with fresh seaweed and—in an homage to the Troisgros brothers—made a version of their famous salmon fillets, cooked for ten seconds per side in a nonstick pan and served with a low-calorie version of the sorrel sauce.

He was enjoying himself. To apply the same care, finesse, and invention in the service of low-calorie dishes as he did to any others made perfect sense. And indeed, when he thought about it, cuisine minceur was a direct outgrowth of nouvelle cuisine. The lightness, the novelty, the freedom from established culinary tradition—all were essential to Guérard's cooking, dietetic or not.

Guérard's low-calorie menu at Les Prés d'Eugénie was a hit. How big a hit, he could never have anticipated.

In the spring of 1975, Christian Millau came to the spa hotel for eleven days to write his version of the always-amusing food-critic-on-a-diet story for the *Nouveau Guide* (just as Gault had done a few years earlier at the Swiss clinic). He lost a total of fifteen pounds, the cover story proudly announced. "With dry bread?" he asked. "Not at all. On the contrary, I ate lobsters, thrushes, frogs' legs, ducks, and chocolate granita. You don't quite believe me? It is the truth." He went on to describe what he called Guérard's "real revolution" in cooking: "Thanks to his research and his talent, gastronomy and good health are no longer irreconcilable." To prove it, he listed the menus for three days of his daily diet regimen at the resort—a far cry from dry bread or shaved carrots:

MONDAY

Lunch

Crayfish salad

Grilled quail with garlic cream

Celery root puree with parsley

Apple stuffed with fresh fruit

Dinner

Fresh tomato tart with thyme

Sea bream with black pepper–infused sabayon sauce

Pear soufflé

TUESDAY

Lunch

Old-fashioned sweet onion tart

Duck breast slices with green peppercorns

Potato yams

Strawberry and melon salad

Dinner

Vine thrush soup

Roasted lobster with fine herbs

Soufflé of wild strawberries

WEDNESDAY

Lunch

Pâté of three river fish with tomato cream sauce

Cider-poached chicken with apricots

Poached meringue with mangoes

Dinner

Carrot cake with chervil

Sea bass cooked in seaweed with chopped tomatoes and olive oil

Onion marmalade with sherry vinegar

Warm apple tart

This was diet cuisine? Roasted lobster with fine herbs? Warm apple tart? Well, yes, it was, Millau reported. He asked Guérard about his recipes and their development, and delved into the science of metabolism, diet, and health. "I've embarked on a droll adventure," Guérard explained. "In the beginning, it was amusing, but it required such an effort that several times, I confess, I was tempted to give up." He explained his techniques, how he reduced fat, sugar, and calories while preserving taste and flavor. "For a chef," he said, "this is what's most interesting: constantly tending towards a lighter, healthier, more inventive cuisine. A cuisine for everyone and not just a cuisine for dieters."

Guérard's diet cooking received international attention too:

Indeed, American guests were an increasingly common sight in the little village of Eugénie-les-Bains. A few months after the *Nouvelle Guide* story, the chief food and restaurant critic of *The New York Times*, Craig Claiborne, arrived in town to report on the phenomenon of "slimming cuisine." The article was titled "A Practitioner of the New Cuisine Is Still Master of the Old."

> Within a very short span of time, this spa resort has attracted food enthusiasts from all over the world (mostly from the United States) to see what the young French chef, Michel Guérard, hath wrought with what is called la cuisine minceur, or slimming cookery.
>
> That style of cooking has been sanctified recently as a new cuisine that allegedly eschews all forms of butter, eggs, cream and sugar and has been hailed—mostly in American periodicals and in prose as rich and thick as crème fraîche—as the salvation of the gourmet belly.

Claiborne was duly impressed but found it hard to stick strictly with the diet menu. "In that this was our first meal in France in a long time, and in that we have hungered for months for fresh foie gras, we gave in to our baser instincts and appetite. . . . As meal followed meal during our stay, we cheated a good deal." He spent most of the article marveling at such decidedly non-minceur dishes as soft scrambled eggs piled with caviar and served in an eggshell; puff pastry filled with white asparagus tips and hollandaise sauce; and, of course, plenty of foie gras. The minceur dishes, meanwhile, were "quite obviously superior to any diet food" he'd ever eaten, he wrote—"tasty and quite palatable."

The review was a rave, suspicious of the over-the-top claims about cuisine minceur but rapturous about Guérard and his cooking. And if there was some confusion about the difference between nouvelle cuisine and cuisine minceur, that was only an advantage. Harnessing the power of health, diet, and weight loss to the innovations and inventiveness of nouvelle cuisine, Guérard had created a bona fide publicity bonanza.

It was only logical, then, that Guérard was asked to write a cookbook. Claude Lebey, who wrote restaurant reviews for *L'Express* and also worked for the venerable publisher Robert Laffont, approached Guérard with the idea, and soon enough the chef was collating his new recipes, working with a photographer, and preparing to publish *La Grande Cuisine Minceur.* Guérard was by no means the most famous chef in France, but Lebey had seen the potential of the idea. Enough with the typically sad diet recipes. Cuisine minceur was new—of the moment. The seeming contradiction between "grande" and "minceur" was an amusing provocation, Guérard thought. He wrote in the introduction of his own decision to lose weight:

> The beautiful and mysterious Christine, who perhaps had (already?) decided to marry me some months later, had sweetly murmured in my ear, "*Vous savez,* Michel, if you would lose some weight, you'd look great."
>
> What a shock! I realized that I had to get rid of this disgraceful fat, shed this *embonpoint* to win Christine's heart. . . . I began the Long March through fields of grated carrots and other such appealing delicacies that quickly make you sorry you ever saw the light of day and sadistically drive you to despair. . . .

> The punishment was too severe to be borne, some evasive action had to be taken. . . . But I had to solve it in a way that first of all pleased me, and this would entail modifying many of the entrenched practices of our *gourmand* heritage.

The book was published the following year, 1976, and immediately translated into a dozen languages. *La Grande Cuisine Minceur* was a global bestseller (the English-language title was *Michel Guérard's Cuisine Minceur*) and would draw clientele from all over the world to Guérard's restaurant in remote Eugénie-les-Bains. He had moved from the city to the country and now found himself a global celebrity chef.

Soon enough, *Time* magazine would come calling. They wanted to put him on the cover. And soon enough, too, a backlash was brewing. Cuisine minceur had crystallized certain elements of nouvelle cuisine—the small portions, the lack of cream and butter—that lent themselves to criticism and ridicule. "The vain snobbery of slimming cuisine" was how Robert Courtine described it in *Le Monde.* And as for nouvelle cuisine? "Not everything new is good, and not everything good is new." He did not approve.

9

Foreign Correspondents

The Americans were coming, and they were coming in droves. News of the nouvelle cuisine revolution in French cooking had reached sophisticated travelers, and they were booking tables at the anointed restaurants months in advance. Bocuse, Guérard, Troisgros, Senderens, Vergé—they were destinations, worthy of pilgrimage, the chefs' names imbued with totemic power. There was all the thrill of discovery—at tasting, at last, the famous saumon a l'oseille or salade gourmande—and there was also the undeniable cachet of returning from France and talking about what you'd tasted.

Such was the power of novelty, and public relations. Nouvelle cuisine chefs and restaurants had been the subjects of countless articles in French newspapers and magazines over the past few years, led by Gault and Millau's *Nouveau Guide*. Now the international press had caught hold of the story as well.

The first American journalist to report on the new style of cooking in France—even before Gault and Millau had named it "nouvelle cuisine"—was Raymond Sokolov in *The New York Times*. He'd just been named as the successor to Craig Claiborne, the legendary food editor who'd quit the paper to start a culinary newsletter. In March 1972, Sokolov published an article titled "In French Culinary Art: The Beginnings of a Subtle Revolution," calling the cooking of Bocuse and his compatriots "a radical simplification of the grand cuisine of the 19th century, the heavy, formal style of cooking codified by Escoffier." Sokolov described the light sauces and ungarnished, ingredient-focused cooking. He ate Bocuse's signature preparation, the loup en croute, which he said "glorifies the fish, concentrates the mind on one idea." At the Pot-au-Feu he ordered Guérard's foie gras, served "entirely unadorned, without aspic or truffle or even parsley," and at Archestrate was impressed by Alain Senderens's turnips in cider, which he called "a vegetarian triumph."

Eating out in France had become an adventure, Sokolov reported—a "voyage of discovery." Sure, the grand old Lasserres and Tours d'Argents were still grand, but the new generation of restaurants "hum with the excitement of revolutionary cells."

"It is a genteel revolution," he said, "spearheaded by a small number of young chefs who have moved up through the medieval system of apprenticeship that prevails in French restaurant kitchens." Sokolov was most taken with Bocuse, the leader of this new culinary avant-garde. At least in part, this was because Bocuse had mastered the art of being fun to write about—the key to success when it came to garnering good press. He was funny, energetic, and quotable. "Some men have mistresses," he told Sokolov, laughing, as he explained the high costs of his business, "I run a luxury restaurant." His actual mistresses went unmentioned, of course.

Bocuse also made a point of spending real time with any journalists who came calling. He took them into his restaurant kitchen, of course, but also on hunting expeditions, or to visit local vineyards. And invariably, he took them shopping. Sokolov described the experience:

> At dawn most mornings, this baldish, playful man of 46 puts on his suede jacket, gets into a blue Renault van and drives five miles to town to gather in the best of everything.
>
> In the open-air market along the quais, he finds organically grown vegetables picked by hand at local farms. The fish is spectacularly fresh. And, perhaps most important of all, each one of the half dozen wholesalers he visits does business early, so that Mr. Bocuse can supervise all his purchases himself and be back in the kitchen in time to preside over the preparation of lunch.

This scene—Bocuse the master chef trawling the Lyon farmers' market at dawn for the freshest ingredients for the day's cooking—would appear in seemingly every article written about him. In *Vogue* magazine, Quentin Crewe wrote at length of his 7 a.m. excursion with Bocuse: "For two hours he wanders round, choosing and rejecting, prodding and asking." In the *New York Times Magazine*, Waverly Root described his 6 a.m. trip with the chef: "He whips through the market with gusto, like a minor cyclone, sucking up food as he goes. In the time it would take you or me merely to stroll through the market, he emerges from the far end, his shopping finished." *Time* magazine found him at 5 a.m., "searching the local farmer's market for the freshest produce. He avoids supermarkets as he would canned soups."

Whether he was shopping at 5 a.m., 6 a.m., or 7 a.m., Bocuse—and nouvelle cuisine—had broken through in the American press. The New Wave of French cooking was a story, and the woman orchestrating all of the press coverage was, of course, Yanou Collart.

Collart's timing had been perfect. The early 1970s was a period of change and fluidity, in which the old rules of public relations were being rewritten to suit a new generation of actors, rock stars, fashion designers, and yes, restaurant chefs. Collart was at the nexus of press, glamour, and post-1960s French pop culture, and had caught on to the significance and cachet of the new generation of chefs early on. Bocuse, Guérard, the Troisgros brothers, Vergé, and Senderens were all celebrities, worthy of appearing on magazine covers and being interviewed on evening talk shows. Collart knew all the important journalists and radio and television personalities in Paris and, increasingly, the foreign press too.

She represented Bocuse's Association de la Grande Cuisine Française, meant to promote the new generation of French chefs—the Bande à Bocuse—as well as many of the chefs independently. She fielded calls from journalists looking for stories, and from VIPs looking for dinner reservations, and did her best to keep her clients in the limelight. But the sudden surge of interest from the US opened up new possibilities.

What about a press trip? An over-the-top, ultradeluxe, private jet gourmet tour of France for the American press?

The champagne producer Moët & Chandon, recently merged with cognac maker Hennessy, was eager to raise its profile in the States and offered to sponsor just such an expedition. The best restaurants in France, served up for a select group of American food journalists. The restaurant stops along the way would of course all be members of Bocuse's Grande Cuisine association. Collart set about recruiting participants, starting with Danny Kaye, the comic actor, food aficionado, and now good friend. Ever since she'd taken him on the tour of Paris markets and restaurants, he called whenever he was in town. She knew he'd keep the proceedings lively, and the trip would benefit from a bit of Hollywood star power.

Her next call was to Gael Greene, the restaurant critic at *New York* magazine. They'd met in 1971, when Greene was in Paris on assignment and hoping to wrangle a reservation at Guérard's Pot-au-Feu, which was fully booked six weeks in advance.

"When would you like to go?" Collart had asked immediately. "Tonight? Tomorrow? I'll pick you up at your hotel." A friendship was born. Greene was opinionated, amusing, and brash, and so was her writing for *New York*. She would certainly love to come on the weeklong culinary extravaganza. Collart asked her who else she ought to invite—high-profile writers interested in French food. Who came to mind?

Norman Mailer? Truman Capote? Tom Wolfe? John Updike? Greene tossed out the names of some of her literary heroes. None of them were available, it turned out.

Instead, boarding the plane to Paris, the first person she saw was Al Goldstein, the disheveled and amusingly sleazy publisher of the antiestablishment pornographic tabloid *Screw*. Somehow, some way, he'd finagled a ticket for himself and was now sipping champagne in the TWA first-class cabin.

"I'm not supposed to mention *Screw* on this trip," he told Greene, going on to say that he'd recently taken a wine course at the Four Seasons restaurant, that being the extent of his gourmet education. Of the dozen journalists invited on the trip, he said, "I'm probably fourteenth choice." He laughed.

Had Collart been desperate? Or had her daring, antipuritanical Gallic sensibility led her to imagine Goldstein as a kindred spirit? Perhaps both, and in any case it was a stroke of luck for Greene, always on the lookout for material. She was, loosely, a member of the so-called New Journalism tribe, inserting herself casually into her articles, finding the telling, ironic detail for her reporting, and here was Al Goldstein, the notorious publisher of naked paparazzi photos of Jackie Kennedy Onassis, sipping champagne en route to France. What could be better?

Also on the plane: Susan Schraub, a junior-level editor from *House Beautiful*; Jane O'Reilly, correspondent for the recently launched *Ms.* magazine; wine expert Alex Bespaloff, author of *The Signet Book of Wine*; Jackie Lewis, who worked for her brother Bob Guccione's *Penthouse*; *Rolling Stone* writer Timothy Ferris; celebrity photographer Dan Wynn; and Nora Ephron, who wrote for *Esquire* and *New York* and had just returned from covering the "Battle of the Sexes" tennis match between Bobby Riggs and Billie Jean King.

They were a motley crew, to say the least. According to Collart, some of the left-field invitations (representatives from two different sex magazines?) were the fault of Moët & Chandon, whose New York importer had sent them. But no matter. In late September 1973, they landed in Paris and began the most extravagant weeklong food tour imaginable.

The champagne was never-ending, and so were the truffles, and so was the foie gras. Every day, a new restaurant feast late into the night, and the next morning, a groggy brunch (with more champagne) and then a short flight to a new town and a new hotel and another dinner late into the night, and so it went, a gourmet press tour bacchanal that was also punishingly relentless. By the third day, Greene was in a permanent stupor, "never ever totally sober, groaning when the jet fridge yields more champagne . . . and drinking it."

They'd been divided into two small groups, each being flown around France in luxurious ten-passenger Mystère 20 jets. They flew to Biarritz, to Strasbourg, to Tours, to Cannes, to Lyon, crisscrossing the country for dinners at all the best restaurants, greeted every night by a different, beaming chef in his chef's whites: Charles Barrier, Roger Vergé, Pierre Laporte, Paul Bocuse, Jean and Pierre Troisgros, Paul and Jean-Pierre Haeberlin, Michel Guérard.

They ate Belon oysters and giant crab legs, roasted baby shrimp, and langoustines in a pepper and fennel broth at Le Duc in Paris, the seafood restaurant. At Vergé's Moulin de Mougins they ate a stunningly light cream of spinach soup made with almond milk, and an asparagus and sea bass terrine with mousseline sauce. At Troisgros they were served the famous salmon with sorrel sauce, of course, and also thin slices of seared duck liver with turnips. At Bocuse, roasted Bresse chicken with truffles, and an array of fresh green beans, cardoons, and a crayfish salad with mustard cream. At Guérard, Mediterranean sea bass steamed with seaweed and served with finely chopped fresh tomatoes, and puff pastry filled with lobster and sweetbreads with a bordelaise sauce.

There was far, far too much of it, but all the food was inventive and memorable. There was, of course, an epic abundance of foie gras and other traditional haute cuisine preparations and ingredients, but the unmistakable theme of the tour was novelty. A new generation of young chefs, and their embrace of new ingredients, influences, and techniques. For the American press, the excitement was palpable, and about more than food and cooking. What Gault and Millau were calling nouvelle cuisine signaled a larger shift in the culture, all the hedonism and idealism of the post-1960s moment, the rejection of bourgeois tradition, the glamorization of youth. The new French cuisine had sex appeal.

Greene's write-up of the trip in *New York* magazine a few weeks later was detailed in its descriptions of food and menus, the excitement over Guérard's use of seaweed and Vergé's use of almond milk and the Troisgros brothers' newfangled nonstick Tefal frying pan. But her travelogue was equally a testament to the new and slightly risqué glamour of French cooking—the attractive, flirtatious chefs, the late-night high jinks as champagne glasses were balanced into towers and off-color jokes about food and sex and seduction filled the dining room. She described Danny Kaye making eyes at the young editor from *House Beautiful*: "You could get pregnant just drinking this poire," he says. She described Al Goldstein hesitating to eat a pale-pink poached duck liver mousse. "Al, I am shocked," she quotes herself saying to the *Screw* editor.

"A man of your sexual sophistication ought to love this dish." Later, she declares: "Great food is like great sex. The more you have, the more you want."

This teasing, slightly debaucherous atmosphere was a sign of the times, one in which the chef had emerged from the kitchen and into the popular imagination as a creative, sometimes rebellious figure. At Guérard, at the end of the night, at the end of the weeklong tour de France, Greene writes: "There are musicians now—accordion, violin and noisy sing-along—but even in my semi-paralyzed state I know we have just tasted a triumph of taste and intellect."

The dean of the American culinary establishment was Craig Claiborne, who'd been the food editor at *The New York Times* since 1957, apart from his brief and unsuccessful stint publishing his newsletter, the *Craig Claiborne Journal*, in 1972 and 1973. By 1974, he was back at the *Times* and had recently met Yanou Collart in Paris, who promised to introduce him to her friends, the Bande à Bocuse, the chefs who were revolutionizing French cooking. Like everyone else, Claiborne was immediately and completely seduced by Collart's whirlwind of wit and charm.

In June 1974, she invited him to a grand dinner Bocuse was planning in honor of Mado Point, the seventy-five-year-old widow of Fernand Point of La Pyramide in Vienne, where Bocuse had been trained as a chef. Mme Point had been running the restaurant ever since her revered and hugely influential husband had died in 1955.

Point had been the most famous chef in France. A mountainous, larger-than-life figure who drank champagne for breakfast and had taught Bocuse, Pierre Troisgros, and Alain Chapel, among others, how to cook with seasonal ingredients, to respect freshness, and to undercook green beans so they remained crisp. Those fresh haricots verts were now a Bocuse trademark, and Bocuse himself had inherited the role of most famous French chef. The dinner for Mme Point was a moment for Bocuse not only to look back fondly but also to look ahead. The onetime students (many of whom were in attendance at the dinner) were now the well-established new generation, taking French cuisine to new heights.

Claiborne was seated next to Mme Point, who told him, as they drank champagne and ate Charentais melons filled with wild strawberries, and then smoked salmon and Caspian caviar with dill and mustard sauce, that Bocuse was the "fils spirituel" of her husband, Fernand. Claiborne was captivated; by the end of the night, he was enthralled.

Bocuse had served prime rib, roasted over an open coal fire, along with green beans, sautéed wild mushrooms, and Idaho potatoes. "But Idaho potatoes never tasted like this before!" one of the Americans at the table exclaimed, noting the rich cream and fresh tarragon that accompanied the dish. All the food, and all the wine, was marvelous. "I am madly in love with Paul," Claiborne said drunkenly to Collart on the drive back to his hotel late that night. "If I were twenty years younger . . ." Claiborne was more or less openly gay, and fond of this sort of amusing provocation. "Yanou, my dream is to make love to you," he said to Collart when they arrived at the hotel, "but I'm too tired. We'll do that tomorrow!" Instead, he asked for her help typing up his article for *The New York Times*. It was six in the morning by then, and Claiborne wasn't speaking too clearly. The meal was described in loving detail, and Bocuse in heroic terms:

> There are those who declare that Paul Bocuse is flushed with his own image, that he is an aggressive publicity seeker and self serving. As a matter of fact, he is one of the finest ambassadors both of France and his profession. He is a Gallic Ariel, an irrepressible clown who will dance on tables and at the climax of an evening toss champagne glasses into the air. He is also a gentleman, a highly complex human being who plays a calliope to amuse the world. He is an *enfant terrible* who doubtlessly wonders at times why the Lord chose him to wear such a heavy and responsible toque blanche.

Collart was delighted to have won over Claiborne to the cause of nouvelle cuisine; she could not have wished for a more powerful ally. With his help, the Bande á Bocuse would conquer America.

Indeed, the US was ready for nouvelle cuisine. Interest in food and cooking, in restaurants and at home, had been growing exponentially since the early 1960s, as Americans discovered better, fresher ingredients, and abandoned the tuna casserole and Jell-O salad clichés of the 1950s. Julia Child had debuted *The French Chef* on PBS in 1963; cookbook sales were skyrocketing, including Claiborne's definitive *New York Times Cook Book*, published in 1961. The Cook Book Guild book club distributed new titles to hundreds of thousands of subscribers every month. By the late '60s, Nora Ephron was poking fun at what she called "the Food Establishment" in an article in *New York* magazine, describing the inexorable rise of faddish dishes, all starting, she claimed, with the emergence of curry: "The year of the curry is an elusive one to pinpoint, but this much is clear: it was before the year of quiche Lorraine, the year of paella, the year of vitello tonnato, the year of beef Bourguignon, the year of blanquette de veau, and the year of beef Wellington." Everyone was talking about what they were eating. "Food became, for dinner parties in the sixties, what abstract expressionism had been in the fifties," Ephron wrote.

Now, in the 1970s, a new, countercultural element had emerged. Alice Waters launched Chez Panisse in a ramshackle, two-story building on Shattuck Avenue in Berkeley, California, in the summer of 1971, just around the corner from Peet's Coffee, which had opened a few years earlier. With a menu focused on fresh, seasonal cooking, Chez Panisse was a French restaurant, self-consciously informal in style and rigorous about locally sourced ingredients. Waters was not trained as a chef, but it didn't matter: She could sense a new, post-1960s ethos in cooking, in tune with natural food co-ops, organic farming, making your own granola, and baking your own bread. Yes, everyone was baking bread, it seemed—James Beard's *Beard on Bread* was a huge bestseller in 1973. Old-school haute cuisine, meanwhile, was seen as passé, out of touch, both in the US and in France.

It was in this context that the new French cooking arrived in the US, dispensing with formality and flambés and overrich sauces, putting a glamorous and rebellious spin on tradition—it was cooking for and of the moment.

10

Coming to America

In May 1974, Gaston Lenôtre opened a restaurant in New York City called the Chateau France. It was actually more a patisserie than a restaurant—there were eighty seats in the small dining room, but the plan was to sell an enormous variety of pastries, croissants, tarts, canapés, charcuterie, petits fours, chocolates, ice creams, and desserts. The restaurant, on East Fifty-Ninth Street, would also offer catering services.

The French invasion had begun! That was the hope, in any case. Yanou Collart had organized a formal black-tie opening night party and invited "tout" New York. She'd gone so far as to arrange for an actual, live cow to stand in front of the restaurant, signifying the freshest of ingredients and dairy, and offered a prize to any guest who could successfully milk the animal. There were few winners. On the other hand, the party was so crowded there was a long line out the door, and that counted as success. In *The New York Times*, Craig Claiborne described Lenôtre as the "chief wizard of French pastry makers," and also referred to him as a "sorcerer" and a "wand-waver."

Lenôtre was an old friend of Bocuse's who had expanded his patisserie business from a single shop in Normandy to a large catering operation and a well-regarded cooking school in Paris. He was the only member of Bocuse's Grande Cuisine association who was a pâtissier rather than a restaurant chef. He was tall, suave, and very much in tune with the nouvelle cuisine ethos, as promoted by Gault and Millau, who celebrated his inventiveness and light touch in the pages of the *Nouveau Guide*.

Lenôtre's buttercream was famously ethereal, his mille-feuille famously delicate. He pioneered the use of gelatin and other stabilizing ingredients in his dishes, all of which were produced with meticulous, quasi-scientific precision. Starting in the mid-1960s, he'd begun freezing certain ingredients during the production process, allowing him to vastly expand his catering business. He also pushed fresh and seasonal fruit to the forefront of his menu (lots of strawberries and apricots), and invented mesmerizing combinations of almond cake, coffee cream, nougatines and pralines, vanilla and chocolate.

Somewhere between the live cow on the sidewalk and the bal musette quartet playing throwback waltzes in the back of the room stood a few of the current stars of French cooking—Bocuse, Vergé, and Guérard—in attendance to support their comrade Lenôtre.

They were coming to New York and the US more and more often, it seemed.

Bocuse, as usual, was the focal point. He came to promote his new Beaujolais-Villages wine, and to host elaborate private dinners. The previous year, he'd agreed to cook dinner for what turned out to be hundreds over the course of three evenings in Manhattan, hosted by a wine importer, the Four Seasons restaurant, and various socialites. He'd managed to bring all sorts of specialized ingredients on the plane with him. As Gael Greene reported in *New York* magazine:

> In the same spirit in which Americans carry Nescafé to France, Bocuse brings along his own flour, salt, chickens, tarragon, bay leaf, crayfish, petits fours, truffled sausage, tomatoes, string beans, cream, butter, foie gras, woodcocks, a wild duck, sauce base in Baggies, and two kilos of truffles bigger than golf balls. If he seems nervous, it is because he expects that at any moment the notorious American Customs will find his pigs' bladders—hidden now cunningly in the sleeves of his jacket and layered into his underwear. . . . But the welcome is regal, the pigs' bladders diplomatically ignored.

Bocuse would invariably get amused press attention for his food smuggling—accompanied by photographs of him hoisting legs of lamb into his carry-on and grinning. His Beaujolais was available in Japan, too, where he also traveled frequently and planned to open a restaurant. When he came to Los Angeles, he invited a few of his friends along, as always—Roger Vergé and Jean Troisgros—and asked Yanou Collart to arrange the itinerary. She was by now well connected in Hollywood (in part through her boyfriend, Lino Ventura, she'd done work for William Friedkin, José Feliciano, Jack Nicholson, and many others), and she introduced them around. Danny Kaye took the visiting French chefs to the Los Angeles farmers' market and proceeded to cook dinner for all of them in his professionally outfitted kitchen. He was eager to show off his devotion to Chinese cooking, his skill with the wok.

Everywhere they went, the chefs were toasted as conquering heroes, bringing the new French cooking and savoir faire to an eager American public. "Spending a day in Los Angeles with French chef Paul Bocuse requires both the stamina of a marathon runner and a healthy liver," reported the *Los Angeles Times* in 1974, noting his frenetic schedule. "On a recent one-day visit, Bocuse cooked the food for an elegant brunch for about 25 people, went on to a mid-afternoon champagne reception in his honor, then attended a late afternoon wine and foie gras tasting featuring his personal selection of wines and his own hand-made foie gras from his restaurant near Lyon, France. After that he went out to dinner."

That LA trip—like his stops in New York, Chicago, Dallas, and Washington—had been organized to promote Bocuse's wine label, a partnership with Mel Master, a young Englishman who'd discovered Rhône wines and begun exporting them, and Georges Duboeuf, an up-and-coming winemaker from Beaujolais. They'd all decided that putting Bocuse's name on the label was the way to break into the American market. This was one of Bocuse's many ventures as he expanded beyond France.

The culinary world was booming and expanding. Cookbook sales had never been higher. Home cooks were buying nonstick pans, Marcato pasta machines, Cuisinart food processors, and more. They were discovering new and exotic spices and ingredients—green peppercorns, ginger, turmeric, alfalfa sprouts. Julia Child and other TV cooking shows demonstrated the latest recipes, and cooking classes were immensely popular all across the country.

In Napa County, California, for example, Michael James and Billy Cross launched a series of weeklong cooking courses in a large country house, each taught by a famous French chef. "Twelve participants will be accepted for each session," reported Craig Claiborne in *The New York Times*, "and they will be chauffeured from San Francisco to a Victorian 'chateau' on an estate in the wine country. There they will be offered private accommodations with a full staff." The program was called "The Great Chefs of France" and sold out instantly, despite the shockingly high price of $1,500 per person. *NBC Nightly News* sent a camera crew to record the first classes in the fall of 1974.

James and Cross were in their mid-twenties and had met at Chez Panisse, in Berkeley, where Cross was working as a bartender. James had accompanied Simone Beck, coauthor with Julia Child of the seminal *Mastering the Art of French Cooking* books, to dinner at the celebrated restaurant. He was a trained chef and had been working with Beck on her just-published cookbook, *Simca's Cuisine*, translating her recipes from French into English. Soon enough, the men had fallen in love, traveled to France, and lately returned to open a cooking school.

They faced a silent but persistent antigay bias—turned away from multiple possible venues for the school—but finally found the perfect house, owned by a wealthy couple in Philadelphia. They rented it for the year.

Beck—James's mentor—agreed to teach the first rounds of classes, and James and Cross began inviting many of the young impresarios of nouvelle cuisine for the subsequent courses. They enlisted *New York* magazine's Gael Greene to help, since she knew them all personally, hiring her as a translator for the sessions. In the fall of 1975, Roger Vergé arrived in Napa to teach for a week.

James and Cross created a fantastical, bohemian atmosphere at the grand Napa estate. There were flowers everywhere, and beautiful linens, crystal glasses, and antique dishware. The wine was free-flowing. James led the students in the kitchen with Vergé, while Cross took charge of the ever more extravagant decor and staging of the evening dinners. One night, he lit the room with hundreds of beeswax candles of all sizes, and set out dozens of orchids. Candles also lit the paths outside the house. The waitstaff—most of them young gay men James and Cross had hired in San Francisco—were dressed in different outfits every night: black tie, or Moroccan caftans, or French sailors' blue-and-white stripes, or military-style dark green jackets with gold buttons and epaulets.

They were putting on a show, and it was fabulous. Food and cooking had merged with West Coast bohemianism and experimentation at the Great Chefs of France, aligning nouvelle cuisine with American post-1960s cool. Over the coming seasons, all the classes sold out, as the vanguard chefs of nouvelle cuisine—Michel Guérard, Gaston Lenôtre, Jean Troisgros—arrived in Napa to teach, welcomed as the culinary celebrities they were. In 1976, James and Cross partnered with the Mondavi winery, which began sponsoring the program, hosting the classes at its Oakville estate. This was the year Jean Troisgros came to teach. Once again, Gael Greene was on hand, helping translate since Jean spoke only limited English. Also, as it happened, Greene and the older Troisgros sibling had begun an on-and-off affair two years earlier.

Greene was a sensualist—she wrote unapologetically about food and sex, casting herself as the epitome of the "liberated" 1970s woman. She'd just published an erotic, Erica Jong–style novel called *Blue Skies, No Candy*, which had received scathing reviews ("It's a slender line that separates the tacky from the gross, and Miss Greene has crossed it," said *The New York Times*) and then rocketed up the bestseller lists. At the cooking school in Napa, one of the students asked Greene to sign her copy of the book and to read a section to the class. "I needed to find a scene that didn't take place in bed, that didn't rely on my heroine's graphic stream of consciousness and all those four-letter words," Greene realized. There was some embarrassed laughter but mostly cheers and raised wineglasses when she finished. This was the mood at the Great Chefs of France—libertine and celebratory. Greene described the atmosphere in Napa as "wanton luxury."

> Jean was a model of discretion in class, relaxed and proper. At night, he was comfortable and affectionate in the big bed we shared on the open balcony overlooking the soaring living-dining space below. . . . Sometimes the morning light pouring in would wake us. Sometimes it was the bustle of staff setting up breakfast on the table below, shushing one another not to disturb our sleep. Jean would wake as men often do, primed for making love. And I

> would climb on top, riding my own rhythm, my arm pressed against my mouth so no telltale cries could escape. Once my breathing returned to normal, I would call out over the balcony rail, "Good morning, everyone."
>
> Those muffled moments felt naughty and delicious, almost as naughty and delicious as raspberry pie for breakfast.

The great chefs of France had arrived in America—they were celebrities, imbued with sex appeal and glamour, subject to enormous press attention. Nouvelle cuisine was the hot new thing.

Paul Bocuse appeared on the cover of *Newsweek* magazine in August 1975. This was a coronation of sorts, confirmation not only of his status as the most famous chef in the world but of nouvelle cuisine's now undeniable cultural power. *Time* and *Newsweek*, with circulations in the many millions, were the final arbiters of the American national conversation: staid, self-important, resolutely middle of the road, always "big picture." When the newsweeklies noticed something (the miniskirt, marijuana, Bruce Springsteen), the entire country noticed too. And so here was Paul Bocuse, beaming, triumphant in his chef's whites and toque, beneath the *Newsweek* cover headline: "Food: The New Wave."

Like seemingly every other article about Paul Bocuse ever written, this one began at the farmers' market.

> Shortly after dawn, at the Saint-Antoine produce market in the ancient French city of Lyon, a white pickup truck screeches around

> a corner, double-parks impatiently and disgorges a rugged man wearing a rumpled windbreaker. . . . "*Viens ici*, Paul," shouts a fruit vendor, "I've got some melons you won't believe."

As Bocuse sails through the market, picking and choosing the best and freshest ingredients (slicing open and then rejecting those melons, for example), *Newsweek* lays out the tenets of nouvelle cuisine—lighter, fresher, simpler, the new generation of chefs rejecting heavy sauces and striving for invention, embracing new ideas and ingredients.

> Preaching simplicity, they have launched innovations that, while falling well short of such hyperbolic accolades as "the new French revolution" accorded them by Paris food critics Henri Gault and Christian Millau, are nonetheless the first fresh direction French cooking has taken in nearly two centuries.

The article made much of the health benefits of the new style of cooking, how nouvelle cuisine resonated with the current intense interest in diet, fitness, and organic produce ("Au revoir to flour, butter, sugar and cream"). But most of all the article described the spectacular rise in interest in food and cooking in America, both at restaurants and at home. Chicago's Crate & Barrel home and kitchen wares chain had seen revenue triple since 1970. Business at Rockefeller Center's Rainbow Room in New York was up 55 percent the previous year. And more:

> In recent years, cookbooks have burgeoned as one of the U.S. publishing industry's hottest phenomena. Despite the recession, sales

> of such high-priced cheeses as French Brie and Danish Tilsit are skyrocketing. Supermarkets in major cities offer leeks, fresh herbs, and organically grown produce while kitchen supply stores can't keep such exotic cooking implements as a wok (a Chinese cooking pan) in stock.

The article was mostly laudatory, and Bocuse himself was ecstatic—to be on the cover, the center of attention. He was portrayed as a roguish, imperious, charming self-promoter. "In the once-cloistered world of haute cuisine, Paul Bocuse has gone so relentlessly public that he has even hired a public relations agent." This was regrettable and tacky, the authors implied, but Bocuse knew full well that without the efforts of Yanou Collart (the unnamed publicity agent in question), he would not have found himself on the cover of the magazine to begin with. Nor did he mind the disapproving descriptions of the "gigantic 4-foot-high sign" of his name atop his restaurant, or the "massive portrait" of himself hanging in the dining room.

He was larger than life. He was a swashbuckler. He had changed the role of the restaurant chef by making it more public—by leaving the kitchen to greet his guests. "In my father's day," he told the magazine, "the chef was a slave. He lived in a stinking hot kitchen underground. He never saw customers. He became a cretin." Now, the chef was a public figure, on the cover of *Newsweek*. Bocuse roamed the dining room during lunch and dinner service, leaving the cooking to his large staff.

If there were notes of skepticism in the piece, Bocuse didn't mind. Nouvelle cuisine was expensive, *Newsweek* noted, and not always as healthy as it claimed, as when a "sumptuous, foie-gras-laced dish sneaks onto Bocuse's menu." The magazine also made a point of highlighting his unapologetic male chauvinism. He was prone to making outrageous comments about women, always the provocateur. But never before had he done so in an international venue like *Newsweek*. In this case, his comments about womanizing were coupled with facts about his private life that French newspapers and magazines had never reported:

> To relax, Bocuse hunts boar with friends in Alsace, skin-dives, collects antiques, coaches a local boy's soccer team whose jerseys sport his name, and routinely expresses contempt for women in the kitchen. "The only place for them is in the bed," says Bocuse, adding that "anyone who doesn't change his woman every week or so lacks imagination." Living by his own bon-vivant precepts, Bocuse has a 28-year-old daughter by his wife, Raymonde, and a 6-year-old illegitimate son whose mother is a medical technician in nearby Lyon.

How typical for the Americans to be shocked by infidelity, Bocuse thought. In France, private life was private, and mistresses and children born out of wedlock went unmentioned in polite society. He had countless affairs and multiple lovers—his sexual machismo was all part of his charm. He was French, after all, and he made no apologies for that.

But it was the claim about women in the kitchen, that they could not be great chefs, that sparked attention. In the context of the sexually liberated 1970s (and the era's bestselling novels like

Fear of Flying and *Blue Skies, No Candy*), Bocuse's adultery was unremarkable, au courant, even. "Bocuse wouldn't be Bocuse without his women," he would say grandly, speaking in the third person.

Fine. But the status of women chefs went beyond one man's preferences and his wife's and his mistresses' private choices. Bocuse's insistence that the professional restaurant kitchen be a male-only domain was an affront to women's rights and women's equality. And there were many—not least the women currently working as chefs—who were justifiably angry at his blithe sexism.

Bocuse was making a habit of such provocations. In *Le Monde*, Robert Courtine had recently criticized Bocuse for similar statements made on French radio.

And that same summer of 1975, within weeks of the *Newsweek* cover story, Bocuse had been profiled in *The New York Times*. Craig Claiborne invited Bocuse to cook dinner with him and a few friends at his beach house in Long Island when Bocuse was visiting New York. Claiborne wrote up the dinner, with recipes, under the headline "Paul Bocuse, King of Chefs, Creates in an East Hampton Kitchen."

The article noted that Bocuse, "indisputably the most famous chef in the world," who was "tall, broad-shouldered, and handsome," had "doubtless done more to 'propagandize' French cooking throughout the world than anyone else of his generation." Claiborne had invited two well-known New York–based French chefs, his longtime collaborator Pierre Franey, and Jacques Pépin, to the dinner, and together they helped Bocuse make a lobster stew with peas and carrots, and chicken with a fresh tomato, tarragon, and vinegar sauce.

As they were cooking, they talked, and Claiborne raised the question of women chefs, and why there were so few of them. His own theory, he said, was that "in the old days at least the average restaurant kitchen was a fiery furnace only a dumb male would endure," and that professional pots and pans were intolerably heavy. "But that is certainly not the view of Mr. Bocuse," Claiborne wrote, "who is regarded among his colleagues as being heavily macho and with a high profile sex image."

"Women," Bocuse states, "lack the instincts for great cooking. It follows in the same sense that there are so few great women architects and orchestra leaders. Women who become chefs are limited in their accomplishments. They have one or two dishes they accomplish very well, but they are not great innovators."

They all laughed at Bocuse's preposterously retrograde pronouncements, delivered with such confidence. It was 1975, and he spoke about women like a caricature of a man stuck in the 1950s. For Claiborne, this was an oddity and nothing more, mentioned in passing, but the article prompted a huge response. Letters poured in, decrying Bocuse's "ignorance" and "bigotry." "In New York I know of a number of women chefs who are seriously engaged in the creation of excellent and original food, despite the tremendous discrimination against them and despite their lack of training because of such discrimination," wrote one reader. "This prejudice not only hurts women, it ultimately hurts the entire profession."

On the largest stage possible, in the pages of *The New York Times* and *Newsweek*, Bocuse had revealed himself as a dismissive male chauvinist who was also convinced of his own charm and magnetism. One person paying close attention back home in

France was Annie Desvignes, whose plan to launch a culinary association for women now seemed all the more urgent. She was galvanized. Here was the man being celebrated as the great ambassador of French cuisine, the "king of chefs," according to *The New York Times*, publicly and gleefully disparaging women's talent.

With typical bravado, Bocuse embraced the controversy. He was on the cover of *Newsweek*, and that's what mattered. Yes, people would write letters to the editor, and yes, his clients in Lyon would whisper about his wife and his mistresses and his children—he wasn't bothered. "Lyon is upside down," observed his publicist Collart of the fallout, "but Paul does not care." In fact, he was proud. He had no shame—he was virile, he spoke his mind, so be it.

He had the *Newsweek* cover printed on postcards—hundreds of them—which he handed out at the restaurant to everyone he saw.

PART THREE

Enemies

11

Nemesis

The older Courtine got, the more cantankerous he felt. He was in his mid-sixties now. Was he a curmudgeon? Yes, of course. In a way, that was his job: to find fault, to demand perfection and always be disappointed, to uphold the highest of French standards. But there was a certain bitterness creeping in these days. The modern world moved too fast and cut too many corners, he thought. Everywhere he looked he saw impure ingredients, slipshod cooking, uncaring service. In a word: *Americanization*. And it wasn't just restaurants.

He hated to travel, for example.

At every hotel, whether a small country inn or a grand palace, there always seemed to be something missing from the breakfast tray: the sugar, the butter knife, the spoon for his soft-boiled egg. And then again, there was always something extra too: the croissant and jam he hadn't ordered and didn't want, a jug of milk with his coffee when he'd ordered it black. Was it really so hard to get the small things right?

A simple pot of tea: impossible. And decent coffee? Don't even ask. He would never forget the manager of the Hôtel la Cloche in Dijon, some years ago, asking if all was well as Courtine walked into the lobby from his room one morning.

"My God, dear sir, why is your coffee so infernally bad?" he'd said.

And the man had replied, in all seriousness: "But you should have told us that you wanted good coffee—we would have made it for you!"

This was what he was up against.

As for hotel rooms, there was inevitably something wrong, malfunctioning, or poorly designed—the leaking faucet, the bathroom mirror underlit or too far from the sink, and impossible for shaving. No stationery at the desk, no shampoo or soap in the shower after the first day. And worst of all—and this was true in 99 percent of all French hotel rooms—it was all but impossible to read in bed because of the inadequate lighting.

He hated to travel. The food at highway rest areas was miserable. The very phrase "snack food" offended him. The inane babble of conversation among waiters at restaurants and bars—"out loud and without any shame," he thought to himself—irritated him too. Just the other day he'd been forced to endure what seemed like the entire life story of the cashier at a pub while he drank his beer. She spoke interminably to one of the waiters as they stood a few feet away, ignoring him entirely—"as if I'd been an object left there by the decorator!"

Malédictions! he thought. Curses! Curse them all. And yet here he was, on the road, a four-and-a-half-hour drive south of Paris, in Lyon. He'd been invited by an old friend and fellow gastronome, Henry Clos-Jouve, who was a great proponent of Lyonnais cooking, to join him and a few other food critics for a traditional *mâchon.* This was a hearty, workingman's breakfast that included andouette sausages, crispy tripe, fresh cheese, and plenty of Beaujolais. Clos-Jouve was determined to preserve this nineteenth-century custom, which had originated with silk workers—the canuts—who ate after working the early shift.

Beaujolais and tripe for breakfast! The mâchon was a true reflection of old France and its regional culinary idiosyncrasies and traditions. Courtine was adamantly in favor of celebrating just this sort of local cuisine, served in the city's numerous bouchons, bistros known for their Lyonnais specialties. Lyon was of course justly famous for its food, but there were local traditions and specialties like this all over the country, from the cassoulet in Languedoc to the bouillabaisse in Marseille.

Courtine loved all these "vieille France" dishes and traditions. But they were endangered, disappearing, passé . . .

Indeed, Courtine's bitter complaints about the indignities of modern travel, modern hotels, and modern restaurant service were only the tip of the iceberg. Such trivial matters were signs of deeper rot and decadence in French culture and cuisine, he was convinced. He'd written an article a few years earlier, in 1970, titled "*Ou va la cuisine française?*" (Whither French cuisine?). "Crossroads or dead end?" he'd asked. "It's up to the chefs to answer that question. . . . Have they become mere merchants interested in profit alone? Are they, like our era, upside down, protesting and ignorant? Are they simply the victims of a bad education, of a backward-looking cult favorable to laziness of mind?"

Courtine bemoaned entrenched, unimaginative, overcomplicated haute cuisine and its valorization of "luxury" ingredients, the "prodigious intellectual nullity" of chefs who forgot that food should taste like the ingredients it was made from, who "confuse cooking with pageantry, preparation with presentation." True French chefs, he wrote, "must have a feminine conception of cooking, if I may say so, and a traditional one too. This taste of cooking comes to them from their mother or grandmother and clings directly to the ground where they were born."

This was for Courtine the crux of the French cultural inheritance—a connection to the land, the ingredients, the soil—*le terroir.* And he had found reason to hope, in his 1970 article, that the new generation of chefs might find a way to continue the grand tradition. He singled out Bocuse, Guérard, and the Troisgros brothers for praise. "They have, in any case, the youth of the heart and the spirit," he wrote.

That was 1970. Now it was 1975, and 1970 felt like a long time ago. France had changed. It was time, he decided, to write a new, updated article about the state of French cuisine, and to highlight all the ways it was going wrong. The suddenly au courant notion of "nouvelle cuisine" demanded a rebuttal, a correction, a counterargument.

Clos-Jouve had invited a number of prominent food critics to Lyon—charter members of the fanciful but heartfelt fraternity he called the Ordre des Francs-Mâchons. Defenders of the Lyonnais breakfast. The men arrived the evening before the appointed mâchon and decided they'd meet for dinner at Bocuse, of course—where else?—the best restaurant in town. They were five, all well-known, well-fed connoisseurs of grand cooking and the best wines, and so it was no surprise that Bocuse greeted them personally, pouring Dom Pérignon champagne as he announced the menu he had prepared for the occasion:

Crayfish-tail salad with caviar
Mediterranean sea bass in puff pastry
Cardoons with chicken livers
Roast woodcock on croutons
Fresh duck foie gras with truffle salad
Cheeses
Desserts

The dinner was a feast. And of course, mostly what they did was talk about the food. They were professionals, after all. Were crayfish better served shelled or unshelled? What was a cardoon, exactly, some kind of degenerate artichoke? All agreed that the delicate, pale livers from the local Bresse chickens were notably superior to all others, and that the fall woodcock season was a delight.

But Bocuse's signature dish—the Mediterranean sea bass encased in pastry—did not meet with Courtine's approval. The fish itself was banal, swimming as it did "in a calm, over-civilized sea," he said. "To me it is somewhat fallacious fare, lacking in joy and tonicity." And furthermore: "The puff pastry adds nothing to the bass, and the bass adds nothing to the dinner."

Courtine had complicated feelings about Bocuse and his

cooking. The chef's charm was undeniable, and the food he served was of the highest quality. But the popular idea that Bocuse was somehow leading a revolution in French cooking was preposterous. His Association de la Grande Cuisine Française was nothing more than a glorified publicity maneuver, a sleazy commercial venture, "a Grand French racket." The chefs Bocuse had gathered in the group—including Roger Vergé, the Troisgros brothers, Michel Guérard—were perfectly admirable, but the idea that this was a new school of cooking, a nouvelle cuisine, was wrong. And the relentless proselytizers of this movement, the critics Henri Gault and Christian Millau, ought to know better.

They had reached the cheese course, the end of the meal. They were all a little drunk. Courtine emptied his wineglass and closed his eyes.

"That seems like a lot to eat," one of the other critics said, summarizing the multicourse meal, "yet it seems so light . . . for two bits I'd start all over again!"

There was a fire crackling in the dining room's large fireplace. And now someone else at the table spoke up. "What a magnificent log for a side of beef!" he said.

That was all it took. Paul Bocuse, standing at the table, waved to the kitchen and immediately two young commis emerged carrying a huge slab of Charolais beef on their shoulders, along with a cutting board and a large knife. Bocuse sliced off two ribs and threw them on the fire. And so the meal continued.

Bocuse had a knack for this sort of dining-room theater, the grand gesture. He served green salad while the prime rib cooked on the fire, and then sliced the meat at the table. It was perfect—"marbled but not fatty, tender yet not tasteless, and extraordinarily juicy," Courtine exclaimed and, as he did so, also mentioned how good lobsters could be cooked this way on the open flame. No sooner had he said this then Bocuse disappeared into the kitchen and reemerged triumphantly with a basket of live lobsters, which were then also roasted on the fire.

And so it went. More wine, more Dom Pérignon, more food. At some point Bocuse produced another crayfish dish—*écrevisses à la nage*, with a warm, spicy broth. The conversation was free-flowing now, uninhibited.

Courtine held forth poetically—on wine, food, and France. "In the very name Burgundy you can hear the barrels being rolled into the cellar and you can see the ruddy faces of Rembrandt's bourgeoisie," he said. "In one Belon oyster there is all the gray sea feared by Breton sailors. France is a country where seven cities bitterly dispute the origin of the cassoulet as though disputing the birth of Homer. They talk about the regions of France—the real regions are gastronomic. Food doesn't lie. There is the sauerkraut region, the goose-fat region, the beer region, the wine region—that is the real and only France, and the real and only Europe."

But all this was endangered, just like the mâchon breakfast. Endangered by margarine, by industrialization, by the sulfur added to white wine, by adulteration, preservatives, and food coloring. By the infiltration of France by foreigners and foreign food. He was incensed in particular by the proliferation of Chinese restaurants.

"This is the yellow peril, a veritable fifth column," he said. "There were twenty-seven Chinese restaurants in Paris before the war, now there are four hundred." Courtine hated Chinese food: "It's food for sadists. They cut everything up into tiny pieces!"

He laughed raucously. It was difficult, in moments like this, late at night, to be sure how serious he was. The more he drank, the more provocative and polemical and comically hyperbolic he became. "There is nothing worse than hygiene," he said. "If a child drops his lollipop in the mud, let him pick it up and eat it. If he gets sick and dies, it's too bad—it's those that survive that are the ones worth keeping. The trouble with the world today is there's no infant mortality, we're subsidizing millions of cripples."

He laughed again. "Everything is going down the drain," he said cheerfully. "We'll have to start over again when there are ten people left in a cave."

Soon enough, Courtine was talking about politics. He was stridently anti-Gaullist, accusing the war hero, leader of Free France, and former president of ushering in an era of decline and decadence. The Fifth Republic, established by de Gaulle in 1958, was, furthermore, "anti-gastronomic," he claimed. "The Fourth Republic politicians smelled of the provinces, they had peasant origins and big stomachs. According to my personal survey, the average weight of cabinet ministers dropped 26 pounds under Gaullism." De Gaulle himself had eliminated cheese from the menu at the Élysée Palace because he wanted every meal to be over in sixty minutes, Courtine claimed. "They were barbarians at the Élysée!"

He hated de Gaulle with a passion, and had celebrated his death. "In 1970 he surprised us," Courtine remembered. "He died suddenly, without warning, and I was so taken aback that I didn't have the time to buy champagne for my friends." But a year later, on November 9, 1971, the first anniversary of de Gaulle's death, he'd arranged a celebratory dinner in a private room at the Tour d'Argent. They ate foie gras and toasted with a 1920 Château Filhot Sauternes.

Just who were the friends Courtine had invited to that rather macabre celebratory dinner? He didn't say, but the general category of guest was clear enough. Courtine strenuously avoided politics in his newspaper columns, but in private his affection for a strain of French far-right culture and politics was clear. He spoke fondly of his friend Louis-Ferdinand Céline, the prominent novelist who'd died in 1961; of lunches with singers and humorists Jean Rigaux and Pierre-Jean Vaillard; and writers Albert Simonin and Marcel Jouhandeau. He attended cocktail parties and restaurant openings with fellow gourmets and men-about-town Georges Prade and Paul Montaignac de Pessotte de Bressolles, whose nickname was "Divan the Terrible."

This was Courtine's secret world, one of erudite, literary sophistication and lamentations of France's lost glory, culinary and otherwise. And what bound these men together was something they never quite said out loud. The war, and what they had said and done and believed during the war, went unmentioned, always.

They were all former collaborators.

Yes, the rumors were true. When Dominique and Albert Nahmias had opened their Left Bank restaurant Olympe in 1973, they'd been warned about Courtine, and that he might be hostile seeing as Albert was Jewish, and that Courtine had been a collaborator during the war, and that there was a cadre of Nazi-sympathizing food critics in France, Courtine being the most prominent among them. All of this was true, except Courtine hadn't been unfriendly at all and, indeed, had lauded the tiny restaurant and Olympe's cooking.

Like many others in France, Courtine and his circle had been supporters of Philippe Pétain and the Vichy regime and its appeasement of Nazi Germany, and opposed the French Resistance and de Gaulle's Free France. In the end, of course, the Allies liberated Nazi-occupied Paris and all of France; Pétain fled to Germany; and the war was won. In the immediate, tumultuous aftermath, the worst of the collaborators were punished, some executed by firing squad, others sentenced to prison.

By the early 1950s, though, France was moving forward, the economy growing along with the postwar baby boom and a rising middle class, and former collaborators mostly quietly reintegrated in polite society. A convenient mythology about the former collaborators took hold—that they had fought for France in their own misguided ways, that the Vichy regime had never really supported Hitler or his war. Unforgivable offenders had been banished—members of the vicious Vichy paramilitary organization la Milice, for example, which had worked with the Gestapo—but the many ordinary businessmen and bureaucrats who'd sided with Pétain were given a pass, never reprimanded at all.

The sins of the past were best forgotten.

Still, there were consequences to having been deemed a collaborator. The postwar judicial process had meted out a punishment called the "dégradation nationale" to more than one hundred thousand citizens, temporarily restricting their voting rights, banning them from running for public office, stripping them of military honors, and forbidding them from working as teachers, bankers, notaries, and journalists.

For Courtine and others who'd written about politics for pro-Vichy newspapers, this last decree was a problem. The practical reality of the dégradation nationale was a ban on working as an editor or writer covering news and politics. Writing about travel, tourism, gastronomy, and similar topics, on the other hand, was considered politically inconsequential and did not require a press pass or any other official approval.

And so Courtine reinvented himself. He locked away all evidence and memory of his wartime writing. He would never speak of it, publicly or privately. He fashioned himself as a bon vivant, writing cabaret and music reviews, and about nightclubs and restaurants; contributing to *Le Parisien*; and then, starting in 1952, to *Le Monde*.

He was by no means alone in his transformation. It was not uncommon for Courtine, at a dinner or event, to cross paths with other collaborators condemned by the dégradation nationale to labor in the lush, abundant fields of luxury, travel, and food journalism. They greeted each other with convivial, knowing glances. They were now arbiters of taste, defenders of tradition.

George Prade had worked for the collaborationist *Nouveaux Temps* newspaper under the notorious Jean Luchaire (executed in 1946) and now spent his time promoting the subtle pleasures of champagne as the head of the trade group Ordre des Coteaux de Champagne. Paul Montaignac de Pessotte de Bressolles was a minor aristocrat who'd also worked for *Nouveaux Temps* and now wrote about food (*Un Épicurien à Paris*); he was known for his love of the Romanovs and falling asleep after dinner—hence the nickname, Divan the Terrible. Along with Courtine, by far the most prominent and powerful, these three were whispered about in the restaurant business—they were known as the "Trio of Collaborators" even all these years later. These were the whispers Albert Nahmias had heard.

It was a historical irony that in retrospect seemed preordained: that food and luxury lifestyle journalism would be infiltrated by former fascist sympathizers, and a strand of reactionary traditionalism reconstituted and alchemized as "good taste."

As the long dinner at Bocuse came to a close, the men realizing they would be eating a hearty mâchon breakfast in only a few hours' time (they'd agreed to meet at 9 a.m.), Courtine was still talking. "I love Lyon—a secret, gourmandizing, and hungry city. Lyon of my heart," he said grandiosely. "Lyon of the three rivers, Rhône, Saône, and Beaujolais; Lyon, the birthplace of the writer Henri Béraud, who was tried for collaboration and was assassinated by de Gaulle."

Courtine toasted the novelist and self-declared antisemite ("The Jew is the born enemy of national traditions," Béraud had written in 1941), who had in fact been sentenced to death for his collaboration after the war, but whose sentence had been commuted by de Gaulle.

"À la santé de Henri Béraud!" The men raised their glasses. No one else in the restaurant heard them, or took notice.

Michel Guérard at his restaurant Pot-au-Feu in Asnières, outside Paris, 1974.
MICHEL ARTAULT / GAMMA-RAPHO

above

Guérard in the kitchen at Pot-au-Feu.

MICHEL ARTAULT / GAMMA-RAPHO

left

The Troisgros brothers, Jean and Pierre, at their family restaurant in Roanne in the 1960s.

SERGE LIDO / SIPA

Paul Bocuse at a market in Lyon, early 1970s.

MICHEL ARTAULT / GAMMA

Roger Vergé serves soup, late 1970s.
MIKE SLAUGHTER / *TORONTO STAR* VIA GETTY IMAGES

Pastry chef Gaston Lenôtre.
JEAN-CHRISTOPHE MARTIN / AFP VIA GETTY IMAGES

The Association of Women Chefs (the Association des Restauratrices Cuisinières, or ARC) in Paris in 1977, wearing white toques. Left to right, first row: Monique Brisset, Fernande Euzet, Gisèle Crouzier, Georgette Descat, and Jacqueline Libois. Second row: Christiane Massia, Christiane Conticini, Marie-Françoise Lachaud, Carole Beyssier, Fernande Allard, Madée Trama, and Gisèle Berger.
JEAN-CLAUDE DEUTSCH / PARIS MATCH VIA GETTY IMAGES

Olympe in the kitchen at her Paris restaurant, Olympe, in the mid-1970s.
COURTESY OF ALBERT NAHMIAS

ARC pamphlet and guide to member restaurants, late 1970s.
COURTESY OF SIMONE LEMAIRE

"Vive la Nouvelle Cuisine Française," the cover of *Le Nouveau Guide Gault-Millau*, October 1973.
COURTESY OF ALEXIS MILLAU

Food critics Christian Millau and Henri Gault in Paris, late 1970s.
BERTRAND LAFORÊT / GAMMA-RAPHO VIA GETTY IMAGES

left

Le Monde restaurant critic Robert Courtine.

UNIVERSAL PHOTO / SIPA

below

Yanou Collart, press agent for many French chefs and restaurants, in Paris, early 1970s.

GIANCARLO BOTTI / GAMMA-RAPHO VIA GETTY IMAGES

Courtine outside Fouquet's in Paris, 1980.

JAMES / TF1 / SIPA

New York magazine restaurant critic Gael Greene, 1971.
ASSOCIATED PRESS AP PHOTO / RAY STUBBLEBINE

New York Times food critic Craig Claiborne, early 1980s.
PHOTOGRAPH BY MARIO E. RUIZ
ZUMA PRESS / ALAMY STOCK PHOTO

Paul Bocuse and friends preparing lunch at the Élysée Palace, on the occasion of his being awarded the Legion of Honor, 1975.
KEYSTONE-FRANCE / GAMMA-RAPHO

Bocuse serving his truffled VGE soup, named in honor of French President Valéry Giscard d'Estaing, 1976.
MICHEL ARTAULT / GAMMA-RAPHO

Bocuse on the cover of *Newsweek*, August 11, 1975.
COURTESY OF NEWSWEEK

above

Jean and Pierre Troisgros at an outdoor feast, 1976.

PASCAL DELLA ZUANA / SYGMA VIA GETTY IMAGES

left

Bocuse boards a flight for New York City, 1974.

MICHEL ARTAULT / GAMMA

Julia Child, Dena Kaye, Gael Greene, Bess Myerson, and Charlotte Curtis at Bocuse's Dinner for Women in New York City, 1974.
PHOTOGRAPH BY SAHM DOHERTY-SEFTON

Olympe with Roman Polanski, Paul Bocuse, Eve Ruggieri, and Jean Castel at restaurant Olympe, early 1980s.
COURTESY OF ALBERT NAHMIAS

above

Christiane Massia and her all-women kitchen staff at restaurant Le Marché in Paris, 1977.

JEAN-CLAUDE DEUTSCH / PARIS MATCH VIA GETTY IMAGES

left

New York Times restaurant critic Mimi Sheraton, disguised for her televised debate with Paul Bocuse and others in Paris, 1979.

ASSOCIATED PRESS AP PHOTO / EUSTACHE CARDENAS

left

Roger Vergé, Gaston Lenôtre, and Paul Bocuse launch their restaurant Les Chefs de France at Disney World's Epcot Center in Orlando, 1982.

BERNARD CHARLON / GAMMA-RAPHO VIA GETTY IMAGES

below

Lea Linster wins the Bocuse d'Or in 1989, the first woman to do so.

COURTESY OF LEA LINSTER

Funeral of Paul Bocuse at the Saint-Jean Cathedral in Lyon, January 2018.
PHOTOGRAPH BY JOEL PHILIPPON / MAXPPP / ALAMY STOCK PHOTO

Restaurant Bocuse, Collonges-au-Mont-d'Or, near Lyon.
SERGE MOURARET / ALAMY STOCK PHOTO

Courtine soon got to work on his follow-up story in *Le Monde* on the current trends in French cooking. What had changed since his last article, published in late 1970? "I was proud (four years ago, so close and yet so far away!) of the young chefs who wanted to be—and only wanted to be—cooks, and of whom Paul Bocuse was the indisputable leader." He had celebrated the honest, simple cooking of the Troisgros brothers, Guérard, Senderens, and the others. And now, in January 1975?

> Where are we after four years? Bocuse founded, with a few others, the "Grande Cuisine française," which is only a commercial affair and where, curiously, the best and the worst meet. He invests in Japan (small revenge) and inundates it with a Beaujolais which, even with his name on the label, remains miserable. Some chroniclers who discovered this effort at renewal belatedly speak of a "Nouvelle Cuisine Française" with more enthusiasm than serenity, and advocate raw and undercooked fish pell-mell.

He'd been critical of Bocuse's self-promotion and Gault and Millau's nouvelle cuisine cheerleading from the beginning. Courtine was all in favor of fresh ingredients but balked at nouvelle cuisine's implicit rejection of tradition. Did every fish now need to be served pink? Did every young chef now need to train a coterie of even younger followers? "It's crazy how these little prodigies proliferate in fashionable restaurants where you proclaim yourself a chef at twenty!" he wrote. "You don't eat better for that, but it doesn't matter: Go-go rushes in. This is the new French culinary combination."

Nouvelle cuisine was a fad—an expensive fad. It was now being served in nightclubs. And what of the lost art of sensible, natural cooking? It was in the hands of women, Courtine argued: "It is at the market that we distinguish the good housewife. And we can say that good housekeeping corresponds to good cooking. Even if it was simple, modest, economical. Because cooking has been mainly the business of women since Paleolithic times, as Delteil would say. We must return to this Paleolithic cuisine and, from the drugstore to the big restaurant, refuse the civilization of the can opener and endless preservatives."

Courtine had recently received the letter from Annie Desvignes describing her rejection by the Maîtres Cuisiniers de France and the difficulties she and other women chefs faced in the restaurant business. He had immediately agreed to help. For him, women's cooking was at the heart of French civilization. More than that, he now realized, women's cooking must be a bulwark against the decadence of nouvelle cuisine.

He would hold up the tradition and artistry of Desvignes and other women chefs as the embodiment of all that was sacrosanct and truly French. His conservative, reactionary politics would find common cause with the feminist movement when it came to food and cooking. And as it happened, he'd been given the perfect bit of ammunition by Paul Bocuse himself, during a radio interview in early 1975.

"Women," Bocuse declared, "have no place in the professional kitchen, they're underdeveloped and lack both imagination and talent."

This was precisely the prejudice Desvignes had described, and Courtine used the quote in two different articles in the spring of 1975 attacking Bocuse and nouvelle cuisine and defending women chefs, one in *Le Monde* and one in *Cuisine et Vins de France*. "Bocuse should have stirred his spoon ten times in the stew before proclaiming this absurdity," Courtine wrote in the latter, going on to describe cooking as essentially and inevitably the invention of women:

> The man went hunting, fishing, gathering and returned to the hut, the cave, the tent, where the woman, vestal, maintained the fire, the food of the family. Since the discoveries of fire, then of the pot, that is to say grilling, braising and boiling, what have we invented in the kitchen? Nothing!

As an argument, it was preposterously retrograde—women belonged in the kitchen, and should stay in the kitchen—and the very opposite of Desvignes's claim to self-determination as a chef. But no matter. Courtine's articles on the topic were filled with loving descriptions of the dishes served at the women's restaurants. Chez Mado's bouillabaisse, Christiane Massia's duck skin omelet, Annie Desvignes's rabbit with Thiérache cider, and Simone Lemaire's duck pâté with orange jelly . . . Never before had they received such prominent notice in the national press.

Courtine had taken on nouvelle cuisine and its many faults, and would use the women chefs (exemplars of purity and French tradition) to make his case. With or without their permission.

12

The Association of Women Chefs

In December 1975, on a cold and overcast Saturday afternoon, six women gathered in the back of Ty-Coz, a seafood restaurant on rue Saint-Georges in Paris. Midafternoon, and the sky was already dimming, the narrow, single-lane street outside in shadow. The restaurant was closed between lunch and dinner. One by one, the women arrived: Annie Desvignes, Simone Lemaire, Gisèle Berger, Christiane Massia, Fernande Allard, and Odette Kahn, greeting each other politely, some of them meeting in person for the first time. Jacqueline Libois, the chef and owner of Ty-Coz, was their host, hanging their coats and leading them to a table.

The group had no name yet. They'd come together as a result of Annie Desvignes's letters describing her rejection by the Maîtres Cuisiniers de France, barring her from the trade organization because—and only because—she was a woman. Her idea was to launch a new group for women restaurateurs. She'd sent letters to other women chefs, and to *Le Monde*'s Robert Courtine, who had offered his support. It was Courtine who'd introduced Desvignes to Odette Kahn, the editor of *Cuisine et Vins de France.*

Desvignes had touched a nerve. They were there to join forces, to make a statement, to demand recognition and respect. The issue was not simply that Desvignes had been denied membership by one particular powerful institution. That was no surprise. Indeed, it was a wonder she had tried to join the Maîtres Cuisiniers at all. No, the issue was the status of women chefs more broadly—their exclusion from top restaurant kitchens, from apprenticeships, from training positions as stagiaires. By forming their own organization, they could change all that.

Christmas was the following week. Paris was festive, full of shoppers, decorations, and sidewalk vendors selling roasted chestnuts. The mood at Ty-Coz was just as high-spirited, as the chefs laughed at the indignities of being a woman in their profession. The insults and, maybe worse, the seeming invisibility. Here they were at one of the great seafood restaurants in Paris—specializing in the fresh oysters and Muscadet mussels and fish stews of Brittany. The restaurant had received no stars, nor was it even listed in the Michelin guide. Courtine had noted the omission in his recent, glowing review of Ty-Coz in *Le Monde,* calling the snub "mysterious."

Desvignes looked around the table, her eyes flashing. She'd brought the rejection letter from the Maîtres Cuisiniers and now held it up as she read aloud. The "master chefs" association was for men only, a "closed academy where the spirit breathes." The explanation was insulting. Closed to women chefs, and for no reason.

They had all heard the specious arguments over the years. Women were "too weak" to lift heavy pots and pans in the kitchen. Women would be sexually disruptive in the kitchen. ("They'll throw the place in an uproar. The men will feel them up and jump them on the stove," one Paris chef was heard to explain.) Women lacked a keen sense of smell and taste, and thus could never succeed at the highest level as chefs or sommeliers. They had heard it all.

Women were free to enroll in private cooking schools like the Cordon Bleu in Paris, where Julia Child, for example, had taken classes back in the 1950s. But finding a job at a restaurant as a commis or apprentice was close to impossible.

"Apparently, the only women ever offered positions are named Claude or Dominique," said Lemaire—names that could be male or female. And when the applicant showed up in person, well, that was the end of that. The women all laughed bitterly.

Her bistro in Saint-Germain-des-Prés, said Fernande Allard, had recently been honored by the Comité National de Gastronomie. But the certificate, which now hung on the wall at Chez Allard, did not mention her—the chef—and instead listed her husband's name, André Allard.

The women all laughed bitterly, again.

Allard was a venerable Left Bank institution, founded in the 1930s, where a woman had always run the kitchen—first André's mother, Marthe, and then, after she and André were married, Fernande. She'd inherited the family recipes from her mother-in-law and added her own. Her duck with olives and fish with beurre blanc were both noted in the Michelin guide, where Allard had been awarded a star.

Still, it was her husband's name on the restaurant sign—"Restaurant Allard—André Allard," inscribed in gold on the wood paneling above the doors—just as it was her husband's name on that framed certificate. Not that she cared, particularly, about such trivial matters. Still: The second-class status of women chefs, in matters large and small, was pervasive.

There was an undercurrent of anger in the room. Inevitably, the conversation had turned to Paul Bocuse and his recent public declarations about women chefs, their lack of "imagination and talent," their lack of "instincts for great cooking." He was talking about them, the women gathered at Ty-Coz, fellow chefs, women who had toiled and persevered and opened their own restaurants against all odds, and succeeded. And here was the icon of grand French cuisine, the "king of chefs," belittling and insulting them loudly and repeatedly.

It felt personal. And it was infuriating.

Bocuse had been the inspiration they needed, his loud derision spurring the women to action. Everything Bocuse did received outsize attention in the press—his disparaging comments about women chefs, yes, but also his various business expansions, international travels, and publicity stunts.

In January of the previous year, Bocuse had cooked what he called "The Dinner for Women" at the Four Seasons restaurant in New York City. The event was emblematic of his brand of patronizing chauvinism, and a response to the mild criticism he'd received after cooking a grand dinner (also at the Four Seasons) at which every guest but two had been male. This had been pointed out to Bocuse by Gael Greene, the *New York* magazine columnist, who'd been the only woman invited to the dinner. (The other woman in attendance was the socialite Patricia Buckley, who'd come because her husband, William Buckley, was unavailable.)

"I have never minded being the only woman at the party," Greene said. "Actually . . . confession-time . . . I have loved it." Still, when she laughingly complained to Bocuse about "the gastronomic world's disdain for women," his response was immediate. "Next time I come to New York, I'll cook a dinner for women only," he said, "but they must all be women somehow involved with food, as cooks or epicures."

And so "The Dinner for Women" was born. What was the point, exactly? To demonstrate Bocuse's respect for women? To deign to cook for them? The thinking was unclear, but the guest list showed canny self-promotion—the dinner was a press event. The women invited were celebrities, socialites, and prominent journalists, and included Julia Child, playwright Lillian Hellman, sculptor Louise Nevelson, fashion designer Pauline Trigère, opera soprano Margaret Tynes, TV star turned political player Bess Myerson, *New York Times* op-ed page editor Charlotte Curtis, and *Washington Post* and CBS News journalist Sally Quinn, along with a number of magazine reporters, including Dena Kaye and Gael Greene. Quinn arrived with a TV crew in tow, and the local TV news channels were filming in the kitchen.

Bocuse had brought Jean Troisgros and Gaston Lenôtre with

him to help cook. The menu was explicitly nouvelle cuisine, the highlight being a Michel Guérard–style fish with seaweed, served daringly with red wine.

Truffled white sausages, croustades of lobster mousseline, snail fritters

Truffle ragout with foie gras on spinach

Salad of crayfish tails with mustard cream

Sea bass baked in seaweed, with scallops and beurre blanc sauce

Dandelion greens and cardoons

Citrus sorbets

Lenôtre's amuse-bouches were brilliant—delightful—but the rest of the meal was subpar, according to Greene. "There is no question that Bocuse and Troisgros are wizards," she reported. "But I can't believe they would have dared serve the same menu to male muck-a-mucks of haute cuisine circles." The fish was overcooked. The crayfish salad was bland. The dandelion greens were old and the cardoons were starchy. As for the conversation among the dozen women around the table, it was pleasant, staid, unremarkable. "It's rather like a class reunion at Smith," said Julia Child; the dinner had "nothing whatsoever to do with serious gastronomy, and everything with publicity and promotion, which, of course, all of us were quite well aware of."

In her *New York* magazine column, Greene summed up: "There were few great victories for feminism at the Dinner for Women. Paul Bocuse adores women in the classic sexist way. He would probably roar if anyone ever sat down and outlined the women's movement to him."

Bocuse's roguish, macho persona was self-consciously a bit of a performance, tempered by his humor, his winking, flirtatious charm with both men and women. He was the most famous chef in the world, and he played the role perfectly. Always engaging, flattering, magnetic. His womanizing was brazen, and his many outrageous comments about women were made with a smile on his face. His sins, it seemed, were easily forgiven, shrugged off, not taken seriously.

But for the women meeting at Ty-Coz, Bocuse's insults had not been forgotten. And it seemed that the more he repeated them, the more famous he became. His "bad boy" persona was good copy, and his now global celebrity as the standard-bearer of French cuisine had rendered him unassailable. Earlier that year, in February 1975, he'd been awarded the French Legion of Honor by President Valéry Giscard d'Estaing, presented at the Élysée Palace. Bocuse had arranged to cook lunch for the president and invited the Bande à Bocuse to join him: Jean and Pierre Troisgros, Michel Guérard, Roger Vergé, Alain Chapel, Louis Outhier, and Paul and Jean-Pierre Haeberlin. The Troisgros brothers would make their salmon with sorrel sauce, Guérard his duck fillets with foie gras, Vergé his salades du Moulin, and Bocuse himself would be presenting a truffle soup, newly invented for the occasion.

It was a grand, triumphant celebration.

It was also a circus: the stars of nouvelle cuisine shopping together at the Rungis food market, trailed by camera crews and photographers, then cooking together at the presidential palace, all in their chef's whites and toques. Bocuse was the first chef to receive the high honor since Auguste Escoffier in 1919, and after Giscard d'Estaing pinned the medal to his chest, he presented his truffle soup as the first course, each bowl topped with a pastry dome.

The press was full of pictures of Bocuse at the Élysée Palace, surrounded by his loyal friends, shaking the president's hand, sitting at a long table in the ornate dining room. The wines were the best of France, including a 1970 Montrachet and a 1926 Château Margaux. The truffle soup was magical and a little mystifying, according to reports, the president asking: "But Monsieur Bocuse, how should we eat it?" *"L'on casse la croute, Monsieur le President,"* he replied. Let us break bread. Once the crust was broken, the intoxicating aroma of the soup was revealed. Bocuse added the soup to the menu at his restaurant the very next day, renaming it "Black Truffle Soup VGE," in honor of the president.

Bocuse had reached the pinnacle of his profession, heroic and indomitable.

But here was the detail that Annie Desvignes and the other women chefs had noticed: There were only two women in attendance at the Élysée Palace lunch that day, and of course neither of them were chefs. An entire dining room of French culinary celebrity, from all over the country (many of whose restaurants, including those of Bocuse, Guérard, Vergé, Outhier, and the Troisgros brothers, were run with the help of their wives), and the only women at the table were the first lady, Anne-Aymone Giscard d'Estaing, and Bocuse's wife, Raymonde.

"A very masculine lunch," *Le Monde* later noted, dryly.

There was no doubt about it: The Bande à Bocuse was a boys'

club, and any attempt to include women only made that more obvious.

Theirs would be a women's club. A rebel alliance. They called it the "ARC," the Association des Restauratrices-Cuisinières—the Association of Women Chefs.

Annie Desvignes felt a surge of optimism, the thrill of taking action, of fighting back. All the women chefs in France, unrecognized and unacknowledged by the Maîtres Cuisiniers, would now have their own forum. They had taken matters into their own hands, and nothing Bocuse or anyone else could say would stop them.

At Ty-Coz, Jacqueline Libois poured glasses of champagne for her guests, and they toasted the future, and the ARC. They were full of ideas, all speaking at once: The ARC should have placards and window stickers for member restaurants to display. What about a guide to member restaurants, with maps and telephone numbers? How would they recruit new members to begin with? This was crucial. They were only seven that day in Paris, but between them they knew dozens of women chefs who might join them.

Odette Kahn, the editor of *Cuisine et Vins de France*, took charge of logistics. Kahn was steely and sophisticated, her hair swept back in a short, authoritative bouffant, her jewelry conspicuous but tasteful. She was in her fifties, older than the other women at the meeting, and well established in the food world. They would need to register the ARC as a nonprofit organization, she explained, with each of them designated as officers. Kahn herself would be secretary general, Libois the treasurer, and Gisèle Berger, they decided, would be president. Berger's small seafood restaurant, La Bonne Table, was in Clichy, on the outskirts of Paris; she was voluble, cheerful, ready for the task. Desvignes, Allard, Massia, and Lemaire would serve as vice presidents and regional representatives.

When they met again a few weeks later, this time at another Paris seafood restaurant, Le Pistou, ARC's numbers had grown—they were now eleven chefs around the table. They agreed on a few basic rules of membership: ARC restaurants must be woman owned and run; must use fresh ingredients, not frozen; and must be vouched for by two current members—"god-mothers." They would visit any woman who applied to join the ARC and see her at work in her kitchen. It didn't matter how large or small the restaurant, how elaborate or simple the menu, as long as she cooked with quality.

Over the coming months in 1976, ARC grew to forty-five members, and the meetings continued. They designed a logo (a simple, graphic dinner plate with the letters *ARC* in the center and "cuisine de femme" written underneath) and printed window stickers for each member.

They contacted Bragard, the premier French supplier of chef's whites, aprons, and uniforms, and asked the company to make a women's chasuble, a kind of tunic, more feminine than the standard apron, and this became the ARC's official garment.

This was, after all, a key function of the group—to open doors in the culinary world for women, even the most mundane of doors. Why shouldn't women chefs have an appealing apron? More consequentially, the ARC also promoted the hiring of women commis and junior cooks. Many of the kitchen staff at ARC restaurants were men, but that was changing. The women of ARC were all self-taught as cooks and as restaurateurs, and they wanted to make pathways into the profession easier for the next generation. To offer guidance, advice, and training—all the things they had been forced to figure out for themselves.

Kahn had convinced Champagnes Mumm, one of the great champagne producers in France, to sponsor the ARC's directory, a small booklet listing each of the member restaurants. The advertisements for Mumm would pay for the printing of the pamphlet, which included photographs of each of the chefs alongside information about her restaurant. On the first page of the directory was the group's credo, a mission statement:

> This association, created in 1975 for the defense and the promotion of the profession of women chefs and the safeguard of the traditions of fine cookery, is exclusively composed of women chefs who own their restaurant and exercise in it their culinary art.

The success of the ARC, Annie Desvignes knew, would depend on publicity. The purpose of the group, after all, was to tell the world that women chefs existed, that their restaurants were worth seeking out—whatever Paul Bocuse said, and whatever the Michelin guide decreed. And press attention was also how the ARC would attract new members and gain momentum. Fortunately, the women had Courtine in their corner, and he now wrote frequently and enthusiastically about "les dames d'ARC," as he called them.

In his weekly column, he'd written about Desvignes's rejection by the Maîtres Cuisiniers ("Well! Imagine that Mme Desvignes asked to be part of the Maîtres Cuisiniers and that she was told that 'it was not for women!' There it is, segregation! . . . And since these gentlemen chefs have the nerve to refuse these ladies, why not create an association of women cooks?") as well as the eventual founding of the ARC. He had traveled north to Vervins to stay at Desvignes's small inn and restaurant, La Tour du Roy, recommending its "very comfortable rooms" and praising her cooking.

Whether it was in roundups of Parisian bistros or of regional specialties, Courtine made a point of including ARC member restaurants in his columns, and championing women chefs. He also helped recruit other food writers to the cause, including his friends Henry Clos-Jouve (who'd organized the traditional mâchon breakfast in Lyon), Michel Piot (restaurant critic at the newspaper *Le Figaro*), and Philippe Couderc (restaurant critic at the weekly *Nouvel Observateur*). All of them wrote approvingly of the ARC. The word was getting out.

Courtine also volunteered to write a brief introduction for the opening pages of the ARC directory. In typically grandiose style, he described women's cooking as the essence of life:

> Because in the beginning, there was the maintenance of the fire, a vital necessity. . . . Because they were gathered around her, the

> children, and the children's children. . . . Because there was the land that does not lie, the sky and its promises, the sea that comes from afar. . . . The woman is the mistress of the home, and the kitchen is women's business. This is the "nature of things"!
>
> Because women's cuisine, I've already explained, is quite simply THE cuisine. The real! The first in date, but also the first in friendship. That of the heart, that of the hand on the heart, that of sincerity.

Desvignes was thrilled, of course, to receive this support. Any attention for the ARC was welcome. And Courtine was by far the most influential gastronomic writer in France. Still, she couldn't help but notice the sentimental, traditionalist, reactionary argument he was making and wonder how it would suit the ARC in the long run.

13

Experiments

Michel Guérard stood on the scale in his white chef's jacket and toque, arms akimbo, beaming. There was something faintly comical about the scene—the small man (five foot three inches), the large toque (almost reaching the low, stucco ceiling), the industrial, upright scale, the stationary bicycles in the background. Guérard was posing for a photograph in the gym at his hotel and spa in Eugénie-les-Bains, promoting his immensely popular "cuisine minceur." Slimming cuisine, à la Guérard, offered the delicacy and quality of haute cuisine with a fraction of the calories. It was a hit: His cookbook, *La Grande Cuisine Minceur,* was on its way to selling a million copies, translated into multiple languages.

In February 1976, Guérard appeared on the cover of the European edition of *Time* magazine, under the headline "The New Gourmet Law: Hold the Butter."

> A veritable blasphemy is threatening some of the world's best kitchens. It is the notion that people—even the French—can enjoy

> a memorable meal that contains only 500 calories instead of the 3,000 or more that tradition demands. No longer, as the old adage had it, need a Frenchman dig his grave with a fork. The blasphemer is an impish, outgoing, pint-sized ex-pastry chef named Michel Guérard, 42, who has invented la cuisine minceur—the cuisine of slimness.

He was famous, but he didn't take himself too seriously. Every article about Guérard invariably described him as "impish." He was charming, playful, and witty; he joked about his weight loss, about how his wife had prodded him to slim down. As a child, he'd wanted to be a comedian, or maybe a priest, or maybe a doctor . . . Now he was a chef, and also a bit of a comedian, a priest, and a doctor. "Or maybe a bad comedian, a bad priest, and a bad doctor!" he would say, laughing. He entertained his guests, he kept them healthy, and he cooked delicious meals.

He did not make grandiose, Bocuse-like statements about women and cooking. He generally ignored Bocuse's provocations, even when they were aimed at him. "When you go to eat at Guérard," Bocuse joked to his friends, "remember to bring all of your medical prescriptions!" Guérard's diet cooking was an easy target for ridicule, but he didn't mind. He was pushing his cooking in new directions. And as Bocuse told *Time* magazine: "Michel is the one who is doing something really original and new. He's the most imaginative of us all."

While Bocuse had taken on the mantle of Escoffier, representing French cooking in all its self-important, chauvinistic glory, receiving the Legion of Honor, cooking for the president, upholding nouvelle cuisine as a modern interpretation of "La Grande

Cuisine Française," Guérard was still experimenting. He was convinced that whatever he learned as he developed low-calorie recipes for his cuisine minceur would prove useful for his cooking in general. He was interested in new techniques, new technologies, in the science of cooking. And this was what had led him to the sacrilege—the blasphemy—the heresy—of the frozen supermarket entrée.

Yes, Michel Guérard, celebrated Michelin-starred chef, charter member of the Bande à Bocuse, *Time* cover subject, had agreed to consult for Nestlé, the Swiss food giant, and to help devise the lowliest of meals.

He'd been approached by Pierre Liotard-Vogt, the managing director of the company, who asked if Guérard might want to help develop a line of frozen diet food. "I just bought your cookbook," he explained. Vogt was a corporate titan, overseeing everything from baby food and canned soup to chocolate bars and instant coffee, as well as a vast selection of frozen Stouffer's, Libby's, Buitoni, and Findus-branded meals, sold the world over. Vogt was also a gastronome, a member of the exclusive Club des Cent, which met weekly at Maxim's and required each associate (there were only ever one hundred, all men) to pass a detailed culinary examination. Vogt was elegant, sophisticated, and well connected.

"I will understand completely if you refuse," he said to Guérard, "knowing the likely backlash of your fellow chefs."

But Guérard was curious and agreed to visit the Nestlé Grand Froid frozen food plant in Beauvais, an hour north of Paris. This was a massive industrial complex and warehouses, all windowless, corrugated steel walls and loading docks, surrounded by parking lots. The epitome of faceless, intimidating corporate food production, in other words. There were large placards advertising Nestlé ice cream cones on the outside walls.

Inside was a whole new world. Huge assembly lines and conveyor belts, unfathomable machines, laboratories, and kitchens. In the research and development department, Guérard met with chemists, physicists, nutritionists, and cooks, and was immediately won over. There was so much to learn here.

Since Les Prés d'Eugénie was closed during the winter months, Guérard had time to work for Nestlé and visit the plant in Beauvais frequently. He learned about simple and complex carbohydrates, about milk proteins, about pasteurization, about Maillard reactions—"exciting things that are not taught in the kitchen," Guérard thought, "a completely unknown universe."

He would present his ideas for recipes, all the while learning the science and the constraints of industrial food production. He'd been hired to work on Nestlé's diet cuisine but quickly found himself immersed in all aspects of frozen food, and mostly preoccupied with making it taste better.

Guérard's frozen entrée invention—"a small miracle," he called it—happened by accident. A simple idea that worked. He'd been preparing to make a pastry filled with almond cream for a TV appearance (cooking shows being increasingly popular), and was shopping for ingredients at a Prisunic supermarket in Paris. Into his cart went almonds . . . eggs . . . butter . . . cream . . . and then, passing by the frozen food aisle, looking at the array of offerings, he noticed a fish gratin dinner. And he thought: Why not fill his puff pastry with fish instead of almond cream? And might this work as a frozen dish?

He made his pithivier, a dome-shaped pie, and filled it with white fish in a beurre blanc sauce, baked inside puff pastry, and served it with pureed watercress. He brought the idea to Beauvais, and this would be his breakthrough. Indeed, Guérard's fish pithivier brought about a change in perception. "We have discovered that a frozen entrée can actually be good!" he declared. The crust browned in the oven, while the lemony beurre blanc sauce stayed inside the savory pie. Soon boxes of his dish, complete with a small photograph of the smiling chef and his signature, began appearing in supermarkets all over France.

There was immediate skepticism and suspicion from other chefs, as Vogt had predicted. But the reaction was muted. For one thing, some of them, notably Gaston Lenôtre, had also been experimenting with frozen ingredients. And the truth was the frozen entrées on the market were mostly bland and bad; Guérard had found a way to make them better, and that was admirable. Alain Senderens, for one, immediately leaped to Guérard's defense.

More Guérard-inspired Nestlé frozen dishes followed, including a top-selling seafood savarin with crab legs. He learned to work within strict limits—none of the ingredients could be rare or expensive, for example, but the key was to be "intransigent about quality." And at the same time, Guérard's understanding of the science of industrial-scale cooking began to influence his cooking at Les Prés d'Eugénie. The mass production of béarnaise sauce, for example, could not rely on whisks and whipping; other methods of introducing air bubbles (using pressurized gases) were required. Not that Guérard was producing mass quantities of béarnaise sauce at his restaurant, but his eyes had been opened to the chemistry of cooking, and its manipulations. How to distill flavors, how to invent new textures . . . A door to the future had been opened.

In Roanne, Jean and Pierre Troisgros were also experimenting. The brothers had recently completed a massive modernization and full electrification of their restaurant kitchen, at an enormous cost. (Their accountant had protested, calling the plans "*IRREMBOURSABLE*" in all capital letters—"UNPAYABLE." And what about the possibility of power outages? They went ahead anyway.) The large room was now air-conditioned and sunlit, with a wall of windows overlooking the gardens outside; they had banished coal and installed electric burners and ovens instead; the ovens had precise temperature controls and were shoulder-high with glass windows to see inside; all the countertops were steel and easy to clean.

The wide-open kitchen meant that Jean and Pierre could survey each of the stations at a glance, like "soccer coaches overseeing our players," Pierre said. "We have always been crazy about modernity, new tools and new architecture." It was, in 1976, the most modern kitchen in France, state of the art.

The Troisgros brothers had embraced technology, everything from Teflon pans to Robot-Coupe food processors. And they had recently stumbled on something entirely new: A young chef and friend of the brothers named Georges Pralus had recently returned from a visit to the US, bringing with him a vacuum-packing device. Its purpose was food storage and preservation, but Pralus had the idea to use it for cooking foie gras.

Foie gras prepared in the traditional manner, placed in a terrine and cooked in a bain-marie, lost 40 to 50 percent of its weight in the process. Pralus, who was infectiously good natured and enthusiastic, began tinkering with Cryovac and Multivac machines. He tried vacuum packing the foie gras, compressing the goose liver into its terrine, and cooking it as usual. This reduced the weight loss by a bit. Next, he tried cooking the foie gras inside the sealed plastic bag, but the bag split—exploded. The same thing happened when he used two bags. But three layers of vacuum-sealed bags did the trick. And the foie gras that emerged hadn't lost any of its weight in the process. The texture was perfectly smooth, the flavor delicate: an ideal foie gras.

Cooking with steam had recently become a nouvelle cuisine mainstay—cuisine à la vapeur—allowing delicate, precise control of the heat, preserving color and flavor. Cooking with submerged, vacuum-sealed bags in water was an extension of the same idea. Pralus ran numerous experiments, adjusting temperatures and cooking times, until he hit on the perfect recipe for the dish. Long submersion in hot—but far from boiling—water was best, yielding a smooth but firm, cooked but still pink foie gras.

Sous vide cooking had made its debut, invented in the kitchen at Troisgros, and the chefs began applying the technique to fish and chicken breast, as well as to endives and artichokes. The low cooking temperature preserved the texture and bite of vegetables, and there was no oxidization, meaning colors stayed bright.

And the colors were important. Nouvelle cuisine had allied itself with the auteurist avant-garde, the chefs seen as artists, and none more so than the Troisgros brothers, whose extravagantly large plates served to highlight the artful presentation of their cooking. The thin slice of salmon floating on a pale-yellow pool of sorrel sauce. The trio of broiled tomatoes stuffed with egg, spinach, and fresh cheese, presented in ceramic egg cups. The slices of vegetable terrine with cross-sections of carrots, green beans, and artichoke hearts served on a thin layer of fresh tomato sauce. The dishes resembled modern, abstract painting—shapes, colors, and geometry revealing a new culinary sophistication.

The pages of Gault and Millau's *Nouveau Guide* were full of news of culinary trends and technological advancements. The editors taste-tested frozen dinners and tried new kitchen gadgets, reported on the science of nutrition and food preservation, investigated kitchen cleanliness, and explained "microbes." The ethos of the magazine, like nouvelle cuisine itself, was relentlessly modern.

A few years earlier, in 1972, Gault and Millau had launched an annual guide to restaurants in France, called Gault & Millau, in direct competition with the Michelin and Kléber guides. Like the magazine, the guide was casual, witty, and opinionated. And it was selling: For the 1976 edition, they had printed more than one hundred thousand copies. Unlike the Michelin, which Gault and Millau considered staid and conservative, and which "rewarded seniority," the Gault & Millau guide had its eye on new talent. They awarded not stars but toques, one to five, and rated food on a scale of 1 to 20, like French school grades. (The highest grade was never given: "Only God can achieve 20, and He is rarely to be found at the stove.") The guide printed its coveted toque ratings in two colors: black ink for the standard, old-school restaurants serving the classics and red ink for the avant-garde, nouvelle cuisine establishments. Every year, there were more red toques.

Gault and Millau had named nouvelle cuisine, outlined its tenets and commandments, and nurtured its development in the pages of their magazine and guidebooks; now a new wave of chefs and restaurants was following in the Bande à Bocuse's footsteps. In January 1976, the *Nouveau Guide* published a cover story titled "Bocuse, Here Are Your Children," profiling twenty-three "young wolves of French nouvelle cuisine," including Georges Blanc, Frédy Girardet, Bernard Loiseau, and Michel Rostang. The chefs posed for a group portrait, all smiles. Some things never changed—they were still all men.

"Even if it annoys some," the editors wrote, "we must objectively recognize that, thanks to this new trend, in France in 1976, we don't eat quite as we used to. Lightness, simplicity, and invention have driven out, at least in part, routine and bad habits."

Gault and Millau were riding high, taking on Michelin and winning, defining French food and cooking for a new generation. Nouvelle cuisine combined rebellious, post-1960s rule-breaking with technological and scientific mastery; the *Nouveau Guide* published profiles of up-and-coming chefs and their restaurants, their new dishes and innovations, and multipage advertisements for the latest nonstick pans. "Nouvelle cuisine adapts particularly well to non-adhesive coating," the Tefal ad copy announced. "Simpler preparations, stripped down, without the patina of tradition, allow ingredients to retain all their original flavor. Fish no longer need to swim in fat, meats are seared without having to be immersed in a pound of butter."

In the spring of 1976, Gault and Millau decided to publish a grand assessment of nouvelle cuisine: What had the new cooking achieved, what was its significance, where was it going? The cover story was, inevitably, a celebration of both nouvelle cuisine and Gault and Millau's role in promoting it:

> October, 1973. On the cover of *Nouveau Guide*, a large headline: "*Vive la Nouvelle Cuisine Française.*" A profession of faith but also an act of baptism for three small, inoffensive words: French nouvelle cuisine.
>
> More than two years have passed, and we have never talked about it more than now. The movement has indeed traveled beyond our borders. In Belgium and in Switzerland, countries with conservative culinary cultures, some of the best chefs have joined. In the United States and Great Britain, in Germany and Japan, "nouvelle cuisine" is the subject of an extraordinary number of articles and reports, and our great cooks are welcomed as ambassadors of a new way of life.
>
> Certainly, twenty-nine months is short compared to the long history of our gastronomy, but isn't it sufficient time to recognize that "nouvelle cuisine" is more than a passing fashion, and to wonder if it is not a small revolution—palace coup?

Nouvelle cuisine had managed to "liberate a cuisine that was too pompous, too routinized, unnatural, full of prohibitions and conventions, and which corresponded less and less to our modern way of life." The new cooking was "anti-Grand Bouffe," the editors explained, and offered chefs an escape from conformity.

Accompanying the article was a comprehensive listing of the

best nouvelle cuisine restaurants in France, Belgium, and Switzerland, ninety-five in all, a who's who of the chefs changing French cooking. There was only a single woman chef listed: Olympe Nahmias.

Olympe was not interested in the latest kitchen technology, nor in nouvelle cuisine particularly. Still, she was happy to be included among the Gault-Millau vanguard. She was exploring new ingredients and combinations in the kitchen, experimenting with spices, adding turnips and purple artichokes to her spring salad, for example, and using mint and cumin in her vegetable terrine. She made her own flavored vinegars; she served a "sour and sweet" sauce with her roasted duck; her curried crayfish was one of her signature dishes.

"I've never liked the pomp and shackles of classic cuisine, and even less the inept heaviness of bourgeois cooking," she said. "My cuisine is the cuisine of freedom: spontaneous, unschooled, vivacious, eclectic, tasty and gourmet, a bit iconoclastic and without frills."

The tiny restaurant on rue Montparnasse was more popular than ever, something of a clubhouse for the Paris film, theater, and music scenes. Here were Michel Serrault and Jean Poiret, stars of the long-running hit *La Cage aux Folles* at the Théâtre du Palais-Royal, and the comic actors Coluche and Miou-Miou. And here was Daniel Toscan du Plantier, head of Gaumont films, and singer-songwriters Julien Clerc and Jean-Jacques Goldman, and, every so often, Hollywood royalty—Orson

Welles, Francis Ford Coppola, Miloš Forman—or an actual rock star like Mick Jagger or Johnny Hallyday.

It was down to good fortune: being in the right place at the right time. The Left Bank in the early 1970s, a young and rebellious chef. Olympe was glamorous. And this was what Bocuse was denying the women chefs, Olympe realized: glamour. In his conception, women chefs were dowdy and old-fashioned, and so was their cooking. The great men of the Bande à Bocuse, meanwhile, were modern and scientific, forward-looking. "We are experimenting and making the most of what our century has to offer us," said Raymond Oliver, one of Bocuse's compatriots. "It is this curiosity that characterizes the new spirit."

The men were unbound by tradition or taboos; they were dashing, womanizing, rule-breaking revolutionaries, and at the same time they were cool, technological, and cerebral. Whereas women—they cooked their grandmother's recipes, guided by tradition and intuition.

Olympe didn't like this dichotomy. It felt like a trap.

But perhaps the ARC was a way out. At exactly the same time that Gault and Millau were celebrating the triumphs of nouvelle cuisine in the spring of 1976, the ARC was signing up new members and preparing a public debut for later in the year. Women's cooking could be whatever they made it—that was the idea insisted upon by the association. And for Olympe, a charter member, that was the future she wanted, her cooking liberated and iconoclastic.

14

Battle of the Sexes

The ARC was on top of the world—at least that's how it felt. A whirlwind of press coverage and feature stories, interviews and photo shoots starting in the fall of 1976 had lifted the profile of the women chefs and broadcast their critique of the male-dominated French food establishment far and wide. "The Revolt of Women Cooks" was the headline in *Paris Match* in January 1977, accompanied by a large group photograph of twelve of the founders, all smiling. The organization had been created to battle "phallocratic toques," the article explained, which was why the women were photographed wearing tall white chef's toques, which they never wore in the kitchen. The racy men's magazine *Lui* also ran an article with a picture of the ARC chefs—fully clothed, of course—among the naked pinup girls that filled its pages.

The story of the ARC quickly went international as well. "Female French Chefs Push for 'Kitchen Lib'" reported the UPI newswire: "The great cuisine of France is more or less a man's world. Now the few women chefs are winning recognition for their own style of cooking." In February 1977, *The New York Times* ran a story about the ARC under the headline "Women Restaurant Cooks in Paris Strike Back."

> PARIS—Female cooks in restaurants in France are successfully using their own national association to further the cause of women's haute cuisine.
>
> Leading male cooks oppose the presence of women in the kitchen, arguing that haute cuisine is a man's world, and that view has been repeatedly expressed by Paul Bocuse, the master cook.
>
> Mr. Bocuse, who has not only professional prestige but also official authority as the gastronomic adviser to the Government tourism department, declared that women were not qualified for haute cuisine because (a) they lacked imagination, (b) they weren't able to direct a kitchen staff and (c) they just weren't as good as men.
>
> Not so, say the women cooks.

The president of the ARC, Gisèle Berger, was the face of the organization and appeared in many of the articles. She was generally portrayed as modest, hardworking, and—contrary to Bocuse's caricature—inventive. Women's cooking might be simpler, more traditional, passed down from mother to daughter, but it was also capable of exploring new ideas. The *Times* noted some of the items on the menu at Berger's restaurant, La Bonne Table:

> Mrs. Berger said she had taught herself to cook. "I have it in my hands," she said. But she expressed regret that young women had difficulty finding a cooking school. One of the aims of the associa-

> tion, she said, is to teach cooking and to arrange for young women to become assistants to established cooks.
>
> Mrs. Berger's menu alone would disprove Mr. Bocuse's thesis that women lack culinary imagination. The menu includes lasagna stuffed with seafood and fish, seafood on sauerkraut and a seafood cassoulet.
>
> What's more, Mrs. Berger claims to be the inventor of an extraordinary seafood and fish sausage, "stuffed also with spinach, celery and . . ."
>
> Mrs. Berger suddenly stopped and said, blushing: "I can't tell you, because it's my secret."

In *Le Monde*, Courtine also took aim at Bocuse's claim that women restaurant chefs were subpar. "After all, in Paris alone," he wrote, "there are still a few left at the stove, women for whom cooking is love, respect, and imagination and who, if they had heard Mr. Bocuse's rantings, would have hurriedly laughed . . . for fear of being forced to cry! We salute them here." Courtine described Berger as a woman who cooked with "intelligence and mischief but never gratuitously," and steadfastly defended the women of the ARC. "Not only are women capable of invention, but also of preparing a cuisine of lightness, common sense, and decency."

Bocuse was enjoying himself. Cast as the villain in all the stories about the ARC, he embraced the role with devilish gusto. He decided to write a letter to the women's chef group, sending copies to Berger, the president, as well as to the other founding members, including Christiane Massia and Annie Desvignes. The letter was addressed to "Mesdames les cheftaines"—the "lady chieftains" of the ARC, the greeting meant as a sly insult, since "cheftaines" was generally used to mean "girl scout leaders" or "den mothers." He signed the letter "Paul Bocuse, king of pranks." The tone was tongue in cheek.

> Mesdames les cheftaines,
>
> All my compliments on the double-page spread in *Paris Match*. It is simply to be deplored, this illegal wearing of toques, exclusively reserved for us phallocrats who have not yet worn a garter belt, but who would be immediately seduced if one of you had that day, being great amateurs and connoisseurs in this area.
>
> Wishing my wife to improve her culinary knowledge, and having no background in this area, I would like to know the conditions for admission to your association (training, number of years in the profession, etc.) with a view to a future name for my restaurant, which I am thinking of perhaps renaming "Chez la Mère Bocuse."

Bocuse ended the letter reiterating his opinion that women chefs lacked creativity:

> I would like to repeat here my conviction that women are certainly good cooks for so-called "traditional" cuisine: Mère Filloux, Mère Brazier (seventy-five years of cooking between them) but only one menu: artichoke stock with foie gras; Lyonnais quenelle (much appreciated by my friend Courtine), chicken in half-

mourning; chocolate mousse. Cuisine not at all inventive in my opinion, I regret to say.

Paul Bocuse, roi de canulars

The letter was deliberately preposterous—accusing the women of "illegally" wearing toques, and then asking about his wife joining the ARC, and musing about changing the name of his restaurant. It was all a joke for Bocuse, an amusement. "Chez la Mère Bocuse." Cue the uproarious laughter.

Bocuse's mocking, teasing letter was accompanied by his continued attacks in the press, always with a wink and a smile. "I would rather have a pretty woman in my bed than behind a stove in a restaurant. I prefer my women to smell of Dior and Chanel than of cooking fat," he told *People* magazine. "Women are good cooks, but they are not good chefs. Women who systematically want to do what men do just end by losing their femininity, and what I adore most of all is a feminine woman."

There were no women working in Bocuse's kitchen, needless to say. "Here, it is a man's job," he said.

"I am reproached for taking poses like Caesar, but that's just theater," he told Gault and Millau's *Nouveau Guide*. "In fact, I am very shy. I never know where to put my hands. Except with women."

Christiane Massia decided to write back to Bocuse on behalf of the ARC. She was young, chic, full of confidence, and her Paris restaurant, L'Aquitaine, specialized in the food of southwest France. She served classics—rillettes of eel, brandade soufflé—but put her own twist on the recipes. Her focus on vegetables—delicate pureed Jerusalem artichokes or pureed lettuce—was noteworthy. So was her determination to hire as many young women cooks to work for her as she could. Her goal, one day, was to run an all-female kitchen. She wore her long blond hair in a single braid.

Bocuse's over-the-top male chauvinism made her angry, but his schoolboy humor made him difficult to rebut. He had the advantage of insincerity. Or rather, the women of ARC had the disadvantage of earnestness: His insults were a game, and to respond entirely seriously would be a losing gambit. Bocuse would always claim to be only kidding (he'd signed his letter "king of pranks," after all), and if they couldn't take a joke, well . . . Massia addressed him with ironic deference as "Maître-queux"—master chef—in her reply.

Cher Maître-queux,

So sorry to have pained you by daring to wear the white toque, the phallic symbol of your science, your authority, your virility.

We owe you so much, we female cooks. Without you, each of us would still be isolated in front of her little wood or coal stove. Today, we are banded together, and famous; the great Paul Bocuse writes to us, TV reporters from all over the world clutter up our tiny kitchens.

If Robert Courtine is the founder of the ARC, then you are its instigator.

And now your wife wants to join us. She likes to cook, and learned from her mother your beautiful Lyon family cuisine: this will be enough knowledge if her customers think so; then I will have as much pleasure at the table of "la Mère Bocuse" as I had at Paul Bocuse, and that is saying something!

You quote the menu of two eminent cooks, one long dead, the other in retirement. . . . We today are thousands and very much alive, and full of creativity. I invite you to visit the restaurants of the ARC, and judge their culinary imagination for yourself. But as long as you maintain that they have none, a black flag will fly over our pots.

Let's reconcile, Paul Bocuse, and let's make those who come to us happy.

Christiane Massia

She received no reply.

The "women wearing chef's toques" controversy caught the attention of French women's magazines, *Marie Claire*, for example, which quoted Bocuse's litany of complaints. The white toque was "a male appendage," he declared. Women chefs "have no culinary imagination," he declaimed. Was he serious? No. Was he joking? No. This was Bocuse the prankster, the smart aleck. The popular feminist writers Marianne Antoine and Florence Rémy responded with a public letter taking him to task. They were the authors of bestselling books like *Comment Élever et Soigner son Mari*

(*How to Raise and Care for a Husband*), the cover of which showed a smiling woman pushing a baby carriage occupied by a man smoking a pipe.

Bocuse was "blowing up his own stars," Antoine and Rémy wrote, by "displaying an elevation of thought unworthy of a snack bar boy," let alone the spokesperson for French gastronomy. And as for the toque question: "One would like to believe that you're joking; your tone forbids this reassuring hypothesis. We only know of laws forbidding the unauthorized wearing of military decorations or weapons: would you by any chance take your headgear for a medal of honor or a 22 long rifle?"

Gault and Millau addressed the creation of the ARC with a cover story in the *Nouveau Guide* on the best women chefs in Paris. They generally saw the women as relics of the past. "Never has the number of restaurants been so great, no epoch has known such an explosion of talent, such a celebration of invention and such a frenzy of novelties," they wrote. "Why is it, then, that this shower of graces has not been able to touch women as well? Exceptions, glimmers, hopes, we certainly find some here and there—an association of women chefs, the ARC, has even just been created, bringing together the last of them across France."

Gault and Millau sided with Bocuse on the essential inferiority of women chefs. As much as they admired the "mères" of Lyon and the other iconic, traditional women chefs, they considered them lacking:

> Women—in the kitchen at least—do not know how to command. They only have authority over themselves and are tragi-

> cally unskilled in leading a brigade. It is a sociological observation confirmed, for example, by their absence from hotel and cooking schools. And which also explains to a certain extent their terribly touchy nature, and their obsessive desire to want to do absolutely everything in the kitchen themselves: in Lyon, Mère Léa does not even allow her young daughters to peel the cardoons.

The ARC hoped to change attitudes about women chefs (and win entrance for them in apprenticeship programs and associations), but they clearly had a long way to go: In the eyes of Gault and Millau, women were hopelessly weak, touchy, and obsessive.

Still, a cover story in the *Nouveau Guide* was to be welcomed; the group photograph included Massia, Berger, Allard, Libois, and Olympe, among others, and the reviews of each restaurant were quite detailed. They gave Allard high marks for the "perfection" of her classic Burgundy cooking, her coq au vin and rare-cooked duck with turnips. Christiane Massia's southwestern French cuisine was a bit heavy but "opulent" and made with supremely fresh ingredients. Some of the women, Gault and Millau discovered, were "even cooking nouvelle cuisine. . . . The classic complaint that women's cooking lacks invention finds some scathing denials here." Gisèle Berger's La Bonne Table was "joyous and original," they wrote, her fish always "irreproachably fresh," and her cooking displayed "an inventive ardor full of intelligence and mischief." Olympe's cooking was based in nouvelle cuisine, the magazine wrote, her sauces light and her dishes—crispy baked artichokes and sautéed crayfish and rare fillets of beef—"audacious and inspired."

Olympe read the Gault and Millau article with some irritation. The entire debate about women chefs, and women's culinary creativity, and women wearing or not wearing the toque, and whether women were cooking "nouvelle cuisine," seemed ridiculous. Of course women could cook, and of course they could cook creatively, and for that matter they could wear whatever they wanted in the kitchen. The very idea of the ARC was to demand recognition for their talents, and equal access to culinary institutions like the Maîtres Cuisiniers de France. Instead, they were now embroiled in arguments about styles of cooking, and whether women were innately "touchy" and "obsessive."

Who cared what a buffoonish Bocuse had to say about her cooking or anyone else's? The editors of the *Nouveau Guide* had given her a rave review, and for that she was grateful. But the gist of the article seemed to be that most women cooked in the old-fashioned, bourgeois style, with a few "nouvelle cuisine" exceptions. She was one of the exceptions, and therefore embraced by Gault and Millau, who also made a point of calling her "the most beautiful woman chef in Paris."

Was that flattering, or was that demeaning?

Courtine, meanwhile, saw the ARC as a bulwark against nouvelle cuisine, defending national traditions, the glories of "real" French cooking. "The defenders of the great, noble, haute cuisine contemptuously call women's cooking 'simple'!" he wrote. "But women's cuisine has its nobility: that of the heart. It is bourgeois in the best sense of the term, and tinged with regionalism, because it originates in the very products of the soil where it was born. It is robust and healthy. It is honest, and nothing is hidden."

But this was not how Olympe saw her cooking. She wanted to be free of the past, not wallow in tradition, however noble. Courtine, she feared, was hijacking the ARC for his own purposes. He saw the new generation of women chefs as inheritors of the mères of Lyon, nationalist symbols of matronly abundance, cuisine of "the old Gallo-Latin land," as he would say.

Olympe and her husband, Albert Nahmias, were well aware of the connection between Courtine's archconservative culinary opinions and his politics. The rumors about Courtine's collaborationist past continued to circulate, and, more and more, so did stories about his present-day opinions and attitudes. Albert heard that Courtine had been seated next to the Israeli ambassador at a press lunch at restaurant Laurent in Paris, for example, when the ambassador asked, teasingly: "You're with *Le Monde*, so you must be a socialist?" (The newspaper was considered left wing.) Courtine's deadpan reply: "National socialist."

Courtine apparently made a pilgrimage every spring to Vichy, taking the waters at the Hôtel du Parc, where Pétain had kept an apartment during the war. This was seen as a sign of his devotion to the memory of the war, and his Nazi sympathies. At *Le Monde*, there were also whispers. Holding the door for Courtine one day, the legal columnist Jean-Marc Théolleyre, a former Resistance fighter who'd survived Buchenwald during the war, was rumored to have said: "After you, dear collaborator." Another staff writer apparently protested: "If guys like him had won the war, the newspaper would be printed in Gothic type!"

Rumor, anecdote, gossip: Much of the talk about Courtine was unsubstantiated. Still, the culture of French silence on the topic of collaborators was changing. *The Sorrow and the Pity*, the searing documentary by Marcel Ophuls, challenged the French myth that they'd all (with a few exceptions) heroically resisted the Nazi occupation. The film had been commissioned by French television in 1969 but never aired; instead, it played in small movie theaters in the early 1970s and had won international acclaim. Similarly, Robert O. Paxton's history of the era, *Vichy France*, was translated and published in France in 1973 and revealed the awful depth of French collaboration.

Would the truth about Courtine ever be known? Olympe wondered. What was that truth, exactly? In any case he was now leading the way at the ARC. He was not the founder of the organization (as Massia had stated in her letter to Bocuse), but he'd been instrumental. And after Bocuse's repeated attacks on women chefs, Courtine had leaped to their defense.

Courtine—and Courtine's ARC—made Olympe slightly queasy.

The Bocuse affair turned out to be—perversely but perhaps not unexpectedly—phenomenally beneficial for the ARC. The press loved a controversy, and in France, everyone had an opinion about food. The countless articles and TV spots had brought the women of the ARC and their restaurants into the public consciousness to a degree they had never foreseen.

They were the subject of two different cookbooks published

that year, in 1977. The first was written by Courtine and published under his *Le Monde* pseudonym La Reynière and titled *200 Recettes des Meilleures Cuisinières de France* (*200 Recipes of the Best Women Chefs in France*). Each of the forty-five chefs, all members of the ARC, was given a brief biographical introduction, followed by a handful of her recipes. Simone Lemaire's Easter pot-au-feu, Annie Desvignes's rabbit with apple cider, Olympe's curried crayfish, Christiane Massia's orange-marinated turbot cutlets. Courtine had written an introduction about the true superiority of women's cooking, recounting Paul Bocuse's insults, and the founding of the ARC.

Grandes Dames de la Cuisine, by *Elle* magazine writer Madeleine Peter, followed the same format, with longer profiles and recipes. "Men can acquire their science in schools which prepare them for their career," Peter wrote in her introduction, "but to this day women are not admitted to these schools. They learn 'on the job' to perfect their gifts." The book was translated and published in the US as *Favorite Recipes of the Great Women Chefs of France.*

The ARC had succeeded in reaching a large audience, both in France and abroad. In May 1977, the group held its annual meeting over lunch at La Croix Blanche, Gisèle Crouzier's restaurant and inn in Chaumont-sur-Tharonne in the Loire Valley. Gathered in the large, warm kitchen, lunch cooking in the oven (one of Crouzier's specialties was stewed rabbit with apricots), the women, a dozen or so, welcomed their guest of honor: the First Lady of France, Anne-Aymone Giscard d'Estaing.

This was a symbolic moment, a celebratory lunch very different from the presidential lunch for Bocuse at the Élysée Palace two years earlier, which the First Lady had also attended. There were no awards, no Legion of Honor medals, and there was no press, no photographers, and no interviews. The meal was modest, cooked by Crouzier and her small staff; there was no presentation of any newly invented dish for the occasion. There were also no men.

They stood together, smiling, Giscard d'Estaing in her Chanel suit, Crouzier in her chef's whites, the others in colorful dresses. Someone snapped a photo of the moment—no one posing or even looking at the camera. It was all rather informal, and yet, for Desvignes, Lemaire, Berger, Allard, and the others, a real honor, vindication for the ARC.

Still: The fight would go on. The president of the Maîtres Cuisiniers de France, Émile Tingaud, responded to the founding of the ARC with unapologetic vitriol, telling his members in a private meeting, "As long as I am president, no woman will join this association."

PART FOUR

"Nouvelle Cuisine Is Dead"

15

Trendy

Michel Guérard was suddenly famous, actually famous, strangers-stopping-him-on-the-street famous. Was it the magazine covers and newspaper articles about his restaurant in Eugénie-les-Bains? Was it his newly awarded third Michelin star?

No. Mostly, it was television.

The impresarios of nouvelle cuisine had begun to appear regularly on a half-hour TV cooking show called *La Grande Cocotte*, which aired on TF1, the preeminent national broadcaster, starting in 1976. Guérard, Bocuse, and the Troisgros brothers starred in a majority of the episodes, cooking their favorite dishes for the show's host, the theater and movie star Marthe Mercadier. The show was in color—a relative novelty—and charmingly simple: a set with an oven and stove, a table with the relevant ingredients, the stylish Mercadier asking questions and helping here and there while Bocuse prepared his famous sea bass en croute or Guérard made his "salade folle," or a feuilleté with custard and strawberries.

There was no studio audience; Mercadier, with her elaborate eye makeup and beehive hairdo, kept the show moving briskly.

Guérard didn't mind the fame, not at all. He'd always been a performer; he liked putting on a show. In 1977, he launched another TV cooking program, also on TF1, called *La Cuisine Légère* (*Light Cooking*). The episodes were short, just fifteen minutes long, and aired Saturdays at 12:30 p.m.; Guérard presented simplified versions of his cuisine minceur recipes, and in general emphasized the lighter, fresher, healthier approach to cooking that nouvelle cuisine represented.

Both of these shows were immediately and immensely popular, as was seemingly everything else caught up in the cresting wave of nouvelle cuisine. Chefs, restaurants, food critics—the entire insular world of gourmet cooking had entered into the popular culture and imagination like never before. In Louis de Funès's *L'Aile ou la Cuisse* (*The Wing or the Thigh*) in 1976, the comedian played the role of an all-powerful food critic, one who, like Robert Courtine, could determine the fate of any restaurant with a positive or negative review. De Funès's nemesis in the film was an evil industrial food magnate. In *Who Is Killing the Great Chefs of Europe?*, in 1978, Robert Morley also played a food critic, one whose favorite chefs were being murdered, one by one, possibly by a rival chef. These caper-comedies featured scenes of restaurant critics disguised in drag so as not to be recognized, chefs berating underlings for not stirring their saucepots correctly, a Japanese chef flinging his knives in the air, the proprietor of a vegetarian restaurant panicking about an American steakhouse possibly opening next door, and a blind taste test performed live on a television talk show hosted by the famous Philippe Bouvard, playing himself.

It was all good fun and, soon enough, for Guérard and the other newly prominent chefs, overwhelming. Nouvelle cuisine and, more generally, the meaning and future of French cooking, and the rise of the celebrity chef, were ongoing topics of conversation and discussion and interest. Nouvelle cuisine was of the moment, and it was everywhere.

And this was becoming a problem.

At first, Guérard was flattered: His so-called crazy salad, with green beans, asparagus, truffles, and foie gras, was appearing on menus all over France, it seemed—a tribute to his signature dish. The Troisgros brothers' salmon with sorrel sauce was also suddenly ubiquitous, as were Bocuse's famously al dente green beans.

The Bande à Bocuse had always made a point of sharing ideas and inspiration, but never copying one another. "There is a kind of code of honor," said Alain Senderens of Archestrate in Paris. Now, however, the pioneers of nouvelle cuisine found their cooking subjected to large-scale reproduction. "Culinary espionage in the Paris region has taken on worrying proportions," reported Gault and Millau's *Nouveau Guide* in 1976. If Bocuse and friends were indeed artists, their vast culinary progeny were making the equivalent of cheap, knockoff poster art. "As soon as a more or less nouvelle cuisine dish appears on your menu," Le Camélia's Jean Delaveyne told the magazine, "you can be sure that eight days later it will be served elsewhere, more or less well copied."

It wasn't imitation per se that was the problem; it was *poor* imitation. Le Duc, the Paris seafood restaurant known for its très nouvelle raw fish and ceviche dishes, had seen its "poisson cru" copied by restaurants all over the city, many of them unscrupulous. Week-old dorade and frozen salmon did not make for acceptable poisson cru. There was also a plague of terrible seafood terrines, a dish refined and delicate in the hands of Guérard, but equally easy to botch. Undercooked green beans, often served almost completely raw and barely edible, were everywhere. "So many cooks have jumped on the bandwagon," Gault and Millau reported, "some with talent and imagination, others content to plagiarize and 'steal' ideas. *Let's sprinkle a few green peppercorns on the meat, let's serve puree of sorrel with (frozen) salmon, and voilà, pretend we're making 'nouvelle cuisine.'*"

The proliferation of low-end, low-quality nouvelle cuisine was giving its high-profile practitioners a bad name. This was the price of success, imitation the sincerest form of flattery and all that. But the problems went deeper. The sheer, ubiquitous popularity of nouvelle cuisine was reason enough, in some quarters, to suspect the worst. The cooking was trendy, and that was bad. Similarly, the newfound celebrity of the nouvelle cuisine chefs—their television appearances, their overseas travels—was to some an unmistakable sign of decadence and frivolity.

Bocuse, of course, was a lightning rod for this sort of attention. His self-promotion began to draw ever more criticism. In *Esquire* magazine, Roy Andries de Groot took aim at Bocuse's publicist, the unnamed Yanou Collart: "The Bocuse group hired a high-powered Parisian publicity person whose main claim to fame was the habit of dressing in black while driving around in a white Rolls-Royce." De Groot was an aristocratic Englishman (a baron of some sort) who'd lost his eyesight during the London Blitz, moved to New York City after the war, lived in Greenwich Village, and fashioned himself as a food critic, always accompanied by his seeing-eye dog, a German shepherd named Nusta. He described the nouvelle cuisine chefs as "the Young Turks," "the gastronomic mafia," "the enfants terribles," and "the movement," out for profit and glory. He was interested in their cooking but suspicious of their celebrity. Of Michel Guérard, he wrote: "You can hardly open a magazine without finding his picture and a feature about him. Depending on your point of view, he is either the new Messiah or a publicity-hungry iconoclast."

De Groot thought the nouvelle cuisine chefs had sparked a necessary modernization of French cooking but that they had perhaps gone too far. Certainly the mania for Guérard's cuisine minceur was overblown in his opinion. "Perhaps the Beautiful People of New York would be willing to do their dieting in Paris?" he asked, amused. He noted that Craig Claiborne of *The New York Times* and Gael Greene of *New York* magazine had discovered all the same restaurants at the same time (presumably at the direction of Collart in her white Rolls), both reporting "ravishment and revitalization by such low-calorie items as raw, thinly sliced sea scallops." For his part, De Groot found "diet-chic" nouvelle cuisine wanting.

At *The New York Times*, meanwhile, a new restaurant critic was making a name for herself, and she, too, was skeptical about nouvelle cuisine. Mimi Sheraton, hired in 1976, was no-nonsense, hard-nosed, and rather dyspeptic. She considered herself as much consumer advocate as gourmet, and had no patience for Claiborne's chummy personal friendships with his favorite chefs. (He remained the food editor at the *Times*, and the godfather of the American food establishment.) Sheraton wore elaborate disguises when she reviewed restaurants, including tinted glasses and various wigs, and refused any special treatment. She was rigorous and scientific in her approach, famously, for example, having taste-tested and reviewed all 1,196 items for sale at the Bloomingdale's food department for a single article for *New York* magazine a few years earlier.

In the fall of 1977, Sheraton embarked on a tour of the best restaurants in France. Did they really deserve their three-star reputations? Were the high prices justified? How was the service? All the excitement about nouvelle cuisine—what did it amount to exactly? And what about the old-fashioned, haute cuisine stalwarts that were not at all "nouvelle"?

Sheraton took evident pleasure in answering these questions mostly in the negative. No, many of the three-star restaurants did not deserve their reputations. No, their high prices were not justified. The service was often brusque and dismissive. Both nouvelle cuisine and traditional French luxury restaurant cooking came in for lacerating criticism, as did the Michelin and Kléber guides, for upholding top ratings for restaurants that clearly did not merit the honor.

She took aim, first, at one of the sacred cows of French gastronomy, La Pyramide, in Vienne. This was a legendary place, where Bocuse and many others had worked under Fernand Point, and which was now run by his widow, Mado Point. Fernand had died decades ago, and the restaurant had maintained its three Michelin stars and three Kléber crowns ever since. Sheraton thought La Pyramide was in steep decline: "The *mousse de foie en brioche* was a calamity, with both pâté and brioche dry and stale," she wrote. "The *cassolette St. Jacques* combined leathery scallops and overcooked spinach in sauce that tasted dark brown." And so on. She compared the jambon to "cafeteria ham in gravy." Even the cheese plate selections were banal, "dried out and cracked bits and pieces."

When she confronted the editors of the Michelin and Kléber guides about the discrepancy between the quality of the food at La Pyramide and the restaurant's continued high ratings, Jean Didier, the editor of the Kléber guides, responded: "Your question makes me sad and I am sorry you asked it. Yes, I am aware of what you describe. As for ratings, if I follow my head I do one thing; if I follow my heart, I do another. Fernand Point who founded that great restaurant was the spiritual father of today's greatest chefs and his wife is now an old woman. The reason for the top rating is, of course, sentiment."

Only a few years earlier, in 1974, Claiborne had written the article for the *Times* about Mme Point on the occasion of Bocuse's celebratory dinner for her, full of lavish praise. Was there an element of vindictiveness in Sheraton's scathing reassessment? She and Claiborne did not much like each other; that was well known at the *Times*. (She considered Claiborne and other *Times* staffers to be "a bunch of elite snobs.") Now she was examining the cooking of Claiborne's cherished favorites, traveling France to "sample the highly publicized efforts of superstar chefs (many of whom spend as much time making public appearances abroad as they do home at their ranges)."

Having established her take-no-prisoners approach, dismantling La Pyramide at the beginning of her long survey of three-star French gastronomy, Sheraton turned her attention to the Bande à Bocuse, and to nouvelle cuisine. The new cooking had its moments, she reported—a laudable dinner at the Haeberlin brothers' Auberge de l'Ill in Alsace, for example, where she enjoyed the "celebrated" salmon soufflé and braised slices of pheasant and partridge. The service was efficient, if "impersonal and distracted." Alain Chapel in Mionnay was a mixed bag. The stuffed calf's ear was "not awful, it was just silly," while the mousse of chicken livers and marrow and the pâté of eel in puff pastry were "spectacular."

But at the three most prominent restaurants of the nouvelle cuisine movement—Bocuse, Guérard, and Troisgros—Sheraton found much to criticize: "No man to hide his light under a bushel, Paul Bocuse has his signature traced out in green neon, blazing against the night sky above his restaurant. The dining rooms have been decorated with a heavy hand, in what might be considered baronial bawdy-house style, complete with bad art and lurid red candles. Service was offhand but adequate." As for the food, Sheraton loved the famous sea bass en croute, as well as the mussel soup and various pâtés. The rest was all terrible. The turbot was "overpowered by a stingingly acidic wine sauce." The duck was "tough and salty." The lamb was served in "fatty chunks." The chicken au vinaigre was too sour. The pistachio ice cream was inedible.

At Guérard's Les Prés d'Eugénie, the pot-au-feu (for which he'd named his first restaurant in Paris) was excellent, as expected. But Sheraton found cuisine minceur, the dietetic nouvelle cuisine menu Guérard had made famous in his bestselling cookbook, to be unimpressive. "Along with calories, Mr. Guérard seems to have eliminated flavor," she wrote. "(Or could it be the calories themselves have flavor?) . . . A baron of lamb said to have been *braised* with fennel seemed to have been steamed and was uninteresting; alongside it were overcooked, waterlogged slices of zucchini and eggplant."

She was even tougher on the Troisgros brothers' restaurant, finding fault with everything from the "grimy, industrial city of Roanne" to the dining room with "all the charm of a restaurant in a German railroad station" to the "sleazy" curtains and the tables that were too close together and the "brusque, hectic service." And then there was the food:

> The much publicized mosaic pâté of mixed vegetables was served tooth-achingly cold, the salade nouvelle looked and tasted washed out and the puff pastry with sweetbreads was sodden. Aiguillettes de canard, the sliced boned breast of duck, was dry and overdone, and the legs of the duck served au vinaigre the following day for lunch were stringy and their sauce lacked subtlety and richness.

What had started as a "search for the perfect meal" and a critical look at the top-rated restaurants in France had ended in furious dissatisfaction, especially with nouvelle cuisine. In Paris, Sheraton noted that Alain Senderens of L'Archestrate was not at his restaurant but instead traveling, much like Bocuse and the other celebrated chefs, who spent far too much time away from their kitchens in her opinion. (This was one of Sheraton's ongoing and oft-repeated annoyances.) "Prices here are exorbitant for portions that are almost laughably small," she wrote of Archestrate—and the food was too sweet. The duck and lobster appetizer tasted like dessert, and the duck fillets were "as caramelized as candy apples, almost inedibly so."

The backlash had begun. The reassessment. On French television, a top-rated Friday night program, *Apostrophes*, a kind of literary talk show, had recently hosted a panel discussion entitled "Does French Nouvelle Cuisine Exist?" Filmed live at the gilded, belle epoque Train Bleu restaurant in the Gare de Lyon train station in Paris, the ninety-minute-long episode featured representatives from both sides of the "debate." French haute cuisine was changing, everyone agreed, but changing for the better or the worse?

Henri Gault and Christian Millau were on hand to make the case for nouvelle cuisine, as they had been for years in the pages of their magazine and guidebooks. Robert Courtine took the role of stern skeptic. And Paul Bocuse, naturally, was the star of the show, introduced as the face of modern French cooking. The host of *Apostrophes*, Bernard Pivot, noted that Bocuse had appeared on the cover of *Newsweek* magazine, and was a kind of culinary diplomat—"the Kissinger of French cuisine in the US and in Japan," he said.

Pivot was quick-witted and amusing, his dark, bushy eyebrows flickering expressively as he led the conversation about the state of French cooking, trying his best to provoke all sides and also keep the large group under control. There were eight guests, also including Gaston Lenôtre, and two authors of recent cookbooks, Ginette Mathiot and Lise Marie, both women mostly ignored by Pivot as Gault, Millau, and Bocuse faced off against Courtine and Denis Lahana, the chef and proprietor of the Paris restaurant Chez Denis.

Lahana was an ideal representative for the anti–nouvelle cuisine position: His restaurant was traditional and well regarded without being stodgy or ornate. It was a small place on rue Gustave Flaubert, near the Arc de Triomphe, made famous (or perhaps infamous) by Craig Claiborne on the front page of *The New York Times* in 1975. "Just a Quiet Dinner for Two in Paris: 31 Dishes, Nine Wines, a $4,000 Check" was the headline. The article was a stunt: Claiborne had won a charity auction prize of a dinner for two paid for by American Express and had gone out of his way to find the most extravagant menu possible. Lahana served plate after plate of caviar, sweetbreads, quail, oysters, Bresse chicken, partridge, fillet of beef, ortolans, wild duck, roast veal and truffles, foie gras, woodcock, pheasants, and more, along with an array of famous wines including a 1947 Château Lafite-Rothschild, a 1961 Château Pétrus, and a 1929 Romanée-Conti. Then came the desserts, many of them—and about a week later came the letters to the editor, many, many, *many* of them. In an age of inflation at home and famine abroad, Claiborne's article struck a nerve. "How can anyone reconcile this smugly decadent story and almost daily reports of worldwide hunger and starvation?" asked one reader. "Is the *Times* reduced to pandering to the tastes of those who thrive on tales of extravagance, wasteful luxury, and extreme frivolity?" asked another.

In any case, Lahana served high-quality French haute cuisine, the best ingredients, the classic preparations. And it was his contention that nothing about nouvelle cuisine was new. The lightness of the sauces touted by Gault and Millau, for example—he'd been making light sauces when it suited him at Chez Denis for years. "All these so-called advances are not actually new at all," he said. "Light sauces—they already existed. Al dente vegetables—already existed. Raw fish—already existed!"

Not true, as a general matter, replied Millau. How could Lahana deny it? Sure, perhaps he personally prepared wonderfully light sauces and had never overcooked his vegetables, but restaurants all over France had been serving heavy, insipid, too-rich dishes and sauces for decades.

Gault and Millau took turns laying out their argument. "Grand French cuisine has become a vulgar caricature of itself," said Millau. The old, royal, complicated cooking had given way to something new. "Nouvelle cuisine is to classic cooking as chamber music is to a symphony," said Gault. "Each element is distinct, not covered in sauce. We leave things to taste as they truly are."

Bocuse emphasized the changing role of the chef. "Today, chefs are also proprietors—owners," he said. "It wasn't that way fifty years ago. Chefs were servants. Today, we're the bosses. And in the kitchen, we do what we want."

Bocuse seemed cocky, as he always did, but let Gault and Millau do most of the talking. They were well practiced and relaxed on camera, trading jibes with Lahana and Courtine. Millau lit a large cigar and waved it around as he made his points. "Nouvelle cuisine is a refutation of pedantism, of doctrine, of dogmatism."

Courtine was scornful. "For me, nouvelle cuisine is just a publicity gimmick, nothing more," he said. "There are really only two cuisines—the good and the bad!" He wore his shirt unbuttoned with a string tie, and a gold signet ring on his pinky finger. His sideburns were long, and the overall effect was somewhere between bohemian academic and louche aristocrat. "For me, a fillet in a pan with olive oil, cooked over a wood fire, and bread and unpasteurized butter—for me, that is grand cuisine." And what about cassoulet, which had existed for centuries and continued to evolve? Was that also nouvelle cuisine? Courtine asked rhetorically.

"People who reject the idea of nouvelle cuisine are the same people who reject the idea of cooking as art," Millau responded. "If everything has already been done, and all we can do is go back to original sources, then all we can do is repeat traditions over and over!"

Toward the end of the show, Pivot asked Courtine about his latest book, *Madame Maigret's Recipes*, a tribute to the food described in the bestselling detective novels of Georges Simenon. Inspector Maigret was forever eating delicious filleted herrings and veal stews accompanied by a nice Châteauneuf-du-Pape as he solved his cases—always just the sort of old-fashioned French cooking Courtine so admired. Mme Maigret was a fictional character, but Courtine had written a cookbook for her.

"In his preface to your book, Simenon calls you the 'last classic,'" said Pivot. "Are you indeed a *classic*, compared to these men here?" He gestured across the table to the comparatively younger Gault and Millau.

"No," said Courtine, a small smile flickering disdain, "I'm a *reactionary*—that's a little different."

An awkward pause, then everyone laughed.

"Is it a hoax, a public relations snow job, this *nouvelle cuisine française*?" asked Julia Child in an article in *New York* magazine in the summer of 1977. The article was titled "'La Nouvelle Cuisine': A Skeptic's View." No, nouvelle cuisine was not a hoax, she wrote, reporting from France, but nouvelle cuisine was certainly faddish. She described a meal at an unnamed restaurant that had lost one of its two Michelin stars, causing the chef to suffer a nervous breakdown. He'd just been released from a clinic and was now "bravely setting out on a *nouvelle* course," she wrote, and seemingly headed for disaster. She tried his nouvelle cuisine–style braised duck with *espagnole* sauce (made without flour): "The sauce tasted for all the world like liquefied bouillon cubes, utterly drowning the flavor of that *magret de canard*."

Child was not in favor of newfangled sauces, nor did she appreciate some of the other recent trends in fashionable cooking. "Among the many ideas springing to life during this fruitful period," she wrote, "some will stay, others will disappear."

> One that I nominate for oblivion is the penchant for undercooking. For instance, I do not like blood-rare domestic duck; but blood-rare duck, quail, pigeon, and underdone fish are some peo-

> ple's nouvelle cuisine. . . . I don't like "crunchily underdone vegetables" either: Let them be frankly raw, as served in crudités, or let them be properly cooked through, to show forth their taste.

(Simone Beck, Child's coauthor of *Mastering the Art of French Cooking*, felt the same way. "If some hapless cook should happen to serve me crunchy, half-cooked vegetables," she declared, "I say, 'Cook it some more, please. I'm not a rabbit.'")

Child also took aim at what she called the "certain sameness of menu in the new-cuisine offerings," finding the same dishes everywhere she went. What she really craved was an old-fashioned bistro meal, a blanquette de veau and a green salad and a strawberry tart. "It's not that I don't appreciate the nouvelle cuisine," she wrote. "I love it! We need it! It's a shot in the arm to good cookery. But please, let's not throw out the comfortable old glories, at least not while I'm still around."

Nouvelle cuisine was under attack from all sides, it seemed. It was trendy and undercooked, according to Julia Child. It was a publicity stunt, and didn't even really exist or matter, according to Robert Courtine. It was overpriced, too dry, too soggy, and badly cooked, according to Mimi Sheraton. And so on.

The tide was turning.

In France, it was the Sheraton review that got the most attention—an American critic, dismissing both the icons of grand French cooking like La Pyramide (along with Vivarois, Baumanière, and Taillevent, for good measure) and the celebrated nouvelle cuisine restaurants of Bocuse and his friends. *Le Monde* referred to Sheraton as "the tigress of the *New York Times*." The Bande à Bocuse were outraged: A number of the insulted chefs, including Alain Chapel and Michel Guérard, claimed Sheraton had never actually set foot in their restaurants. (Of course, how would they know? Sheraton did not reserve under her own name, in marked contrast to French restaurant critics like Courtine.) Yanou Collart, the publicist, took issue with Sheraton's pretentions to anonymity: "I don't think anybody has to wear a mask to go into a restaurant . . . she's not honest," Collart said. "And if she was a great eater, she would not be that fat."

Things were getting personal.

Bocuse was dismissive, vindictive, and outrageously sexist, as always. "She must have a very unsatisfactory sex life," he said of Sheraton, smirking.

Claude Lebey, a food critic and cookbook editor (he'd published Guérard's hugely successful cookbooks), wrote an open letter criticizing Sheraton for being so hard on Mado Point and La Pyramide. The food magazine *Opinions Gourmandes* also went on the attack, calling her "Mimi Hilton" and "Mimi Holiday Inn," and running photographs of a naked woman in a swimming pool, purportedly of Sheraton but obviously a juvenile insult, and claiming that she must be a stripper at the Crazy Horse Saloon.

The dispute concluded with a televised debate on another of France's innumerable literary talk shows, this one called *Les Dossiers de L'écran* (*Notebook of the Screen*), which invited Sheraton to face her critics, including Bocuse, Pierre Troisgros, Christian Millau, and Jean Didier of the Kléber guides. She agreed to appear in disguise and was outfitted with a blond wig and a lacy black satin eye and face mask. She looked ridiculous, but she held her own, speaking in English with a live translator.

Sheraton summarized her disappointments with nouvelle cuisine, and with three-star French restaurants, many of them overrated in her opinion. She also went after Bocuse for not being in his restaurant often enough. He and the other celebrated nouvelle cuisine chefs were too busy traveling the world to do much cooking anymore, she presumed. Maybe he ought to fly a flag over his restaurant when he was there, announcing his presence, "like Buckingham Palace does when the queen is in residence."

After the show, Bocuse approached Sheraton on the set and tried to snatch the mask from her face. She pushed back firmly, sending him tripping over an electric outlet box and to the floor. Not long after, *People* magazine ran an article on the affair, complete with a large photograph of Sheraton in her disguise. "Who's killing the great chefs of France?" the magazine asked. "Mimi Sheraton proves they can dish it out but can't take it."

16

The Backlash

There was, once upon a time, a real estate developer named Adrien. He was smug and successful, a man about town, hosting lunches and dinners with clients at the best restaurants in Paris. Adrien considered himself a gastronome, a man of refined taste, and as he once again paid another astronomical dinner bill, he thought to himself: places like this must make a fortune! And then he thought to himself: "Why not me?" Pourquoi pas?

Robert Courtine cackled to himself as he wrote. He'd been waiting for this moment for years, for the inevitable backlash against nouvelle cuisine. Now, in 1978, as he worked on a chapter for his new book, *Gourmandissimo*, a collection of light sketches and reminiscences about being a food critic, he found that something had changed. Nouvelle cuisine had run its course, he was sure. There'd been a subtle but unmistakable shift in the atmosphere, and the once chic and au courant glamour of the new cooking was suddenly mockable, maybe even preposterous.

"Chefs are a fractious and insolent race," he said to whoever would listen. "A lot of them, they stick a banana up a duck and call themselves geniuses. Let's get back to the old days when men did the hunting and women did the cooking."

But there was no need for outraged, reactionary polemics (though Courtine did not hold back in private, especially when he was drunk). No, now was the time for wry, sneering comedy, a time for twisting the knife.

Back to the hapless Adrien, the Parisian real estate developer turned restaurateur in Courtine's fable of nouvelle cuisine's terminally shallow gimmickry. He gave Adrien a young mistress—barely of legal age—an ambitious social climber who called herself Sophie, even though her real name was Berthe. Together they planned to take Paris by storm with their new restaurant. But what to call it?

It took forever. They needed a name that would revolutionize Paris. An "in" name, a name that was a little "retro" but also delightfully "kitsch," a name that would entice the "jet set." After much consideration, they decided on a name that said it all. Their restaurant would be called The Restaurant, *spelled in English. Perfect.*

The Restaurant *was now ready to open! The only thing missing was a chef. A mere cook would not do. They needed a chef with a capital "C," a chef as grand as his toque. And there were many applicants. Finally, they hired a twenty-five-year-old who had vaguely peeled vegetables at Guérard before establishing himself in a tiny restaurant devoted to pederastic cuisine. He had long hair and was a connoisseur of terrines and tiny servings of vegetables and rare, undercooked fish. The nouvelle cuisine menu was taking shape. Now they hired an up-and-coming public relations consultant with daring cleavage, and it was she who proposed renaming their dishes. And so the sea bass terrine with lychees became "Terrine Jackie Onassis"; the salmon paupiettes with kiwis became "Paupiettes à la Mitterrand"; the shark fins were baptized "Fins à la Chirac"; and the mayonnaise with chocolate and Davidoff tobacco leaves became "Castro's dessert."*

Courtine reveled in his satire: the preposterous celebrity dishes, the hippie chef cooking disgusting nouvelle cuisine (mayonnaise, chocolate, and tobacco leaves?) for the glittering Parisian socialites, politicians, and aristocrats—tout Paris—who attended the new restaurant's launch party. But Adrien and Sophie's restaurant was of course doomed to fail. He concluded his story in Q and A style:

> *They served us Krug in magnums, not skimping on anything. They served us caviar by the ladle.*
>
> *And then? What happened next?*
>
> *Well, there were the endless, delirious articles, gossip and more gossip about the launch party of* The Restaurant, *which was booked solid for several weeks.*
>
> *And after that?*
>
> *Well, that was six months ago.*
>
> *OK, fine. And now, today?*
>
> *Today? Well,* The Restaurant *is sadly bankrupt. In its place—just opened—is a Chinese restaurant called* À la Tour de Khong.

This was for Courtine the ultimate punch line. The failed, flash-in-the-pan nouvelle cuisine hot spot turned into another outpost of the Chinese restaurant invasion, what he sneeringly called the "yellow peril." Everything wrong with France and French cooking was contained in his short story.

Courtine did not blame Bocuse, the Troisgros brothers, or Guérard for their successes. He enjoyed eating at their three-star restaurants well enough. No, he blamed Gault and Millau first and foremost, for the "disastrous fallout of nouvelle cuisine, multiplying everywhere, producing insipid 'crazy salads,' badly prepared raw and smoked fish, coarse 'fine stews' surrounded by small, bogus vegetables."

Gault and Millau had created a monster, and now every "back road bistro" was serving "fillet of sea bass with raspberries, salad of mutton's feet with kiwis, and mesclun beans with honeyed duck breast," Courtine wrote in *Le Monde* in September 1979, his latest attack on the state of French cooking. "The Truth is a strong liqueur which is not suitable for delicate stomachs," he wrote. "The effeminate people of taste reject it and this is quite normal." (Courtine often described those he considered overly trendy using antigay slurs and innuendo, referring, for example, to "these men who multiply without reproducing.") He warned about the dangers of imagination and creativity in the hands of bad cooks, bad cooks cheered on by stupid critics, bad cooks serving bad food to a gullible public, tricked by a "bombardment of publicity to forget natural common sense . . . to believe they are gourmets by rehashing advertising clichés and preconceived ideas."

"Where is French cuisine going?" Courtine asked dramatically. "To the most unthinkable, the most unforgivable of places given what it was, what it could still be, what the terroirs remain: to mediocrity!"

In the fall of 1979, Gael Greene of *New York* magazine traveled to France and reported back with bad news. "The nouvelle cuisine is dead. *Finie. Morte. Tombée*," she told her readers. That's what everyone in Paris was saying.

> I nibbled my kiwi in puzzled dismay. The glorious nouvelle cuisine . . . grand lightener of sauces, liberator of cuisinary imaginations, glorifier of the homely turnip . . . the chariot that carried the chefs of France to stardom, that made the stove more glamorous than a politician's podium or a wide-angle lens. How could that be . . . such swift and total annihilation?

Late 1970s malaise had come for nouvelle cuisine, it seemed. "Alas, toque-hungry chefs without the nouvelle sensibility began to play the nouvelle game," Greene explained, "committing unforgivable atrocities. And clever amateurs faked it prettily with a minimum of serious technique. The backlash was inevitable." The glamour was gone. The copycats had arrived. The party was over.

"So what have we got for dinner?" Greene asked her savvy French friends.

Well, there was "la cuisine bourgeoise," she was told, and "la vrai cuisine du terroir," all back-to-basics and simple, just the sort of cooking that Courtine advocated for so relentlessly in *Le Monde*. Still, there was plenty of foie gras to be had, thankfully—her favorite—and plenty of talented chefs, too, cooking inventive dishes even if they weren't calling it "nouvelle cuisine." In the same column, Greene turned her attention to Olympe and Albert Nahmias, whose chic restaurant had just moved to a new and larger space on rue Nicolas Charlet, a few blocks from its original location.

The 1930s art deco dining room—all shiny black paint and red velvet—was as crowded as ever. The restaurant served its famous crayfish with curry butter, along with cold duck and fried cucumber, an artichoke ragout, sautéed wild cèpes, and scallops with foie gras. In the kitchen, Olympe, glamorous in her high heels and accompanied by two female sous-chefs, denied that she was cooking nouvelle cuisine, despite being lauded as a nouvelle cuisine chef by Gault and Millau.

"It's not nouvelle cuisine," she told Greene.

Olympe was self-trained and intuitive, Greene reported, and everything was cooked to order. It sounded, in other words, very much like nouvelle cuisine—quick, light, inventive, and fresh. But no: "It's not nouvelle cuisine," Olympe insisted. "It's cuisine de femme."

The "nouvelle cuisine" label had gone out of fashion, and Olympe had never had much use for labels anyway. And what was "cuisine de femme"? It was whatever she wanted it to be.

Olympe was by now only peripherally involved with the ARC, the association of women chefs. But she wholeheartedly endorsed the idea of "cuisine de femme," in the sense that it represented self-determination. She did not cook traditional "mère de Lyon" dishes, but for Olympe, cuisine de femme had taken on a feminist valence—liberation from the male chauvinism of the haute cuisine kitchen.

She had just started making weekly appearances on a TF1 television show called *Le Regard des Femmes* (*The Women's View*) hosted by longtime radio and TV personality Ève Ruggieri. On Tuesday afternoons Olympe presented a recipe live on the air for fifteen minutes: something simple—as few ingredients as possible—and not overly expensive. The point was to offer viewers new ideas and approaches. She was also working on a cookbook, a collection of her recipes called *La Cuisine d'Olympe: Une Grande Cuisine Toute Simple*, highlighting dishes at once grand and uncomplicated.

Olympe had taken her bohemian, free-spirited version of nouvelle cuisine and remade it as something accessible to any home cook. Her restaurant, meanwhile, remained Left Bank chic, full of celebrities and "serious foodies," Greene wrote in *New York* magazine, and later at night, "tout Paris, the men as flashily beautiful as their beautiful women."

In New York City, meanwhile, nouvelle cuisine was still a novelty, appearing on French restaurant menus with increasing frequency, dazzling customers and mostly infuriating Mimi Sheraton of *The New York Times*. There was Claude's on Lexington and Seventieth Street, newly opened, spectacularly crowded, serving salmon scallopine with sorrel sauce, for example, in the style of Troisgros, except the fish was encased in pastry, in the style of Bocuse—a "dried out, almost inedible combination," Sheraton wrote in her review. "When the food did arrive, it veered from excellent to mediocre, and a few dishes were failures, primarily because they were ill-conceived."

Claude's opened in late 1978 and closed a few short months later after a dispute between Claude Baills, the French-born chef, and his backers. Quickly renamed, the restaurant reopened as Le Plaisir, now serving salmon ceviche and poached oysters, everything rare, seared, barely cooked, and very nouvelle. Baills in turn reopened Claude's on Eighty-First Street in June 1979, and was hailed for his sophisticated nouvelle cuisine dishes, including Bocuse's famous truffle soup under a pastry dome.

But it was the arrival of the Quilted Giraffe, also in the summer of 1979, that epitomized nouvelle cuisine in America, and that captured the city's imagination. The restaurant was run by Barry and Susan Wine, husband and wife, who'd opened the original Quilted Giraffe in New Paltz, eighty miles north of the city in the Hudson Valley, in 1975, and recently moved to Manhattan.

This was nouvelle cuisine, American style, embracing all the freedom and showmanship of the original, but relatively untethered to classic French cooking. Barry ran the kitchen and was entirely self-taught; Susan baked the bread and made desserts. The prices were sky-high. In her *Times* review, Sheraton described the cooking at the Quilted Giraffe as "contrived" and noted how insistently and annoyingly her waiter used the phrase "nouvelle cuisine"—seven times during her first visit.

She didn't like it:

> Combining beautifully fresh chunks of lobster and the white fleshed fish lotte in a cream sauce with cantaloupe balls and raspberries is just a little too much gastronomic fun for us. So is the serving of sautéed chicken breasts with blueberry vinegar, blueberries, a puree of beets and flowerettes of broccoli. Less bizarre but still disconcertingly sweet was the pear puree underlining an appetizer of cold lamb with a basil filling, the lime juice that accented absolutely raw and unflavored sliced scallops on a bed of toughly chewy seaweed, and whatever it was that added a sugary, winey accent to the attractively served onion soup.

For Sheraton, as for Robert Courtine, nouvelle cuisine was a fad. "It is probable that many people, anxious to be seen eating the right thing in the right restaurant," she wrote, "are swallowing hard-to-down rare fish, almost raw vegetables, white chocolate mousse that tastes like sweet fat and exotically aromatic seasonings they secretly consider to be as appealing as moth balls."

Whatever the truth of Sheraton's "Emperor's New Clothes" critique of the Quilted Giraffe's cooking, it made no difference. The restaurant was a hit, leading the way as American cooking entered the 1980s. Was it in fact a "nouvelle cuisine" restaurant? Not really. But it was the hot new thing and had many of the now well-known signifiers. Celebrities and socialites filled the place, which had made a kind of playacted decadence its calling card. The signature dish was called the beggar's purse, a small crepe filled with crème fraîche and caviar, tied with chives and topped with a gold leaf. The bite-size, extravagantly priced appetizers were served on a candelabra, and Barry would sometimes roam the dining room with a pair of handcuffs and playfully lock guests' hands behind their backs, forcing them to eat the crepe in a single bite amid the cocaine-fueled laughter.

It was that kind of restaurant.

In the spring of 1981, Gault and Millau published their first guide to New York City restaurants, expanding their footprint internationally. The edition was in French but sold well in New York anyway. "New French Guide to New York City Stirs Controversy," reported *The New York Times*, accompanied by a photograph of

Gault and Millau posing with the book on Fifth Avenue and Central Park South.

The controversy, according to the *Times*, was that the men were possibly prejudiced against classical French cooking and eager only to promote nouvelle cuisine. They had invented the term, after all, and the guide continued their practice of honoring nouvelle cuisine restaurants with red toques, their symbol of an innovative kitchen. The Quilted Giraffe, Claude's, and Le Plaisir all received high marks, unsurprisingly, while more staid and old-fashioned French restaurants had fared poorly, with wan, lukewarm reviews for La Grenouille, La Caravelle, and Le Cygne.

"What the Americans call haute cuisine is expensive, old-fashioned, decadent and academic," Millau told the paper. "Nouvelle cuisine is simply classic cooking with different spirit and technique. It is not replacing pot-au-feu with salmon in strawberry sauce."

Gault and Millau were fighting the good fight, but it was a losing battle. Or maybe it was simply no longer relevant. Nouvelle cuisine had been reduced to a cliché—salmon in strawberry sauce, as Millau told the *Times*—and there was no going back. Sure, French cooking had changed, modernized, evolved, even at classic places like La Grenouille and Lutèce, where the new, lighter cooking was on the menu. But nevertheless: Nouvelle cuisine as a grand, revolutionary idea was dead, just as Gael Greene had decreed.

That same spring of 1981, 130 top French chefs arrived en masse in New York for the annual meeting of the Association de Maîtres Cuisiniers de France. The idea was to promote French cooking, and give the chefs a taste of America. The meeting was also a chance for the practitioners of haute cuisine to take stock, to discuss the future of the restaurant business. It was the first meeting of the association to take place overseas, a sign of the ever-increasing global influence and cultural importance of French cooking; so much had changed in the previous ten years, with Paul Bocuse in particular leading the way.

And yet: The chefs were on the defensive right from the start. At the Maîtres Cuisiniers' press conference, the first questions were about whether French cooking was in decline.

"Most certainly not" was the reply from the president of the group, Émile Tingaud. The problem was nouvelle cuisine, he said, which had run its course. The unceasing and vigorous promotion of the new cooking by Gault and Millau had caused a glut and then a backlash, and indeed there was much more to French cooking than the limited inventions of nouvelle cuisine.

The annual meeting itself took place at the Pierre hotel, and was followed by a black-tie gala. There was also a buffet dinner at the Tavern on the Green restaurant, which included American specialties: eleven varieties of clams and oysters, crab claws, chili, fried chicken, New Orleans gumbo and jambalaya, Kansas City spare ribs, corned beef, pastrami, and lox and bagels. The chefs would then travel to Washington, DC; San Francisco; the Grand Canyon; and Las Vegas, on an extravagant and well-funded tour sponsored by Champagnes Mumm, Seagram and Sons liquors, Rougié foie gras, and Bragard, the makers of chef's whites.

Paul Bocuse said his favorites of the American dishes were Paul Prudhomme's gumbo and jambalaya. ("That's like Shakespeare reappearing and telling you your writing is super," said

Prudhomme when he heard the compliment.) Bocuse had no interest in discussing nouvelle cuisine, and yet the talk was incessant.

"With nouvelle cuisine," said one chef dismissively, "two things are large: plates and price. The rest is small." Everyone laughed. In *The Washington Post*, food critic Phyllis Richman reported on the chatter: "Nouvelle cuisine died March 22, 1981, at the annual meeting of the Maîtres Cuisiniers de France, after a long and painful illness. It was mourned by none." *The New York Times* also reported on the meeting of the French chefs: "The only target of criticism was nouvelle cuisine, characterized by some as ridiculous, by others as nonexistent."

Nouvelle cuisine may have been dead and done with, but the Bande à Bocuse were as celebrated as ever. Bocuse, Roger Vergé, and Gaston Lenôtre were toasted everywhere they went, from the roller disco at the Roxy that Saturday night to lunch at the Parker Meridien hotel, where Alain Senderens was the consulting chef. For a few days in New York City, French chefs were everywhere, at Windows on the World, at the Grand Central Oyster Bar, at the Quilted Giraffe.

The Maîtres Cuisiniers president, Tingaud, was promoting the idea of "regional specialties" as the way forward for French cooking in the wake of nouvelle cuisine. A focus on craft and tradition. There was also talk of "personal cooking." And what about "cuisine de femme"? This, like nouvelle cuisine, remained a contentious topic.

Women ran a majority of the restaurants in France, explained one of the chefs, and should be commended for their homestyle cooking—a valuable weapon in the fight against the spread of fast food. But no, there was a difference between cuisine de femme and "professional" gourmet cooking. And this was why, needless to say, the association had no female members.

Tingaud had, in previous years, lashed out at the women who had founded the ARC, saying his group would never admit a woman chef, and at the annual meeting in New York he now reiterated this policy. The Maîtres Cuisiniers were men, and men only.

All the familiar arguments were rehearsed. "I have fifteen chefs in the kitchen," said one of the owners of Taillevent. "How can you put a woman with fifteen chefs?" Another of the association's functionaries explained: "It's not good for women to get up at four in the morning and do a lot of heavy lifting." Some of the chefs insisted, only half joking, that they could tell whether a man or a woman had cooked a dish from taste alone.

Such was the state of the French haute cuisine establishment: happy to move on from the brash and overpromoted nouvelle cuisine, and still convinced that women had no place in the gourmet restaurant kitchen.

Michel Guérard did not attend the Maîtres Cuisiniers meeting in New York or the chef association's grand tour of America. He continued to work on his menus at Les Prés d'Eugénie, finding inspiration from his travels, and also to work on his frozen food entrées for Nestlé. There were other projects as well: consulting with his old friend Régine Zylberberg about the food served in her Manhattan nightclub, Régine's, and developing a line of

Michel Guérard–branded, low-sugar diet chocolates to be sold in the US. And of course there were the demands of the press—TV appearances, photo shoots, and interviews. He was busy.

He was also tired of being asked about nouvelle cuisine. Not that his philosophy or approach to cooking had changed. He was committed to invention and experimentation, to the best and freshest ingredients. But the nouvelle cuisine label now signaled homogeneity and sameness. "Today, everywhere you go in France, you find the same menus, the same dishes with even the same names, the same flavors," he told *The New York Times.* "There is nothing original."

The March 1981 article was headlined "Guérard Rethinks Nouvelle Cuisine," and in it, the young genius of nouvelle cuisine, the man who epitomized playful, brilliant, and effortlessly irreverent cooking suddenly sounded like an acolyte of Robert Courtine. Nouvelle cuisine had become a gimmick, a fad.

"Where is the originality?" Guérard asked. "Everything is cooked in either raspberry vinegar, strawberry vinegar or pumpkin vinegar. It's sad. . . . Not long ago, I sat down to a meal in a New York restaurant. Everything served me was raw. It had no taste. I asked 'What is this?' They responded, 'Nouvelle French cuisine.' It's not true."

His friend Pierre Troisgros agreed. "Right now," he said, "nouvelle is at a dead end." Both chefs were moving in new directions, turning away from overly familiar nouvelle cuisine tropes, adding classic dishes. Guérard had been devoted to nouvelle cuisine from the beginning, he said, "But I would like to offer a warning: The qualities brought in by the new style do not negate the positive qualities of the old cuisine."

He'd added roasted chicken and sautéed sole to his menu, alongside his nouvelle cuisine dishes—an element of "cuisine paysanne," or peasant cooking, he called it. "When a chef has lost contact with popular cooking, he can rarely produce a cuisine that is truly fine," he said.

They were all in the same boat, looking for a way forward, a way to preserve the excitement of invention but to ground it in tradition. Maybe not even French tradition: Guérard had recently traveled to China and found himself amazed at the dumplings and the crispy duck. He sought inspiration wherever he could.

Paul Bocuse, on the other hand, was less concerned about the future of his cooking, and instead focused on the business of cooking. He was an impresario; the greatest achievement of nouvelle cuisine, in his view, was the fact—as he pointed out repeatedly in interviews—that he and his fellow chefs now all owned their own restaurants.

And Bocuse wanted more. After the meeting of the Association de Maîtres Cuisiniers in New York, Bocuse, Vergé, and Lenôtre skipped the rest of the American tour and flew on their own to Florida. They had business in Orlando, at Disney World, business that might be surprising to some, but was also, perhaps, inevitable: An ambitious new theme park called EPCOT Center (the name stood for "Experimental Prototype Community of Tomorrow") was under construction, and they were going to open a restaurant there.

17

The Truth About Courtine

Simone Lemaire had moved from the north back to the countryside near Vichy, in central France, not far from where her career as a chef had begun. The state contract for her restaurant in Normandy at Le Pin-au-Haras, the royal stables, had expired quite suddenly in 1978. (No explanation was given.) And so she had left Normandy and reopened her restaurant, now called Le Haut Tourne Bride, in the small town of Busset.

Busset was picturesque and prosperous, a rural village centered around a medieval castle called the Château de Busset; Lemaire's restaurant was in a sprawling estate not far away, set in a large, shaded garden. She was cooking the sort of normande and Bourbonnais dishes she always had—ever since she'd started at her sister's Reine Jeanne restaurant all those years ago. Wild boar and other game in season; seafood cassoulet with homemade fish sausage served with green beans from her garden; frog's legs with pearl onions and cider; poached peaches with crème anglaise. As always, everything was cooked to order, "à la minute."

Business at the restaurant was brisk, and Lemaire had also agreed to take on a new job: the presidency of the ARC. The women chefs who founded the organization had always rotated various responsibilities, and now, in 1980, it was Lemaire's turn to step up.

Apart from the usual bureaucratic tasks like arranging the printing of the annual directory and hosting ARC meetings, Lemaire was now suddenly a minor public figure—a spokeswoman for women's cooking.

It was strange, she thought, how the conversation had changed. Only a few years earlier, in the mid-1970s, women chefs had struggled for recognition and respect, variously ignored or disparaged by the culinary establishment and by the Bande à Bocuse. The spectacular rise of nouvelle cuisine had cast them in the shadows.

But nouvelle cuisine, a victim of its own success, had fallen from grace. And so Lemaire found herself gleefully on the attack. After all, nouvelle cuisine was still on menus in trendy restaurants all over France, and proved a useful foil for the ARC. Women's cooking was authentic and down-to-earth, Lemaire told *Le Monde* reporter Michel Castaing, whereas nouvelle cuisine was "spineless and aestheticized," the result of what she called the "disease of creation—a fatal mania."

She was speaking hyperbolically, of course, damning Gault and Millau and nouvelle cuisine's obsession with novelty. Christiane Massia, another of the founding members of the ARC (it was she who'd written the biting public letter to Bocuse after his attack on the group), was also quoted in the same article. "I do not create to create," she said. "I dare to be simple." Lemaire explained that her signature pan-fried Saint-Jacques scallops with bolete mushrooms was "a creation, without being a complication."

Nouvelle cuisine was too fussy, and too pretentious. You could sense the chefs' fingers all over the food, Massia said, building little pyramids of vegetables on the plate. "It ruins my appetite," she said. Menu descriptions, meanwhile, were overwrought. "A woman chef offers a 'salad with croutons,'" said Lemaire. "The male chef calls it 'a small autumn salad with hazelnut oil, and grilled country bread.' The woman: 'pheasant salad with lentils.' The man: 'lentils in salad with pheasant aiguillettes in vinegar and olive oil.'" She laughed. "These days, young restaurateurs seem to write the menu before they know how to cook."

Lemaire's and Massia's attacks on nouvelle cuisine echoed those of Robert Courtine. Indeed, Courtine's attacks on nouvelle cuisine were relentless, and even more so now that the style was no longer in vogue. Portions were too small—finely sliced carrots "sold at the price of caviar." Nouvelle cuisine chefs were nothing more than "manipulators," he sneered in a recent column—"kitchen decor workers," all style over substance.

> This is truly where the problem lies with these gentlemen: they do not create, whatever they think; they present, wrap, escort, and embellish the main product. They play "plate painters." In their kitchens, the little robot assistants learn to paint—sorry, to arrange—on the plates, just as the chef designed it in his brilliant inspiration, the three peas, the turnip in ten slices and the top of

> chervil. If you asked them to make a soft-boiled egg, they wouldn't know how.

Lemaire enjoyed Courtine's snide insults, putting trendy chefs in their place, defending old-fashioned French cooking. Just as she defended the honor of the ARC, so did Courtine. And yet: She was aware of the irony. The ARC had been founded in the spirit of protest and defiance, of women's liberation; Courtine, on the other hand, represented French culinary chauvinism and archconservatism. And while Lemaire's jabs at nouvelle cuisine were generally lighthearted and mild, Courtine's condemnation of overly trendy cooking seemed mean-spirited and scornful.

They made for strange bedfellows, that much was clear to Lemaire. Every year, Courtine wrote a brief introductory letter for the ARC directory, a flowery ode to women's cooking and French tradition. ("Guests will be astonished as childhood memories come flooding back, spurred by the taste of the best ingredients prepared in timeless fashion—rediscovering the true nature of things.")

And it was true: Most of the ARC restaurants served traditional French food, "cuisine de bonne femme" as it was called, just as the famous mères of Lyon and elsewhere did. But the idea of the ARC was never based on any particular style of cooking. Many of the women prided themselves on their creativity in the kitchen, and Lemaire hoped to expand the ARC membership to include chefs who specialized in foreign cuisines. There were a growing number of North African restaurants in Paris, for example, some run by women, serving dishes that did not match Courtine's idealized vision of ARC cooking, not at all.

Lemaire wondered: Had her organization allied itself too closely with Courtine and his retrograde culinary philosophy? Had they doomed themselves to a kind of sentimental irrelevance, destined to be seen as bastions of tradition, "mères" turning out unambitious childhood favorites?

No, not if she could help it.

In May 1980, Robert Courtine turned seventy years old and celebrated with a grand lunch in his honor at Fouquet's, on the Champs-Élysées, the entire Parisian food establishment in attendance.

He was on top of the world. So why did he feel so . . . bitter?

Courtine had reached the valedictory stage of his career—feted everywhere he went, respected, revered, the great food and restaurant critic, proud upholder of French culinary heritage. He had not softened with age, however. He had curdled, somehow, his grievances more powerful than ever.

He woke up at six every morning and squeezed his favored lemon juice for breakfast, writing his weekly *Le Monde* column in his tiny apartment in Bois-Colombes, on the outskirts of Paris. At Fouquet's, Courtine was immediately surrounded by well-wishers, and nodded and smiled tightly. He was immaculately dressed and looked younger than his age. "He lives a disciplined life," said the chef Jacques Manière, who ran the restaurant Dodin Bouffant. "He never eats too much. The dinner table is always a bit like the Last Supper for him: ritual and asceticism."

Courtine remained vigilant in his warnings about industrial

agriculture, about the "large plates and minuscule portions" at nouvelle cuisine restaurants, the insidious effects of "glutamate" in Chinese food, and the ongoing invasion of "Sino-Vietnamese cuisine" in Paris. He was busy working on various cookbooks, and a neighborhood guide to the city, "Géographie Gourmande de Paris." He appeared on television every so often, most recently on *Apostrophes* to criticize the author of a cookbook for including ketchup among the ingredients for a recipe. "I saw the word 'ketchup,' and I closed the book," he said, dismissively, even angrily. *"Le ketchup, c'est du barbarisme!"* he said. Ketchup is barbarism! He said the words with a smile on his face, but meant every one. He was comically strict and uncompromising.

The weekly newspaper *Le Nouvel Observateur* sent a reporter to write a profile of Courtine on the occasion of his birthday, an article titled "The 70 Stars of Robert Courtine." The restaurant critic was duly lauded as powerful, feared, erudite, and old-fashioned. A curmudgeon. A man with no television in his home, and who avoided the telephone. A man who hated nouvelle cuisine and was devoted to the traditional cooking of his grandmother, who was from the Ardèche region, south of Lyon.

The *Nouvel Observateur* story was a warm portrait of a prickly man, par for the course for Courtine. But there was something new, something that sent a chill down his spine—a brief reference to his politics, and to his past:

> Those who really know him know that his heart stopped a long time ago. In 1715, perhaps, supporting the ultra-royalists, the year Dom Pérignon and Louis XIV died. Having left the ranks of

> Maurrassisme, lost in the collaboration press, a moment forbidden from politics, he has to be content with the restaurant.

Of course, everyone at that birthday party knew of Courtine's history as a collaborator, and his pro-monarchist, pro-Catholic, pro-Vichy-regime sentiments. "Maurrassisme" referred to Charles Maurras, who had led the far-right, antidemocratic Action Française movement for decades, from its anti-Dreyfusard beginnings until his imprisonment in 1945. Like many others, Courtine had written for Nazi-supported newspapers during the war (his name had been mentioned in passing in historian Pascal Ory's 1976 book *Les Collaborateurs*), and he was subsequently forbidden to cover politics by the dégradation nationale. Hence his career as a gourmet.

This was all common knowledge but not openly discussed—that would be gauche—and certainly not written about in *Le Nouvel Observateur.* The author of the article was Alain Schifres, known for his witty cultural commentary, in this case connecting the previous generation's icon of culinary rectitude with his collaborationist past, all in the spirit of an entertaining magazine profile. It was wryly amusing, was it not, that the stern enforcer of French culinary tradition had been condemned to a life of restaurant criticism because of his traditionalist, far-right politics?

Still: For Courtine, the *Nouvel Observateur* article was a warning. The rules had changed; the code of polite silence had been breaking in recent years and now it was broken. Whispered gossip had become printed fact, and Courtine's secret history was in danger of being revealed.

And so it was that at the very moment of his greatest triumph, at the peak of his powers, having vanquished all that was unholy in French cooking—the trendy, soulless, overpriced nouvelle cuisine—and celebrating his seventieth birthday surrounded by all of beau monde gourmet Paris, Courtine was afraid. Afraid of being exposed. Yes, everyone knew that he'd written for the collaborationist press, but they could not fathom the pitch-black malevolence of what exactly he'd written.

His past was coming to haunt him.

Slowly, in fits and starts, France was coming to terms with its Vichy history, the post-1968 generation more inclined to question the self-serving mythologies of wartime France. No, every collaborator had not also secretly been a member of the Resistance. Yes, the Pétain regime had eagerly registered and then deported more than seventy thousand French Jews to their deaths in Nazi concentration camps. Now, decades later, a handful of politicians and businessmen who had long escaped scrutiny were being called to account. In 1979, the well-known Nazi hunter Serge Klarsfeld had founded the Association des Fils et Filles des Déportés Juifs de France (Sons and Daughters of Jews Deported from France), demanding that collaborators René Bousquet and Jean Leguay, both of whom participated in the infamous Vél d'Hiv roundup in Paris in 1942, be tried for their crimes.

After the war, Bousquet had a long career in the press and in politics, working for *La Dépêche du Midi* in Toulouse, and was an early supporter of François Mitterrand. Leguay had found success in business, as an executive at Nina Ricci perfumes in New York and at Warner-Lambert pharmaceuticals. Klarsfeld led a noisy protest outside Leguay's home in Paris; a charge of crimes against humanity soon followed.

In 1982, Nicolas Brimo, a young reporter at the satirical and investigative weekly *Le Canard Enchaîné,* published an exposé of Maurice Papon, the French budget minister, accusing him of direct involvement in the deportation of Jews from Bordeaux in 1943 and 1944. Thus began the "Papon Affair," years of legal wrangling, investigations, and indictments. Brimo had previously revealed the sordid history of Robert Hersant, the newspaper magnate (he owned *Le Figaro*, *France-Soir*, and numerous regional dailies) who'd founded the far-right Jeune Front party in 1940 and published the pro-Nazi newspaper *Au Pilori* during the war.

Powerful men were being brought low, wartime secrets revealed. A new generation of writers and reporters were taking on the French establishment, reasking questions about history, national identity, and personal responsibility. Like Alain Schifres at *Le Nouvel Observateur* and Nicolas Brimo at *Le Canard Enchaîné*, Pierre Assouline was an up-and-coming journalist interested in the ironies and occlusions of the current moment, and it was he who stumbled onto the truth of Robert Courtine, entirely by accident.

Assouline was in his late twenties, writing for magazines and newspapers, and making a name for himself as a biographer. He was Jewish, born in Casablanca, raised in Paris, and he was working on an article for *Les Nouvelles Littéraires* about famous writers and their assistants. There was Voltaire and his faithful secretary Jean-Louis Wagnière; Anatole France and Jean-Jacques Brousson; André Gide and Béatrix Beck . . . A friend recommended Assouline track down a man named Lucien Combelle, who'd worked for Gide as well as for Pierre Drieu la Rochelle, the novelist turned fascist intellectual.

Combelle was a striking figure, heavy and tired and massive and athletic all at once. He spoke loudly and slowly, with careful, old-fashioned diction. Assouline couldn't help but like him, even as Combelle's past became clear. He was a former collaborator, a friend of the antisemetic novelist Louis-Ferdinand Céline, follower of Drieu la Rochelle, and the editor in chief of the pro-Nazi newspaper *Révolution Nationale* during the war.

They became friends. A strange sort of friendship, the disgraced former collaborator, an old man, and the worldly, Jewish reporter, meeting for coffee, taking walks around Paris, discussing politics and literature. Combelle was for Assouline a mystery, a man who'd been caught in the sulfurous undertow of twentieth-century politics, who was essentially and unchangeably antidemocratic, and yet intelligent, even decent. They met in 1980 and stayed in regular contact over the years, as Assouline's star continued to rise, writing a biography of Marcel Dassault, the French aviation pioneer and Buchenwald survivor, and a book about the purge of collaborationist intellectuals after the war.

One day, Combelle and Assouline were discussing the prevalence of antisemetic "*délations*"—"denunciations"—during the occupation, the usually anonymous letters sent to authorities exposing supposed Jewish criminality, and often leading to arrest. Marcel Ophuls's *The Sorrow and the Pity* had exposed the practice in detail.

Combelle was circumspect. As the editor of *Révolution Nationale*, he said, there were writers he had refused to publish. He remembered one in particular, a vicious young polemicist who'd come to his office in the hope of getting his columns into the paper. Combelle read them and was repulsed: the articles were denunciations of Parisian Jews who'd escaped the Nazi roundups. With names and addresses. Combelle had thrown the man out unceremoniously.

Soon enough, the articles appeared in the extremist *Au Pilori*, where the writer continued to be published for the duration of the war. And he went on to a long and prominent career. Combelle didn't want to name names, or accuse or "denounce" anyone; the man was still writing today, he said. But Assouline insisted, and Combelle eventually blurted out a familiar name: Robert Courtine.

Courtine—La Reynière—of *Le Monde*? *That* Courtine?

The very same, said Combelle.

A visit to the archives of the Bibliothèque Nationale de France on the rue de Richelieu soon confirmed Combelle's claim. Here, in the vast, resplendent library reading room, ornate, with skylights and oval curves and an almost religious, monastery-like atmosphere, Assouline found himself plunged into the ice-cold deluge of Courtine's *Au Pilori* press clippings. It was overwhelming.

Au Pilori was the worst of the worst of the collaborationist press, pro-Hitler and unapologetically antisemitic. Many of the articles were written anonymously, but "Robert Julien Courtine" published proudly under his own byline. And he had been prolific.

The first articles Assouline saw were benign, almost comical: Courtine had written a regular column called "Spectacles de Paris," reviewing nightclubs, cabarets, and music halls. Here was the future restaurant critic for *Le Monde*, learning his trade: "The audience at the A.B.C. is too good-natured, too inclined to applaud the excellent and the worst, the good and the bad," he wrote. "But what does it matter, program number twelve of the 1942–43 season was perfect. Let's not shy away from our pleasure."

But mostly Courtine wrote about the pernicious dangers of Freemasons and Jews, a litany of propaganda and "Protocols of the Elders of Zion"–style conspiracy.

> Journalists and intellectuals glide over the Jew. They ignore the Jew. They forget the Jew. They do not go (Is it ignorance? Is it tactical?) to the heart of the question. And yet, how could the people of France not understand that at the root of their misfortunes there is the Jew? There is only the Jew. Proof of his malfeasance? It is his power.

All the familiar tropes were present. In one article, Courtine ventriloquized Jewish plotting:

> With gold one buys the most rebellious consciences. Already the main banks, stock exchanges around the world, the debt of all governments are in our hands. The press obey our directives. We will drive Christians to wars by exploiting their pride and stupidity. They will massacre each other and clear space for us. And above all we monopolize teaching and the academy, and we will knead their brains to our liking.

In another, he imagined the origins of the Rothschild banking dynasty:

> In the blackest hovel of the Frankfurt ghetto, a noisy, gesticulating and lousy band of the sons of Israel shouted their joy. Then, scratching his filthy skull under his skullcap, the usurer said to his sweet, cooing companion of their son, "We're going to make him a rabbi!" "I want to be a banker," the son said. "Why not?" thought the loan shark. "Isn't it a profession that suits our race?" The son then married a purebred Jewess who was to bear him a large offspring.

From the perspective of the 1980s, the feverish screeds seemed quaint, preposterous. But as he read, the violence of Courtine's politics became clear. Talk about "hook nosed bankers" and "liquidation." The need to "hunt down" the adversaries of National Socialism, the demand they wear identifying "armbands of infamy." In a discussion of Céline: "There is a Jew in each of us and Céline invites us to kill him. By this he means that a hundred and fifty years of slowly injected venom have rotted and softened our minds and our hearts. And it is after moral hara-kiri that we can lay the groundwork for our future greatness."

Jews had caused the war, and were profiting from the war, and had weakened France. Action was required.

"It is up to us, true National Socialists, to do what is necessary. Either you are a patriot or you are not," Courtine had written. "We demand necessary violence, we want clean-ups, sweeps, sanctions, and executions."

"French honor is at stake."

"These are the true colors of our century. And a race of men forever gone, we hope."

The eradication of Jews.

And here is where Courtine moved from rhetoric to brutal reality, listing the Jews he thought should be targeted. He took on entire organizations: the Union of Jewish Societies of France, the International League Against Anti-Semitism, names, addresses, titles. For various Masonic lodges, the names and addresses of the "depraved Moroccan Jews" who were members. The HEC business school near the Parc Monceau was a hotbed of Jewish resistance, as was the Sciences Po, according to Courtine. "*HEC leads to everything* is the motto of this Jewish lair," he wrote. "Of course it leads to everything: banks, insurance, trade, press, cinema, industry, administration, diplomacy. That's why we are where we are!" He continued:

> The HEC Association of Former Pupils—this is where we could use a good roundup. We talk a lot about the militia. The Revolutionary Front claims to want to act and we admire it. We will admire it even more when a team of militiamen has kicked the ass of the secretary general of this association. . . . This whole tribe can well join the Weill, Bloch, Hass, Israel, Epstein, and Kahn who are neighbors in the HEC directory, and the yids in the shadows, pulling the strings of their jewified comrades, combat bosses, antisocial bosses, Gaullist bosses, saboteurs.

Again, a list of names and addresses. Denunciations and demands for action, for attack. Assouline felt nauseated. He stood up, left the library reading room, and walked in the direction of the bathroom. Among the articles, there was also mention of Jewish nurseries and kindergartens. "To the Germans: you forgot the children. You need to come back and finish the job." Assouline threw up.

What did he do? What could he do?

Assouline knew one thing for certain: He had found his limit. There were collaborators, and there were *collaborators.* He had somehow befriended a onetime fascist, Lucien Combelle, and there were those among his peers who could not understand how that could be, who disapproved. Assouline had always been interested in moral gray areas, and he accepted Combelle's account of himself as essentially different from collaborators like Courtine, who were irredeemable. The true believers, the antisemites, the truly evil. Yes, he had found his limit, a line he could not cross, in the archives of the National Library. There was no moral gray area when it came to a person like Courtine, a person who called for genocide, for murder and death, even of children.

And yet: He did not feel that it was his duty to persecute Courtine or expose the man's forty-year-old sins, as disgusting as they were. He did not feel it was possible. That any public protest by Assouline would only be met by shrugs of indifference. He wasn't cut out to be a gendarme, or a righteous, finger-pointing accuser.

He would make sure their paths never crossed. They traveled in the same literary Parisian circles, but the prospect of coming face to face with the man, of shaking his hand, was unthinkable.

One way or another, he felt sure, the truth would come out.

18

Disney World

In 1979, on a flight from Los Angeles to New York, Yanou Collart ran into an old friend, Armand Bigle. He was the Disney company's man in France and had been for decades, hired by Walt Disney himself and in charge of the studio's promotions and merchandising in all of Europe—magazines, toys, comic books, TV shows, and elaborate PR campaigns for movies like *Cinderella*, *Peter Pan*, and *Davy Crockett*. Bigle was in his early sixties, suave, and flirtatious, sitting across from Collart in first class, and he wanted her advice.

He smiled, and she smiled right back. She knew how to handle men like Bigle, who'd told her more than once that he was madly in love with her, and had offered to buy her an apartment in Paris—and who was of course married. Breezy sparring about the pros and cons of being a kept woman, this was typical, irritating small talk of the late-1970s sophisticated French cocktail party variety. She'd evaded his overtures and laughed him off.

Now, on the plane to New York, they were talking Hollywood business and gossip. She'd been working with Michael Douglas and Jack Lemmon to promote *The China Syndrome* at Cannes, and was well established as a go-to fixer for American movie producers working in France. "If you have any kind of problem, Yanou will solve it!" Sydney Pollack told *The Hollywood Reporter.* Miloš Forman had recently called to ask her advice about how to store his collection of Pétrus and other Bordeaux wines.

Bigle, it turned out, had just been briefed at Disney headquarters in Burbank about the plans for EPCOT Center, an enormous and ambitious project at Disney World just beginning construction in Orlando, Florida. The "Experimental Prototype Community of Tomorrow," as conceived by Walt Disney back in the 1960s, was to be a futuristic, high-tech city, but the idea had evolved over the years. Scheduled to open in 1982, EPCOT would be akin to a permanent World's Fair, divided into two sections: Future World, featuring science and technology attractions, and the World Showcase, with international pavilions from various countries, including France.

And this was where Bigle came into the picture. What attractions should the French pavilion have? Disney was building a replica of the Eiffel Tower and a Parisian-style streetscape, with limestone-colored facades and mansard roofs. And inside? French fashion and jewelry shops? A boulangerie? A cinema? A restaurant?

"You need to talk to Paul Bocuse," said Collart immediately and with great certainty. The new generation of French chefs, that's what Disney's France Pavilion needed—the glamorous allure of the Bande à Bocuse.

As soon as he heard about the opportunity to open a restaurant at Disney's new EPCOT theme park, Bocuse knew he would say yes. How could he say no? This was Disney, this was America, in all its quintessential, outsize glory. America, where everything was bigger—the crowds, the publicity, the money. It was the business deal of a lifetime. Nouvelle cuisine may have lost its luster, but Bocuse was still the most famous chef in the world, and he meant to capitalize on that.

The first thing Bocuse did was get his friends involved. This had always been his approach to commercial ventures, and in this case there would be an added benefit: Bocuse did not speak more than a few words of English, a considerable handicap when opening a restaurant in Florida.

He brought in Roger Vergé, who spoke fluent English, learned as a young man working in hotel restaurants in Casablanca and Jamaica. They flew to Burbank, and in their negotiations with the Americans, Bocuse left the talking to Vergé, only ever visibly reacting when he heard the word "dollars." Bocuse also recruited Gaston Lenôtre, who had experience with large-scale catering and could take charge of desserts. They would call the restaurant "Les Chefs de France," and offer the best of French cooking to the visiting tourist masses.

They would own the restaurant: Bocuse, Vergé, and Lenôtre borrowed money and put up millions for the thirty-year lease, and agreed to pay Disney a percentage of the profits. Les Chefs de France would be the focal point of the France Pavilion, which, in addition to the one-tenth-scale Eiffel Tower, also featured cobblestones, fountains, flower carts, painters with easels, and a very small Pont des Arts–inspired footbridge over a miniature Seine. A Paris stage set, and perfect kitsch.

Bocuse could only chuckle at the earnest American simulation, so deeply preposterous and yet also innocent and sweet. EPCOT Center opened in October 1982 and was a sensation. A $1 billion investment, millions of visitors. In the France Pavilion, Les Chefs de France and its more casual upstairs Bistro de Paris were booked solid for lunch and dinner every day.

The main restaurant was all burnished brass, wood paneling, and burgundy leather banquettes, etched glass and chandeliers, yellow-gold walls, and pressed tin ceilings. The waiters were dressed in black and white, and wore crisp white waist aprons. Every detail was a reasonable facsimile of what you'd find in an authentic French bistro, although the effect was complicated by the appearance of the customers, who favored shorts and T-shirts and even Mickey Mouse ears. This was Disney World, after all!

Still, the smell of garlicky escargots and French onion soup filled the air, and Bocuse could feel the quiet, electric thrum of the new restaurant shifting into gear. The place was enormous—they were serving twenty-five hundred covers on a slow day, and four thousand when it got truly busy, which was often. The three chefs flew in frequently to oversee the operation, sometimes solo, sometimes together. They rented a lakeside house not far from Disney World, and even though they were working, it felt like vacation. They nicknamed themselves "The Three Musketeers"—French swashbucklers in a Disney adventure story.

The food was simple. Everything on the menu was a familiar classic, a cliché: country pâté, quiche Lorraine, vol-au-vent with chicken, blanquette de veau, beef Bourguignon, fillet of beef au poivre with potato gratin. Desserts included profiteroles, pear Napoleon, meringue, soufflé, and various pastries, sorbets, and ice creams. Les Chefs de France also offered a children's menu, "served with fruit cup and beverage."

The cooking was not ambitious, it was not haute cuisine, or nouvelle cuisine, but that wasn't the point. As the *New York Times* food writer Bryan Miller noted:

> Having three of the greatest French chefs collaborate on onion soup might seem like asking Luciano Pavarotti to organize the church supper sing-along, but refined dining is not what Chefs de France is all about. This is Disney, after all, where the image is the message. . . . Visiting the French pavilion at Epcot Center is no more a substitute for a dining pilgrimage to France than a Disney World jungle cruise is for an expedition up the Amazon.

Miller was reasonably good-humored about the sometimes mediocre theme park cooking at the Bocuse, Vergé, and Lenôtre restaurant. The prices were reasonable, the wine list was decent, and the beef fillet was tender, he wrote. But the bread was stale, the duck was dry, and the sauces were bland, "pale-tasting" and "timidly spiced." Bocuse told the paper: "We have had to cut down on seasonings because of the clientele we get at the restaurant. We are not cooking exactly like we do in Lyon, or if we were cooking for New Yorkers. People come here from all over America and they have different preferences."

Le Monde was less forgiving, bemoaning both the impersonal futurism of EPCOT ("We killed Cinderella. Coldly buried under millions of dollars") and the "cardboard and paste" fakery and "bastardized buildings" of the World Showcase. As for Bocuse, Vergé, and Lenôtre: "The obligation imposed on these three prestigious names to stock their kitchen at the Disney World purchasing center seems like a bad joke. We did not find any trace of the taste and talent of these chefs there. It's a shame."

Was this the inevitable, dismal endpoint of nouvelle cuisine? Here were three of the originators of French New Wave cooking, reduced to the mass production of affordable bistro classics. But that's not how Bocuse saw it. He was a chef who understood that restaurants, at some level, were a kind of theater. He was a showman, orchestrating an experience. Les Chefs de France was simply a much larger show, for a much larger audience.

And the money? The money was astronomical.

In southwest France, meanwhile, Michel Guérard was pushing beyond nouvelle cuisine in a very different way. Settled in a far corner of the countryside, he and his wife, Christine, continued to refurbish and renovate their spa hotel, little by little, year by year. Guests traveled to Les Prés d'Eugénie for the hot spring baths, for health retreats, for Guérard's slimming cuisine minceur. But it was his Michelin three-star restaurant that drew most attention, and he was determined to evolve his cooking and his menus. Even if he had now rejected the "nouvelle cuisine" label, he would not give up his creativity.

Guérard found inspiration everywhere: in a Monet painting, in a photograph of a Moroccan garden, in the fleeting smell of his morning espresso. He also opened his cooking to international influences, flavors, ingredients, and techniques. A few years earlier, he and Christine had traveled to Hong Kong and to mainland China, along with Pierre Troisgros, Alain Chapel, and Alain Senderens, and their wives. This was 1978, two years after Mao's death, and post–Cultural Revolution China was only newly open to foreign visitors. It was another world—Guérard found the cooking to be "baroque, unusual, sublime, disconcerting, loving, intriguing, and surprising." He kept a diary:

> CANTON, THURSDAY FEBRUARY 19
>
> It was at exactly 11:30 a.m. that we went to the Canton Friendship Restaurant to enjoy our first real meal of popular Chinese cuisine. Our hosts receive us in a pretty dining room with windows lined with transparent blue and sea green glass, inlaid with delicate animal or floral motifs. The Cantonese meal served to us is a model of its kind and, among the fifteen dishes offered, some delight us like a jellyfish salad cut into crunchy strips seasoned with vinegar and mustard: a wonderful taste. Small pieces of freshwater fish are quickly sautéed with delicious onion sprouts that we don't know in France. To continue to whet our appetite, ravioli in the shape of little white rabbits come out hot from their cooking steam, followed by a fine soup made of snake filaments (yes!) and chicken, but above all garnished with white chrysanthemum petals which add great refinement. And then other little pâtés in the shape of tiny pears, before the arrival of the lacquered suckling pig that we were lucky enough to see prepared in the kitchen. For the first time, we eat a beautiful dish of fried rice with small diced pork, shrimp, peas and beaten eggs: it is the real Cantonese rice which

> only finds its equal in Chinese noodles sautéed and served with onion shoots.
>
> After our toasts with sorghum liquor, we tell our Chinese friends how happy we are to have enjoyed this meal. We are all photographed together under a great Maoist motto which for all we know says that we must fight Western imperialism at all costs. But in any case, we have the impression that French cooks are well loved here.

Guérard was taken with Peking duck, so different and so superior to the sweet, strawberry jam–basted duck served in Chinese restaurants in Paris. He visited numerous kitchens in China to learn the techniques behind the crispy skin and tender meat (a bicycle pump used to inflate and detach the bird's skin during cooking; a bit of water carefully filled in the bird's cavity so the meat was steamed from the inside as the skin was roasting). He also appreciated how every element of the bird was served in different ways, concluding with a fragrant broth, and nothing went to waste.

But it was Chinese dim sum that led him to create what would become one of his most famous dishes. The delicate, steamed dumplings were a revelation, and he decided to make his own, with mushrooms. Somewhere between dim sum and ravioli, Guérard's "oreiller moelleux de mousserons et de morilles" (soft pillow of fairy ring and morel mushrooms) was a single dumpling filled with intensely flavorful wild mushrooms and served in a truffle-infused broth with asparagus. The "soft pillow" went on the menu and stayed there.

Pierre Troisgros, on the same trip to China, was also inspired.

Chinese cooks were "in search of harmony obtained by contrasts: crunchy and soft, spicy and sweet, and with a great concentration of tastes," he said. Many of the ideas of nouvelle cuisine weren't new at all, at least not in Asia.

Troisgros had also spent months in Japan in the late 1960s, and there he had found an elegant minimalism and sense of design in the presentation of dishes. "Very discreet. Just what you need and no more." This, too, had deeply influenced his and his brother's cooking. And so they forged ahead in Roanne—like Guérard, always making improvements to the building and furnishings, and adding new specials to the menu. Dandelion salad with duck cracklings. Shellfish baked with ginger.

But at Troisgros, tragedy intervened. In the summer of 1983, Jean Troisgros died of a heart attack while playing tennis. He was fifty-six.

The sudden, unexpected death of his older brother led Pierre to ask his son Michel Troisgros to return to the family restaurant and join him in the kitchen. Michel had grown up in the restaurant, peeling carrots and washing sorrel on the weekends. He'd gone to culinary school and trained with many of his father and uncle's friends: Guérard, Alain Chapel, Roger Vergé, Frédy Girardet. He was twenty-six, and he returned home to join the family business, a generational shift that came sooner than anyone expected.

Michel would soon put his own imprint on the restaurant. His father and uncle were icons (Roanne renamed the square in front of the restaurant "Place Jean Troisgros" a few years later, with President Mitterrand in attendance), and Michel was steeped in the family lore. But he did not want the nouvelle cuisine that had put the restaurant on the map to become a deadweight. There were already jokes in the kitchen about the signature Troisgros salmon with sorrel sauce, referring to the dish as "un saumon qui amait trop l'oseille"—a salmon greedy for cash—a play on the word *oseille*, meaning "sorrel," but also slang for "money." The dish was a moneymaker.

In any case, Michel Troisgros was looking ahead. In the coming years, he would remove the famous salmon from the menu entirely.

The longstanding knock on Bocuse was that he was never in Lyon, he was always off somewhere else, too busy expanding his global empire and being the most famous chef in the world to actually bother doing any cooking. Of course, even when he was on the premises in Collonges-au-Mont-d'Or, he spent as much time in the dining room greeting guests as he did in the kitchen.

"Who cooks at your restaurant when you're not there?" he was asked.

"The same person who cooks when I *am* there," he replied.

Bocuse had a reliable team, led by his longtime executive chef, Roger Jaloux, his brilliant and trusted right-hand man. Bocuse needed the restaurant to run like clockwork, whether he was there or not, and now more than ever, in the 1980s, his various businesses and projects took him all over the world.

There was Les Chefs de France at EPCOT, already shockingly profitable, grossing $10 million a year, and that number was only going up. There was also the chain of Bocuse-branded

French restaurants in Japan, and his shops selling gourmet specialties and wine at Daimaru department stores there; a hotel restaurant in Rio de Janeiro called Saint Honoré; consulting contracts with Brazil and Venezuela, with Air France's Le Méridien hotel chain (he recommended young chefs for their properties all over the world), and with airlines including TWA, Avianca, and the Concorde. He oversaw state dinners in Brasília and gala dinners at Carnegie Hall, posing for photos with the likes of Frank Sinatra, Jeanne Moreau, Miles Davis, and Isaac Stern.

Bocuse was more than a celebrity chef—he had become a brand. The pope of French cooking. His restaurant in Lyon was a gourmet pilgrimage destination, and always full. Did it matter if he wasn't always present personally? The food was exactly the same. The way he saw it, criticism of his travel and his businesses beyond France was the result of jealousy, resentment, pettiness, or gambits for publicity.

Gault and Millau, for example.

The arbiters and "inventors" of nouvelle cuisine were struggling to adapt to a world that had rendered the term passé. They defended their culinary philosophy as best they could in the pages of the *Nouveau Guide*, but it didn't help that Bocuse had taken to disparaging the cooking as "ethereal food served under a bell jar," distancing himself from the culinary movement that had made him famous. "The baby carrot is next to the fine turnip," Bocuse joked on television, "accompanied by a pea cut into four tiny pieces, all surrounding a fillet of minced bird from which the skin and bones have been removed. Everything comes down to color, to the detriment of flavor."

Was this why Gault and Millau had contrived to punish him

in their ratings? Gault and Millau's guides used a rating system of 1 to 20 points, and had never given any restaurant a grade higher than 19, the idea being that no one was perfect. Bocuse had always received the maximum 19 points. But in the January 1985 issue of the *Nouveau Guide*, Christian Millau announced with much fanfare that the system had changed and that eight French chefs had earned 19.5 points for their culinary excellence, and would be called "super-toques." Bocuse was not among them.

The new top-scoring Gault and Millau chefs all cooked in the modern, nouvelle cuisine style, although the phrase "nouvelle cuisine" did not appear anywhere in the article. Some, like Alain Senderens and Michel Guérard, were long established, while others were younger, the next generation: Marc Meneau, Jacques Maximin, and Joël Robuchon.

Bocuse had been demoted, and as a savvy editor, Millau knew full well that the snub would be the story, that an outcry would result, that Bocuse would defend himself, and that the pot-stirring would sell magazines. Alongside the glowing reviews and group photographs of the "super-toques," Millau also published an article taking on Bocuse directly. Full credit to Bocuse, he wrote, for leading the way to chefs owning their own restaurants, but in delegating the kitchen to Jaloux, he was now more restaurateur than chef:

> We understand perfectly why Bocuse prefers to travel the world and earn money rather than direct his orchestra. He has also rendered an immense service to French cuisine and products by mak-

ing them known well beyond our borders. But, in doing so, he has taken the risk of letting Bocuse happen without Bocuse.

I know his defense perfectly. He's told me a hundred times: "I have a fantastic chef, Roger Jaloux, a sensational team, first-rate products, and I therefore have no reason to be concerned." In a sense, he is right. But, precisely because his team is amazing, everything happens as if Bocuse were no longer at Bocuse, even when he is. . . . As he told me last year: "Jaloux no longer needs Bocuse." It was, possibly, a joke. In any case, it contained a good part of truth.

In typical Bocuse fashion, he laughed off the attack, joking in radio interviews that he'd always been a terrible student and been given bad grades, and 19 out of 20 wasn't so bad. He sent a letter to Millau explaining, tongue in cheek, that since the Gault and Millau guides had raised the maximum restaurant score to 19.51 out of 20, he was awaiting his new score of 19.52! He also noted that the Michelin guide had just given him an award, and would Gault and Millau like a photograph of the trophy for the cover of their next issue?

"I have more respect for Mickey Mouse than for Christian Millau," Bocuse told *Time* magazine. "Critics are like eunuchs. They know how to, but they can't!"

The semiserious feud between Bocuse and the Gault and Millau guides would last for years. But despite the inevitable criticism of his outsize celebrity, his Disney World cooking, his jet-setting consulting work, he embraced his role as a showman. And he would only up the ante.

In 1987, Bocuse launched an international cooking competition called the Bocuse d'Or, a kind of Olympics of cooking to be held every two years in Lyon. He'd been named honorary president of the city's culinary trade fair, the Salon des Métiers de Bouche, which was looking for a way to draw attention to the event.

A cooking competition in front of a large, cheering crowd, pitting promising young chefs from around the world against each other, representing their home countries, making their dishes from scratch, within a strict time limit, using the same ingredients, the results judged by a jury of experts, with figure-skating-style scoring. This was gourmet, haute cuisine cooking as gladiatorial spectacle, with gold, silver, and bronze awards. The brick-like trophy resembled the one given by the César Awards, the French equivalent of the Oscars, and was designed by the same artist, César Baldaccini.

Twenty chefs competed the first year, each assigned a small makeshift kitchen with a gas range, lined up before a grandstand in the convention hall. The theme for the final was Bresse chicken with four garnishes, and the winner, representing France, was Jacky Fréon, a young (male) chef at the Hôtel Lutetia in Paris.

The event drew hundreds of reporters—print, television, radio—and was covered around the world, including in *The New York Times*. *Le Monde* wondered if the "Golden Bocuse" was not a bit too self-promotional, to which Bocuse responded: "I'm not stopping anyone else from doing the same thing . . . They asked me, and my name is more easily pronounced than others."

His critics could say what they wanted. He was the godfather, the king of French gourmet cooking.

Everyone knew.

Everyone knew, but nothing had changed. Courtine was writing his weekly column for *Le Monde* as he always had, telling his readers where and where not to eat, about the glories of true French cooking.

But the talk was louder. The rumors were flying.

Courtine was on the jury for the Marco Polo-Casanova prize, an award given every year to the best restaurant in Paris serving foreign cuisine. The jury was a mix of literary and culinary journalists and writers, the elite of the gastronomic establishment. But when two well-regarded writers were proposed as members, Courtine was vociferous in his opposition and threatened to resign. Gilles Pudlowski was a young food critic who wrote for the *Nouveau Guide* and many magazines and newspapers; Bernard Frank was an author and a prolific columnist for *Le Matin de Paris* and other papers and had been since the 1950s. Both Pudlowski and Frank were Jewish, and saw clear antisemitism in Courtine's veto, and said so.

In the insular world of Parisian gastronomy, Courtine's wartime Nazi sympathies were derided and condemned. As the 1980s wore on, the now septuagenarian *Le Monde* critic's reputation was in steep decline, at least in some quarters.

Jean-Pierre Desclozeaux, the artist and illustrator whose drawings had accompanied Courtine's weekly column for years and were its unmistakable signature, now made a point of never meeting the critic in person. "Otherwise, I would break his face!" he said.

Albert Nahmias at restaurant Olympe heard a rumor that Courtine had traveled to Berlin during the war and marched in a Nazi parade wearing a Nazi uniform. There was apparently a photograph. And he himself had heard Courtine refer to World War II as "my war," and brag (drunkenly) about his Francisque medal, an honor awarded by Pétain's Vichy regime. Courtine had supposedly fled to Germany after the war, and then to Italy, where he was arrested, sent back to France, and sentenced to five years in prison.

Pierre Assouline hadn't gone public with his knowledge of Courtine's pro-Nazi writings, but he did warn others of the truth. When Bernard Pivot invited him to appear on *Apostrophes* to discuss the work of novelist Georges Simenon (Assouline was writing a biography), he was thrilled until he heard that Pivot planned to invite Courtine on the show as well (because of Courtine's Maigret-themed cookbook).

"If you invite Courtine, I won't come," he told Pivot.

"But how can you refuse?" was the reply.

After some back and forth, Assouline finally said: "If you put me on the air with him, I will show, on camera, on live television, what he wrote during the war. And you will see the scandal."

The episode with Courtine did not happen.

Something similar occurred when a friend of Assouline's who worked in public relations told him he was organizing an event for Courtine. He was Jewish, from Tunisia, and Assouline immediately asked him whether he knew Courtine's history. "Of course I know," he said. "Everybody knows he was a collaborator!" To which Assouline replied: "But do you know exactly, precisely, what he did? And what he wrote? I'm not talking about being a Pétainist. I don't mind Pétainists. I'm talking about having blood on your hands. The man is a criminal."

His friend's dinner event for Courtine did not happen.

And this was perhaps the most devastating: Someone—it wasn't Assouline—had made photocopies of several of Courtine's rabid 1940s articles in *Au Pilori*, the pro-Nazi newspaper. The clips were passed around among chefs and restaurant critics like contraband. After a press dinner, after Courtine had left to go home, over a last glass of red wine, someone would unfold a copy of one of the old man's screeds and read a sentence or two out loud. Headline: "The Jew and France," Courtine's wartime review of an anti-Jewish exhibition at the Palais Berlitz in Paris. Quote: "The Jewish peril is not a matter of religion, and it's not limited to France. This is a racial question for all of Europe. It is high time France opens its eyes to the threat of the hordes of Israel that are dragging us to the edge of the abyss."

And so on. Everyone laughed queasily.

Courtine gave no outward sign of noticing the conversations about his past. In his columns, he was erudite and bitter, writing about his usual enemies and hobbyhorses, the deficiencies of the fame-seeking, sellout chefs of the modern era. "Leaving your kitchen, leaving your restaurant to achieve false media glory," he wrote in 1987, "this is now the goal for any cook. It is the triumph of fakery. Which is why chefs who think they are great, aping Bocuse, become traveling salesmen, advertising agents for the 'food industry.'"

But Courtine's power and stature were fading, and he was

afraid. The sight of old Nazis and collaborators being hauled into court in France—an increasingly common sight on the evening news—filled him with terror. And now there was a new rumor making the rounds in the food world: Courtine had apparently confided to a friend that he was prepared to flee to Switzerland at a moment's notice. If he were exposed, or charged, or threatened with a legal proceeding concerning his wartime activities, Courtine would escape to Geneva and hole up at the luxurious Hôtel du Rhône.

This desperate plan was never put into action; Courtine survived in the shadows, in fearful quiescence, for a few more years. A full accounting of his life would occur only after his death.

The initial inspiration for the founding of the ARC had been the sexist, men-only admission policy of the Maîtres Cuisiniers de France. The policy had never changed, and the ARC had only grown, year by year. And it had succeeded: More young women were entering the profession than ever before; many of the member chefs made a point of hiring women to work in their kitchens.

When Olympe Nahmias appeared with Bocuse, Senderens, and others on an episode of *Apostrophes* in 1982 to discuss the state of French cooking (always a hot topic on French literary talk shows), Pivot introduced her as "the best female chef in the world, according to the new Gault and Millau guide," and hailed her success as a "triumph of feminism."

Olympe described how difficult it still was for women to get a foothold in the industry. Five years earlier, at age twenty-five, she said, she'd called a number of the top restaurants and asked about doing a stage, a training apprenticeship: "They all said no, all of them." She looked at Bocuse as she said this, and smiled.

"You should have sent a photograph!" quipped Bocuse, ever the male chauvinist. Everyone laughed.

But the restaurant world was changing for women, in no small part because of the ARC. Now, in the 1980s, it was gradually becoming more possible for women to work as apprentices in professional restaurant kitchens, even those not owned by women.

Simone Lemaire was pushing the ARC forward and out of the shadow of Courtine's narrow definition of "cuisine de bonne femme." The association was adding new and younger members, including women whose restaurants served Hungarian, Italian, Moroccan, Creole, Vietnamese, North African, Turkish, and Middle Eastern cuisines. The ARC would not be limited to traditionalist French cooking, or even to France: Lemaire had invited a few women chefs in England, Switzerland, Luxembourg, and Belgium to join as well.

This new generation of ARC chefs was entrepreneurial and fearless. Fatéma Hal, for example, had grown up in Morocco until the age of eighteen, was sent to France in an arranged marriage, raised children, got divorced, campaigned for women's rights in the Arab community alongside the socialist politician Yvette Roudy, and then decided, at thirty-two, to open a restaurant. Mansouria debuted in 1984, not far from the Place de la Bastille in Paris, with savory pastilla, couscous, and various tagines on the menu. The restaurant served some of the most authentic Moroccan cooking in the city; the kitchen was staffed almost entirely by women.

In Luxembourg, a few miles from the French border, Léa Linster took over the operation of her parents' café-restaurant after her father died in 1982. The place was frantic and utilitarian, combining a gas station, tobacco and liquor store, currency exchange, rooms for rent, and bowling alley under one roof, in addition to the restaurant. Linster was twenty-seven, and set about transforming the property while simultaneously earning a cooking diploma and completing stages with Joël Robuchon and Frédy Girardet, among others. In 1987, her restaurant, now called Léa Linster, was awarded a Michelin star.

Two years later, representing Luxembourg, Linster entered the Bocuse d'Or competition, and won. This was a momentous occasion, for Linster, for the ARC, for women's cooking.

She'd entered on a whim—it was good publicity, even if she didn't win a prize, and she was the sort of charismatic, hard-charging personality destined to excel in a high-pressure cooking competition. Her recipes were eclectic and Luxembourg-accented, with traces of French and German. For the judges in Lyon, she prepared sea bass with a watercress sauce, and her pièce de résistance, a saddle of lamb wrapped in a crisp, rösti-like potato crust, baked, and served in thick slices.

Linster's 1989 Bocuse d'Or win was reported all over the world. Bounding onstage in her chef's whites and tall white toque, she beamed as Bocuse handed her the heavy gold trophy and an oversize $15,000 check, the crowd cheering, flashbulbs exploding, all the winners kissing each other on all of their cheeks, and Bocuse seemed as delighted as Linster. The acrimony and argument about women chefs in restaurant kitchens, let alone their right to wear the toque, was seemingly forgotten.

The next day, Simone Lemaire, now honorary president of the ARC, sent a telegram to Bocuse, striking a tone of sarcastic but heartfelt joy. "Gars Paul," she wrote (*gars* was affectionate slang meaning "guy" or "dude"), "The ARC thanks you for putting an end to five centuries of gastronomy without women."

The moment was, in its way, perfectly emblematic of the triumph of nouvelle cuisine. The phrase itself was now obsolete, and so were the overly mannered cooking clichés and gestures of its 1970s heyday. But the movement to liberate chefs from the past, to introduce new ideas and ingredients and international influences, to question authority and tradition, to open doors to verve and experimentation, had changed the world. The Bande à Bocuse had led chefs out of the kitchen and into the realm of pop culture and celebrity (just as Courtine had bemoaned), but they had also redefined what had been a craft as an art form. The ARC, meanwhile, had demanded recognition and respect for women chefs, for their creativity and talent, for freedom and self-determination. They had fought Bocuse and his retrograde ideas about gender (with the support of Courtine), and they had won. Léa Linster, age thirty-four, standing on the stage with her Bocuse d'Or, basking in the roar of the crowd, was only a sign of things to come, another door opened.

Nouvelle cuisine may have died, but a thousand flowers were blooming.

Epilogue

In January 2018, Paul Bocuse died in his sleep, at home in a bedroom above his restaurant in Collonges-au-Mont-d'Or. He was ninety-one.

The news was not unexpected—he'd been suffering from Parkinson's disease—but it was seismic nevertheless. The grand master of French cooking was gone; an era had ended. Emmanuel Macron, president of France, issued a statement: "Chefs are crying in their kitchens, at the Élysée Palace and all over France. . . . The Nouvelle Cuisine, of which he was a founding father, sometimes criticized or misunderstood, opened a glorious chapter for French cuisine." On the front page of *The New York Times*, Bocuse was described as a "tireless self-promoter" and a "role model for the chef-entrepreneurs of the present day." *Le Monde* estimated the value of his sprawling culinary empire at over 50 million euros.

Outside the front door of the restaurant, the public left bouquets in a growing pile, a spontaneous memorial, while TV reporters set up their cameras. The following week, on a gray, rainy day in Lyon, the Saint-Jean Cathedral filled to capacity for Bocuse's funeral, including 150 chefs in their chef's whites filling the front rows. Everyone was there, it seemed, all of the French culinary elite, and chefs from around the world: Alain Ducasse, Frédéric Anton, Anne-Sophie Pic, Régis Marcon, Yannick Alléno, Christelle Brua, Philippe Etchebest, Daniel Boulud, Joël Robuchon, Gordon Ramsay, Marc Haeberlin, Hiroyuki Hiramatsu, Pierre Orsi, Guy Savoy, Marc Veyrat, and Thomas Keller, among many others.

Of the original Bande à Bocuse, only two now survived: Pierre Troisgros and Michel Guérard. It was Troisgros who took to the pulpit, the first speaker, walking slowly, accompanied by his son Michel. "Paul," he said, "we won't be sad, you wouldn't have wanted us to be, you who had fun all of your life." He reminisced about Bocuse's humor, his talent, his drive.

"But the main thing is what you brought to us cooks," Troisgros continued. "You gave our profession a new value, forcing it to evolve, to come out of the overheated second subbasement and into the light, literally and figuratively. Thanks to your audacity, we entered a new era. No longer lowly cuistot, we are cuisiniers, each responsible for his own performance. The profession thanks you and is grateful to you."

So much had changed over the previous thirty years: waves of international influence, fusion, and experimentation; technological advances and molecular cooking; the valorization of regional cuisines and seasonal ingredients; slow food, bistronomy, gastropubs, New Basque, New Nordic, and other newly labeled food trends; the rise of fantastically expensive tasting menus and the rise of Shake Shack; countless TV cooking shows and competitions and a booming culinary media; and most recently, fallout from the Me Too movement, and the ongoing fight against sexism and abuse in restaurant kitchens.

The food world was a thriving, global cacophony of invention and ambition—new restaurants, new chefs, new dishes, new ideas. And so much of the present could be traced back to the 1970s heyday of nouvelle cuisine, the Bande à Bocuse, the rise of the ARC, the backlash against overly trendy, imitative cooking, and the flood of money, cultural cachet, and celebrity in the food world. Post-1960s, the world had changed, the rules rewritten, and nouvelle cuisine had broken through to the wider popular culture and imagination in a way that food and restaurants never had before.

Nouvelle cuisine was long gone, but the aftereffects of its history were everywhere. And the men and women who had made that history had evolved with the times in the decades since, training the next generation of chefs, seeing progress and change in fits and starts.

The ARC had closed up shop in 1998. Simone Lemaire had retired, and felt the association had served its purpose. Women chefs were succeeding, finding apprenticeships and stages, winning prizes and accolades, opening restaurants. After years of hidebound recalcitrance, the Maîtres Cuisiniers de France had finally decided to accept women as members the previous year, in 1997.

Annie Desvignes applied for membership, as she had more

than twenty years earlier, and this time was rejected because she was too old: Members were required to be between the ages of twenty-eight and fifty-five. The ironies were bleak. Meanwhile, she continued to cook at La Tour du Roy in Vervins, and her son, Fabrice Desvignes, had become the head chef at the Élysée Palace, and unlike his mother, was soon granted membership. Progress was slow, it seemed.

Christiane Massia, Olympe Nahmias, Gisèle Berger, and most of the original members of the ARC had retired, but the next generation was going strong, including Fatéma Hal and Léa Linster. In 2007, Anne-Sophie Pic became the first woman awarded three Michelin stars in over fifty years, at her family restaurant, Maison Pic, in Valance, south of Lyon. Like Desvignes, Pic had been rejected by the Maîtres Cuisiniers de France because she was a woman, although in her case she was eventually accepted. Progress was slow, but it was progressing.

Robert Courtine died in 1998, the same year the ARC disbanded. The great champion of women's cooking and French tradition and onetime Nazi true believer had been quietly but forcibly retired from *Le Monde* in 1993, after protests from other staff members. His wartime writings were by then infamous inside the paper.

Le Monde's very brief obituary for its longtime restaurant critic attempted to set the record straight, and set off a firestorm. "Two Names, Two Lives" was the headline; the revered and feared critic, beloved by *Le Monde*'s readers for decades, had written for the far-right and collaborationist press before and during World War II, had fled to Germany after the war and been caught and punished, and then enjoyed a long career at the newspaper, and written many books. The obituary concluded: "From the most execrable of politics to successor to Brillat-Savarin, the itinerary will surprise only those who have not known the storms of yesterday."

The outraged letters poured in. How could *Le Monde* have kept quiet about Courtine for all those years? How could a newspaper that reported so aggressively about the collaborationist past of President François Mitterrand and his political ally René Bousquet have continued to publish the work of a known collaborator, and only reveal the truth after his death? Many years later, in 2014, *Le Monde* would publish an extensive, detailed accounting of Courtine's past and his career at the paper.

As Bocuse's funeral came to an end, after the tributes and Bible readings from politicians, priests, and family members, his coffin was carried out of the church and into the drizzling rain.

Standing in the pews, the next generation of chefs, many of them trained in the restaurants of the Bande à Bocuse, were left to contemplate how much the world had changed, and how much it hadn't. The icons were mostly gone, their restaurants now grand family institutions—Troisgros, Haeberlin, Guérard, Bocuse—not so unlike the Maxim's, Tours d'Argents, and Lapérouses they had once challenged. And so it would continue, the next new restaurant, the next brilliant chef, emerging in an unexpected place, inspired by—or rebelling against—the legacy of nouvelle cuisine.

A crowd had gathered outside the cathedral, stoic under their umbrellas, and they watched as the coffin was carefully set on a small stand on the front steps. The church organ played a processional; the church bells were ringing. Large screens had been set up outside to broadcast the funeral proceedings, and they showed a still photograph of Bocuse, in his chef's whites and toque. And now the organ music stopped, and over the loudspeakers, echoing tinnily on the cobblestone streets, came Edith Piaf's 1960 recording "Non, Je Ne Regrette Rien," and everyone listened in silence until the song ended, and the coffin was carried to a hearse and slowly driven away.

Non, rien de rien
Non, je ne regrette rien
C'est payé, balayé, oublié
Je me fous du passé

No, nothing at all
No, I regret nothing
It's paid for, swept away, forgotten
I could care less about the past

Acknowledgments

Thank you to Michel Guérard, Pierre Troisgros, Michel Troisgros, Olympe Versini, Albert Nahmias, Simone Lemaire, Annie Desvignes, Yanou Collart, André Gayot, Alexis Millau, Pierre Assouline, Gilles Pudlowski, Jean-Claude Ribaut, Nicolas de Rabaudy, Billy Cross, Gary Jenanyan, Raymond Sokolov, Ruth Reichl, Clark Wolf, Georges Blanc, Guy Martin, Jacotte Brazier, Vérane Frédiani, Gilles Reinhardt, Jean-Philippe Merlin, and Guy Savoy for speaking with me about the time period and events described in this book, and sharing their stories. For invaluable research assistance, I thank Noémie Bablet, Zoë Petit, and Fiona Vilmer. To my brilliant editor, Jill Schwartzman, and also to Brent Howard, Charlotte Peters, Isabel DaSilva, Hannah Poole, and the entire team at Dutton, thank you. My agent, friend, and mentor, David Kuhn, made this book possible; thank you also to Nate Muscato, Allison Warren, Rachel Anne Cantor, and Liana Raguso at Aevitas, and Dana Spector at CAA. For their generosity, insight, and wisdom, I thank my friends Sean Gullette, Adam

Lehner, Albert Wenger, Gigi Danziger, Nancy Novogrod, Mark Leyner, Luke and Vanessa Dawson, Benoît Peverelli, Bruno Maddox and Catrinel Bartolomeu, Adrian Erni, Gerni Jörgler, Adi Schultheiss, Markus Duner, Déborah Burkart, and Jürg Wernli. Finally, I could not have written this book without the love and support of my family, my father, John Barr; my wife, Yumi Moriwaki; and my daughters, Sachi and Emi.

Bibliography

Abidor, Mitchell. *May Made Me: An Oral History of the 1968 Uprising in France.* AK Press, 2018.

Assouline, Pierre. *Le Fleuve Combelle.* Calmann-Lévy, 1997.

Assouline, Pierre. *Simenon: A Biography.* Knopf, 1997.

Aussudre, Matthieu. "La Nouvelle Cuisine Française: Rupture et Avènement d'une Nouvelle Ère Culinaire." Master's thesis, Université de Tours, 2015.

Belleret, Robert. *Paul Bocuse, L'Épopée d'un Chef.* L'Archipel, 2019.

Blake, Anthony, and Quentin Crewe. *Great Chefs of France.* Abrams, 1978.

Bocuse, Paul. *Paul Bocuse's French Cooking.* Pantheon, 1977.

Brazier, Eugénie. *La Mère Brazier: The Mother of Modern French Cooking.* Rizzoli, 2014.

Burns, Jim, and Betty Ann Brown. *Women Chefs: A Collection of Portraits and Recipes from California's Culinary Pioneers.* Aris Books, 1987.

Charretton, Bernard, and Christine Charretton. *Les Nouvelles Bases et Techniques de la Cuisine.* Telecuisine, 1985.

Chatenier, Nicolas. *Mémoires de Chefs.* Textuel, 2012.

Collart, Yanou. *Les Étoiles de Ma Vie: Lino, Jack, Johnnie et les Autres.* L'Archipel, 2019.

Courtine, Robert. *L'Assassin Est à Votre Table.* La Table Ronde, 1969.

Courtine, Robert [La Reynière, pseud.], and Jean-Pierre Desclozeaux. *Autour d'un Plat.* Le Monde Éditions, 1990.

Courtine, Robert. *Feasts of a Militant Gastronome.* William Morrow, 1974.

Courtine, Robert. *Gourmandissimo.* Albin Michel, 1978.

Courtine, Robert. *Guide Courtine, a Guide to Paris Restaurants.* Lyle Stuart, 1976.

Courtine, Robert. *The Hundred Glories of French Cooking.* Farrar, Straus and Giroux, 1973.

Courtine, Robert. *Mangez-Vous Français?* Sedimo Aurillac, 1965.

Courtine, Robert [Savarin, pseud.]. *Real French Cooking.* Faber and Faber, 1956.

Courtine, Robert [La Reynière, pseud.]. *200 Recettes des Meilleures Cuisinières de France.* Albin Michel, 1977.

de Groot, Roy Andries. *Revolutionizing French Cooking.* McGraw-Hill, 1976.

Escoffier, Auguste. *A Guide to Modern Cookery.* William Heinemann, 1907.

Frédiani, Vérane. *Elles Cuisinent: À la Rencontre des Femmes Chefs dans le Monde.* Hachette Cuisine, 2018.

Gramont, Sanche de. *The French: Portrait of a People.* Putnam, 1969.

Greene, Gael. *Blue Skies, No Candy.* William Morrow, 1976.

Greene, Gael. *Insatiable: Tales from a Life of Delicious Excess.* Warner Books, 2006.

Guérard, Michel. *Mémoire de la Cuisine Française.* Albin Michel, 2020.

Guérard, Michel. *Michel Guérard's Cuisine Gourmande.* William Morrow, 1979.

Guérard, Michel. *Michel Guérard's Cuisine Minceur.* William Morrow, 1976.

Hess, John. *Vanishing France.* Quadrangle, 1975.

James, Michael. *Slow Food: Flavors and Memories of America's Hometowns.* Warner Books, 1992.

Kamp, David. *The United States of Arugula.* Broadway Books, 2006.

Klarsfeld, Beate, and Serge Klarsfeld. *Hunting the Truth.* Farrar, Straus and Giroux, 2018.

Mallory, Heather Alison. "The Nouvelle Cuisine Revolution: Expressions of National Anxieties and Aspirations in French Culinary Discourse 1969–1996." PhD dissertation, Duke University, 2011.

Massia, Christiane. *Cuisine Plaisir.* Flammarion, 1987.

McNamee, Thomas. *The Man Who Changed the Way We Eat: Craig Claiborne and the American Food Renaissance.* Free Press, 2012.

Millau, Christian. *Dictionnaire Amoureux de la Gastronomie.* Plon, 2008.

Millau, Christian. *Dining in France.* Stewart, Tabori & Chang, 1986.

Nahmias, Albert. *Petites Histoires de Grands Chefs.* Hugo & Cie, 2015.

Olympe. *La Cuisine d'Olympe: Une Grande Cuisine Toute Simple.* Mengès, 1982.

Olympe. *Ma Cuisine de A à Z.* Albin Michel, 1991.

Ory, Pascal. *Les Collaborateurs, 1940–1945.* Éditions du Seuil, 1976.

Paxton, Robert O. *Vichy France: Old Guard and New Order, 1940–1944.* Knopf, 1972.

Peter, Madeleine. *Favorite Recipes of the Great Women Chefs of France.* Holt, Rinehart and Winston, 1979.

Prud'homme, Alex. *The French Chef in America: Julia Child's Second Act.* Knopf, 2016.

Pudlowski, Gilles. *À Quoi Sert Vraiment un Critique Gastronomique?* Armand Colin, 2011.

Rabaudy, Nicolas de. *Mémoires d'un Gourmet à Table.* Les Éditions du Mécène, 2021.

Sheraton, Mimi. *Eating My Words: An Appetite for Life.* William Morrow, 2004.

Sokolov, Raymond. *Steal the Menu: A Memoir of Forty Years in Food.* Knopf, 2013.

Troisgros, Jean, and Pierre Troisgros. *The Nouvelle Cuisine of Jean & Pierre Troisgros.* William Morrow, 1978.

Troisgros, Pierre. *Itinéraire d'un Cuisinier Gâté.* Privately published, 2017.

Vergé, Roger. *Ma Cuisine du Soleil.* Robert Laffont, 1978.

Viard, Henry. *The Gourmet's Tour de France.* Little, Brown, 1983.

Zizza-Lalu, Ève-Marie. *Paul Bocuse, Le Feu Sacré.* Glénat, 2005.

Notes

INTRODUCTION

xi **"A Grand Menu in the Sky":** "La Grande Carte du Ciel," *Le Nouveau Guide Gault-Millau*, April 1974, 102.

xiv **"women have no imagination":** Robert Courtine, "Ces Femmes aux Fourneaux," *Le Monde*, April 19, 1975.

xv ***"Voilà la nouvelle cuisine française!":*** Paul Bocuse interview, Nicolas Chatenier, *Mémoires de Chefs*, 37.

CHAPTER 1: 1965

5 **Cook what you like:** author interview with Michel Guérard, 2018.

10 **"The perfection of details" and subsequent quotes in this section:** Courtine, "Lasserre," *Le Monde*, May 6, 1965.

12 **"What do you have there?" and subsequent quotes in this section:** author interview with Simone Lemaire, 2018.

15 **"There will now be twelve":** Courtine, "Du Michelin au Kléber-Colombes," *Le Monde*, March 27, 1965.

18 **"So, Marie Laforêt":** author interview with Yanou Collart, 2018.

CHAPTER 2: THE POT-AU-FEU

23 **"Listen, Michel":** Guérard interview, Chatenier, *Mémoires de Chefs*, 95.

23 **"No more sandwiches":** author interview with Guérard, 2018.

24 **"For the first time":** Guérard interview, Chatenier, *Mémoires de Chefs*, 95.

24 **"This is a crime!":** author interview with Guérard, 2018.

24 **"lifeless, inert, and apathetic":** Guérard quoted in Bernard and Christine Charretton, *Les Nouvelles Bases et Techniques de la Cuisine*, 1985.

26 **"You want lamb?":** Guérard interview, Chatenier, *Mémoires de Chefs*, 97.

27 **"What goes through my head!":** Guérard interview, Chatenier, *Mémoires de Chefs*, 97.

29 **"Michel, I want you":** Guérard interview, Chatenier, *Mémoires de Chefs*, 96.

31 **"little pub on a sad street" and subsequent quotes in this section:** Courtine, "Le Petit Bistrot d'Asnières," *Le Monde,* June 9, 1967.

32 **"Delaveyne saved me":** Guérard interview, Chatenier, *Mémoires de Chefs*, 95.

33 **"We'll meet in the evening":** Guérard interview, Chatenier, *Mémoires de Chefs*, 97.

CHAPTER 3: TRUE FRENCH CUISINE

36 **"Whenever in the civilized world":** Courtine, *Real French Cooking*, 15.

36 **"With a very sharp knife":** Courtine, *Real French Cooking*, 168.

36 **"Soak for a few hours":** Courtine, *Real French Cooking*, 188.

36 ***"Listen, waiter":*** Courtine, *Real French Cooking*, 188.

37 **"Provided there is no successful politician":** Courtine, *Real French Cooking*, 346.

38 **"Will we keep our heads":** Courtine, *L'Assassin Est à Votre Table*, 27.

38 **"Synthetic meat":** Courtine, *L'Assassin*, 30.

39 **"The tragedy is not":** Art Buchwald, "Europe's Culture Falls to Hot Dog," *New York Herald Tribune,* June 5, 1955.

39 **"We are in the days of snacks":** Courtine, *Mangez-Vous Français?*, 65.

40 **"More and more" and subsequent quotes in this section:** Courtine, "Anti-Snacks," *Le Monde*, May 23, 1963.

40 **"The French are bored":** Pierre Viansson-Ponté, "Quand la France's Ennuie," *Le Monde*, March 15, 1968.

44 **"But of course, monsieur!" and subsequent quotes in this section:** Courtine, "Les Grands: Maxim's," *Le Monde*, March 1, 1968.

47 **"How often have we found":** Courtine, "Les Grands: Premières Conclusions," *Le Monde*, April 5, 1968.

47 **"You pay a lot more":** Courtine, "Les Grands: La Tour d'Argent," *Le Monde*, March 8, 1968.

48 **"among the best small restaurants" and subsequent quotes in this section:** "Nos 100 Meilleurs Restaurants de France," *Le Nouveau Guide Gault-Millau*, April 1970.

48 **"We did not have the right":** Alain Senderens interview, Chatenier, *Mémoires de Chefs*, 226.

48 **"little too sophisticated":** Courtine, "L'Archestrate," *Le Monde*, October 9, 1971.

49 **"The *palme* for originality":** "Ces Bistrots Feront Courir Paris," *Le Nouveau Guide Gault-Millau*, October 1969.

50 **"She never ate with the men":** Sanche de Gramont, "French Cooking à la Courtine," *New York Times Magazine*, July 6, 1969.

CHAPTER 4: "THE DINNER OF THE CENTURY"

53 **"Elga Andersen would be perfect" and subsequent quotes in this section:** Yanou Collart, *Les Étoiles de Ma Vie*, 46.

55 **"Monsieur Bouvard":** Collart, *Les Étoiles*, 51.

58 **"Paul Bocuse is something of a phenomenon" and subsequent quotes in this section:** Quentin Crewe, "Paul Bocuse and His Restaurant," *Vogue*, June 1968.

59 **"What can we do?":** Bocuse interview, Chatenier, *Mémoires de Chefs*, 37.

65 **"bland and over rich":** John Hess, "7 Chefs Cook 'Dinner of Century'—Were There 6 Too Many?" *New York Times*, September 8, 1971.

65 **"Don't those gentlemen" and subsequent quotes in this section:** Courtine, *Feasts of a Militant Gastronome*, 104.

66 **"Coming back on the plane":** Courtine, *Feasts*, 104.

66 **"You've got to beat the drum":** Bocuse quoted in Rudolph Chelminski, "Secrets of France's Super Chef," *People*, September 6, 1976.

CHAPTER 5: BANDE À BOCUSE

70 **"Ah, that's better":** author interview with Pierre Troisgros, 2018.

70 **"liters and liters":** Bocuse interview, Chatenier, *Mémoires de Chefs*, 33.

72 **"It's all I could find":** author interview with Pierre Troisgros, 2018.

72 **"an absolutely fabulous atmosphere" and subsequent quotes in this section:** Christian Millau, "Super Tocques," *Le Nouveau Guide Gault-Millau*, January 1985.

73 **"We're stronger together":** Bocuse interview, Chatenier, *Mémoires de Chefs*, 38.

74 **"I adore women":** Colin Randall, "We Live Too Long to Have Just One Woman," *Daily Telegraph*, December 15, 2005.

74 **"Voilà la nouvelle cuisine française!":** Paul Bocuse interview, Chatenier, *Mémoires de Chefs*, 37.

76 **"The menu usefully specifies":** Courtine, "Cuisine Normande et Normandie," *Le Monde*, July 20, 1974.

78 **"What if I set up a restaurant":** Élisabeth Bourgeois interview, Vérane Frédiani, *Elles Cuisinent*, 91.

80 **"Novelty is the universal cry":** Auguste Escoffier, *A Guide to Modern Cookery*, xii.

81 **"People are not against these small audacities":** Michel Guérard, *Mémoire de la Cuisine Française,* 78.

82 **"Do not break the crust":** Auguste Escoffier, *A Guide to Modern Cookery*, 248.

83 **"Finally, an intelligent salmon":** quoted in Pierre Troisgros, *Itinéraire d'un Cuisinier Gâté*, 86.

83 **"a filet of Loire salmon":** John Hess, "Michelin vs. Kleber: The

Knife and Fork Duel Is Growing More Heated," *New York Times*, February 23, 1966.

84 **"We share a respectful creativity":** Guérard interview, Chatenier, *Mémoires de Chefs*, 98.

84 **"Matisse and Picasso":** Alain Senderens interview, Chatenier, *Mémoires de Chefs*, 227.

CHAPTER 6: THE TEN COMMANDMENTS

88 **"Michelin is mute" and subsequent quotes in this section:** Christian Millau, *Dictionnaire Amoureux de la Gastronomie*, 381.

89 **"The truth is that":** Courtine, "Les Grands: Premières Conclusions," *Le Monde*, April 5, 1968.

91 **"Innovations must be tested":** "Lenôtre: Le Cesar de la Ganache," *Le Nouveau Guide Gault-Millau*, October 1969.

92 **"eliminating the slightest fault":** "L'Encyclopedie des Grandes Villes," *Le Nouveau Guide Gault-Millau*, December 1970.

92 **"transforming within a few months":** "L'Encyclopedie des Grandes Villes."

93 **"To cook like the bird sings!":** Millau, *Dictionnaire Amoureux de la Gastronomie*, 405.

93 **"astonishing, inventive":** "A L'ouest du Nouveau," *Le Nouveau Guide Gault-Millau*, March 1973.

93 **"chef among chefs":** "L'Expédition Chez Paul Bocuse," *Le Nouveau Guide Gault-Millau*, October 1970.

94 **"I ate very recently at Bocuse":** "Nos Lecteurs Nous Ecrivent," *Le Nouveau Guide Gault-Millau*, June 1970.

95 **"Ten Days, Seven Kilos":** Henri Gault, "Dix Jours, Sept Kilos au Moins," *Le Nouveau Guide Gault-Millau*, June 1972.

96 **"Everything seems to be done" and subsequent quotes in this section:** Millau, "La Grande Cuisine, Quel Sport!" *Le Nouveau Guide Gault-Millau*, October 1972.

98 **"I am ashamed to be French!":** "Le Scandale de La Grande Bouffe à Cannes," Archive video, INA, Institute Nationale de l'Audiovisuel.

98 **"Shame on the producers":** "'La Grande Bouffe' et le Sentiment National," *Le Monde*, June 2, 1973.

98 **"What Makes 'The Grande Bouffe' Different from a Porno Movie?":** *New York Times*, October 14, 1973.

100 **"But who drives this thing?":** Collart, *Les Étoiles*, 101.

100 **"Yanou, you must meet my father":** Collart, *Les Étoiles*, 120.

103 **"Here are our ten commandments!":** Raphaëlle Bacqué, "Quand Gault et Millau Lançaient la Nouvelle Cuisine," *Le Monde*, July 22, 2016.

103 **"mafia of good taste":** "La Bande à Bocuse," *Le Nouveau Guide Gault-Millau*, September 1973.

104 **"We are not iconoclasts" and subsequent quotes in this section:** "Vive la Nouvelle Cuisine Française," *Le Nouveau Guide Gault-Millau*, October 1973.

105 **"First Commandment":** Each of the commandments was accompanied by a paragraph of explanation; the quotes here are excerpts.

108 **"slender young girl":** Tim Carman, "Paul Bocuse, French Chef Who Popularized Nouvelle Cuisine Movement, Dies at 91," *Washington Post*, January 20, 2018.

CHAPTER 7: CUISINE DE FEMME

110 **"No problem, just pay me when you can":** Albert Nahmias, *Petites Histoires de Grands Chefs*, 17.

116 ***"Je suis completement autodidacte!"* and subsequent quotes in this section:** Bourgeois interview, Frédiani, *Elles Cuisinent*, 91.

119 **"The Master Chefs":** Froissand quoted in association history, maitrescuisiniersdefrance.com.

119 **"closed academy":** Courtine, "Voilà la Cuisine des Femmes," *Le Monde*, May 4, 1985.

121 **"All this food":** author interview with Albert Nahmias, 2018.

122 **"youngest and prettiest":** Courtine, "Trois Hommes et Une Femme," *Le Monde*, January 7, 1978.

CHAPTER 8: THE SLIMMING DIET

124 **"My name is Christine Barthélémy":** Guérard, *Mémoire de la Cuisine Française*, 112.

126 **"You almost feel" and subsequent quotes in this section:** Guérard, *Mémoire*, 119.

128 **"lost corner in the middle of nowhere":** Guérard, *Mémoire*, 124.

133 **"With dry bread?" and subsequent quotes in this section:** Millau, "J'Avais Quelques Kilos en Trop, Je Suis Allé les Perdre Chez Michel Guérard," *Le Nouveau Guide Gault-Millau*, June 1974.

135 **"Within a very short span" and subsequent quotes in this section:** Craig Claiborne, "A Practitioner of the New Cuisine Is Still Master of the Old," *New York Times*, October 29, 1975.

136 **"The beautiful and mysterious Christine":** Guérard, *Cuisine Minceur*, 5.

137 **"The vain snobbery":** Courtine, "Restaurants de Banlieu," *Le Monde*, October 26, 1985.

137 **"Not everything new is good":** Courtine, "La Cuisine aux Trois Quarts du Siècle," *Le Monde*, January 11, 1975.

CHAPTER 9: FOREIGN CORRESPONDENTS

140 **"a radical simplification" and subsequent quotes in this section:** Raymond Sokolov, "In French Culinary Art: The Beginnings of a Subtle Revolution," *New York Times*, March 30, 1972.

140 **"entirely unadorned" and subsequent quotes in this section:** Sokolov, "Off on a Gastronomic Voyage of Discovery," *New York Times*, April 6, 1972.

141 **"For two hours":** Crewe, "Paul Bocuse and His Restaurant," *Vogue*, June 1968.

141 **"He whips through the market":** Waverly Root, "The Restoration of French Cooking," *New York Times Magazine*, December 17, 1972.

142 **"searching the local farmer's market":** "Modern Living: The Simple Lion," *Time*, April 9, 1973.

143 **"When would you like to go?":** Gael Greene, *Insatiable*, 85.

144 **"I'm not supposed to mention" and subsequent quotes in this section:** Greene, "Nobody Knows the Truffles I've Seen," *New York*, November 12, 1973.

148 **"But Idaho potatoes":** Claiborne, "Noted Chef's Widow Gets Signal Honor," *New York Times*, June 10, 1974.

148 **"I am madly in love" and subsequent quotes in this section:** author interview with Collart, 2018.

149 **"There are those who declare":** Claiborne, "Noted Chef's Widow," *New York Times*, June 10, 1974.

150 **"The year of the curry":** Nora Ephron, "Critics in the World of the Rising Souffle," *New York*, September 30, 1968.

CHAPTER 10: COMING TO AMERICA

152 **"chief wizard of French pastry":** Claiborne, "An 80-Seat Restaurant Is Just a Front—In the Kitchen, Mon Dieu!," *New York Times*, May 25, 1974.

153 **"In the same spirit":** Greene, "Paul Bocuse: Trial by Pig's Bladder," *New York*, February 5, 1973.

154 **"Spending a day":** Betsy Balsley, "Three-Star Visit by Bocuse," *Los Angeles Times*, January 31, 1974.

155 **"Twelve participants will be accepted":** Claiborne, "Another Simone Beck Disciple Is Ready to Pass on the Word," *New York Times*, August 12, 1974.

157 **"It's a slender line":** Donald E. Westlake, "Blue Skies, No Candy," *New York Times Book Review*, October 10, 1976.

157 **"I needed to find a scene" and subsequent quotes in this section:** Greene, *Insatiable*, 251.

158 **"Shortly after dawn" and subsequent quotes in this section:** "Food: The New Wave," *Newsweek*, August 11, 1975.

162 **"Bocuse wouldn't be Bocuse":** Chelminski, "Secrets of France's Super Chef," *People*, September 6, 1976.

162 **"indisputably the most famous chef" and subsequent quotes in this section:** Claiborne, "Paul Bocuse, King of Chefs, Creates in an East Hampton Kitchen," *New York Times*, June 30, 1975.

163 **"In New York":** quoted in Claiborne, "De Gustibus," *New York Times*, July 21, 1975.

164 **"Lyon is upside down":** Collart, *Les Étoiles*, 170.

CHAPTER 11: NEMESIS

168 **"My God, dear sir" and subsequent quotes in this section:** Courtine, "Malédictions," *Le Monde*, July 22, 1972.

169 **"Crossroads or dead end?" and subsequent quotes in this section:** Courtine, "Ou Va la Cuisine Française?" *Le Monde*, December 12, 1970.

171 **"in a calm, over-civilized sea" and subsequent quotes in this section:** Courtine, *Feasts of a Militant Gastronome*, 134.

172 **"a Grand French racket":** Courtine, *Feasts*, 103.

172 **"That seems like a lot to eat" and subsequent quotes in this section:** Courtine, *Feasts*, 134.

173 **"In the very name Burgundy" and subsequent quotes in this section:** Sanche de Gramont, "French Cooking à la Courtine," *New York Times Magazine*, July 6, 1969.

174 **"In 1970 he surprised us":** Courtine, *Feasts*, 15.

178 **"Trio of Collaborators":** author interview with Jean-Claude Ribaut, 2018.

178 **"I love Lyon":** Courtine, *Feasts*, 133. .

178 **"The Jew is the born enemy":** Henri Béraud, "Et les Juifs?" *Gingoire*, January 23, 1941.

179 **"I was proud" and subsequent quotes in this section:** Courtine, "La Cuisine aux Trois Quarts du Siècle," *Le Monde*, January 11, 1975.

180 **"Women," Bocuse declared:** Courtine, "Ces Femmes aux Fourneaux," *Le Monde*, April 19, 1975.

180 **"Bocuse should have stirred his spoon":** Courtine, *Cuisine et Vins de France*, May 1975.

CHAPTER 12: THE ASSOCIATION OF WOMEN CHEFS

184 **"closed academy":** Courtine, "Voilà la Cuisine des Femmes," *Le Monde*, May 4, 1985.

185 **"They'll throw the place":** Jim Burns and Betty Ann Brown, *Women Chefs*, 1987.

185 **"Apparently, the only women":** author interview with Simone Lemaire, 2018.

187 **"I have never minded" and subsequent quotes in this section:** Greene, "More Confessions of a Sensualist: The Dinner for Women," *New York*, January 28, 1974.

188 **"It's rather like a class reunion":** Alex Prud'homme, *The French Chef in America*, 193.

190 **"But Monsieur Bocuse":** Ève-Marie Zizza-Lalu, *Le Feu Sacré*, 155.

190 **"A very masculine lunch":** Stéphane Davet, "En 1975, l'Invention de la Soupe VGE," *Le Monde*, August 22, 2020.

193 **"This association, created in 1975":** ARC directory, collection of Simone Lemaire.

194 **"Well! Imagine that Mme Desvignes":** Courtine, "Devoirs de Vacances," *Le Monde*, August 23, 1975.

194 **"Because in the beginning":** ARC directory, collection of Simone Lemaire.

CHAPTER 13: EXPERIMENTS

197 **"A veritable blasphemy":** "Hold the Butter! Dam the Cream!," *Time*, February 9, 1976.

198 **"Or maybe a bad comedian":** author interview with Michel Guérard, 2018.

198 **"When you go to eat at Guérard":** Kate Samuelson, "Q&A: Michel Guérard, Pioneer of Low-Calorie Cuisine," *Time*, February 10, 2017.

198 **"Michel is the one":** "Hold the Butter! Dam the Cream!," *Time*, February 9, 1976.

199 **"I just bought your cookbook" and subsequent quotes in this section:** Guérard interview, Chatenier, *Mémoires de Chefs*, 100.

200 **"a small miracle" and subsequent quotes in this section:** Guérard, *Mémoire de la Cuisine Française*, 141.

202 ***"IRREMBOURSABLE":*** Pierre Troisgros, *Itinéraire d'un Cuisinier Gâté*, 68.

202 **"soccer coaches overseeing our players":** Pierre Troisgros interview, Chatenier, *Mémoires de Chefs*, 255.

204 **"Only God can achieve 20":** Paul Levy, "Christian Millau Obituary," *The Guardian*, August 24, 2017.

205 **"young wolves of French nouvelle cuisine" and subsequent quotes in this section:** "Bocuse, Voici Vos Enfants!" *Le Nouveau Guide Gault-Millau*, January 1976.

205 **"Nouvelle cuisine adapts":** Tefal advertisement, *Le Nouveau Guide Gault-Millau*, January 1977.

206 **"October, 1973":** "La 'Nouvelle Cuisine Française': Une Révolution de Palais," *Le Nouveau Guide Gault-Millau*, March 1976.

207 **"I've never liked the pomp":** Olympe, *Ma Cuisine de A à Z*, 8.

208 **"We are experimenting":** "La 'Nouvelle Cuisine Française': Une Révolution de Palais," *Le Nouveau Guide Gault-Millau*, March 1976.

CHAPTER 14: BATTLE OF THE SEXES

209 **"phallocratic toques":** "La Revolt des Femmes Cuisinières," *Paris Match*, January 13, 1977.

209 **"The great cuisine of France":** Aline Mosby, "Female French Chefs Push for 'Kitchen Lib,'" UPI, May 1, 1977.

210 **"Female cooks in restaurants" and subsequent quotes in this section:** Andreas Freund, "Women Restaurant Cooks in Paris Strike Back," *New York Times*, February 17, 1977.

211 **"After all, in Paris alone" and subsequent quotes in this section:** Courtine, "Ces Femmes aux Fourneaux," *Le Monde*, April 19, 1975.

212 **"Mesdames les cheftaines":** La Reynière, *200 Recettes des Meilleures Cuisinières de France*, 285. This is not the entire letter; the first section was quoted in the ARC cookbook written by Courtine.

212 **"I would like to repeat":** Courtine, "Ces Dames aux 'Piano,'" *Le Monde*, May 21, 1977. A second section of the letter was quoted in a column written by Courtine.

213 **"I would rather have a pretty woman":** Chelminski, "Secrets of France's Super Chef," *People*, September 6, 1976.

213 **"Here, it is a man's job":** Crewe, "Paul Bocuse and His Restaurant," *Vogue*, June 1968.

213 **"I am reproached for taking poses":** *Le Nouveau Guide Gault-Millau*, January 1981.

214 **"Cher Maître-queux":** La Reynière, *200 Recettes des Meilleures Cuisinières de France*, 283. This is not the entire letter; the full letter was published in the ARC cookbook written by Courtine.

216 **"blowing up his own stars":** La Reynière, *200 Recettes*, 286.

216 **"Never has the number" and subsequent quotes in this section:** "La Cuisine de Femme," *Le Nouveau Guide Gault-Millau*, October 1976.

218 **"The defenders of the great":** Courtine, ARC directory, collection of Simone Lemaire.

219 **"You're with *Le Monde*":** Gilles Pudlowski, *À Quoi Sert Vraiment un Critique Gastronomique?*, 85.

219 **"After you, dear collaborator":** Raphaëlle Bacqué, "Le Jour Où: Les Lecteurs du 'Monde' Découvrent qu'ils Lisaient La Reynière," *Le Monde*, July 29, 2014.

221 **"Men can acquire":** Madeleine Peter, *Favorite Recipes of the Great Women Chefs of France*, xiv.

222 **"As long as I am president":** Courtine, "Voilà la Cuisine des Femmes," *Le Monde*, May 4, 1985.

CHAPTER 15: TRENDY

227 **"There is a kind of code":** Senderens interview, Chatenier, *Mémoires de Chefs*, 227.

227 **"Culinary espionage" and subsequent quotes in this section:** "La 'Nouvelle Cuisine Française': Une Révolution de Palais," *Le Nouveau Guide Gault-Millau*, March 1976.

228 **"The Bocuse group" and subsequent quotes in the section:** Roy Andries de Groot, "French Cooking Is Dead, The New French Cooking Is Born," *Esquire*, June 1975.

231 **"The *mousse de foie*" and subsequent quotes in this section:** Mimi Sheraton, "Touring France's Three-Star Restaurants," *New York Times*, June 7, 1978.

231 **"a bunch of elite snobs":** Mimi Sheraton, *Eating My Words*, 89.

232 **"the highly publicized efforts" and subsequent quotes in this section:** Sheraton, "Touring France's Three-Star Restaurants," *New York Times*, June 7, 1978.

234 **"the Kissinger of French cuisine":** "Existe-il une Nouvelle Cuisine Française?" *Apostrophes*, aired March 26, 1976.

235 **"Just a Quiet Dinner":** Claiborne, "Just a Quiet Dinner for Two in Paris: 31 Dishes, Nine Wines, a $4,000 Check," *New York Times*, November 14, 1975.

235 **"How can anyone reconcile":** "That $4,000 Dinner for Two: Letters from Readers," *New York Times*, November 20, 1975.

236 **"All these so-called advances" and subsequent quotes in this section:** "Existe-il une Nouvelle Cuisine Française?," *Apostrophes*, aired March 26, 1976.

238 **"Is it a hoax" and subsequent quotes in this section:** Julia Child, "'La Nouvelle Cuisine,' A Skeptic's View," *New York*, July 4, 1977.

239 **"If some hapless cook":** Prud'homme, *The French Chef in America*, 273.

240 **"the tigress of the *New York Times*":** Michèle Champenois, "New-York La Cavalle," *Le Monde*, June 6, 1981.

240 **"I don't think anybody":** author interview with Collart, 2018.

240 **"She must have":** Sheraton, "My Love-Hate Relationship with Chef Paul Bocuse," *Daily Beast*, January 22, 2018.

241 **"like Buckingham Palace":** Sheraton, *Eating My Words*, 126.

241 **"Who's killing the great chefs of France?":** Sheraton, *Eating My Words*, 126.

CHAPTER 16: THE BACKLASH

243 **"There was, once upon a time":** Courtine, *Gourmandissimo*, 107.

243 **"Chefs are a fractious and insolent race":** Sanche de Gramont, "French Cooking à la Courtine," *New York Times Magazine*, July 6, 1969.

244 **"It took forever" and subsequent quotes in this section:** Courtine, *Gourmandissimo*, 108–111.

246 **"disastrous fallout of nouvelle cuisine" and subsequent quotes in this section:** Courtine, "Cuisine Française: Même La Médiocrité est Servie . . . Les Dangers de l'Imagination," *Le Monde*, September 29, 1979.

246 **"The nouvelle cuisine is dead" and subsequent quotes in this section:** Greene, "What's Nouvelle? La Cuisine Bourgeoise," *New York*, June 2, 1980.

249 **"dried out, almost inedible":** Sheraton, "The Latest Thing on the East Side," *New York Times*, January 26, 1979.

250 **"Combining beautifully fresh chunks":** Sheraton, "Newest Outpost of Nouvelle Cuisine," *New York Times*, July 20, 1979.

251 **"It is probable that many people":** Sheraton, "Fashions in Food, Like Those in Clothes, Follow the Trends," *New York Times*, August 1, 1981.

251 **"New French Guide":** Moira Hodgson, "New French Guide to New York City Stirs Controversy," *New York Times*, May 17, 1981.

253 **"That's like Shakespeare" and subsequent quotes in this section:** Phyllis C. Richman, "Flashes in the Pan," *Washington Post*, April 2, 1981.

254 **"The only target of criticism":** Florence Fabricant, "French Chefs' Group Convenes in the U.S. to Dine and Debate," *New York Times*, March 25, 1981.

255 **"How can you put":** Richman, "Flashes in the Pan," *Washington Post*, April 2, 1981.

255 **"It's not good for women":** Fabricant, "French Chefs' Group," *New York Times*, March 25, 1981.

256 **"Today, everywhere you go" and subsequent quotes in this section:** Patricia Wells, "Guérard Rethinks Nouvelle Cuisine," *New York Times*, March 18, 1981.

CHAPTER 17: THE TRUTH ABOUT COURTINE

260 **"spineless and aestheticized" and subsequent quotes in this section:** Michel Castaing, "Ça Va Pas La Toque!" *Le Monde*, November 15, 1986.

261 **"sold at the price of caviar" and subsequent quotes in this section:** Courtine, "L'Assiette aux Leurres," *Le Monde*, November 15, 1986.

262 **"Guests will be astonished":** ARC directory, collection of Simone Lemaire.

263 **"He lives a disciplined life":** Alain Schifres, "Les Soixant-dix Étoiles de Robert Courtine," *Le Nouvel Observateur*, May 19, 1980.

264 **"I saw the word 'ketchup'":** "Au Bonheur des Gourmandes," *Apostrophes*, December 5, 1980.

264 **"Those who really know him":** Schifres, "Les Soixant-dix Étoiles de Robert Courtine," *Le Nouvel Observateur*, May 19, 1980.

270 **"The audience at the A.B.C.":** Courtine, "Spectacles de Paris," *Au Pilori*, February 1943.

270 **"Journalists and intellectuals":** Courtine a.k.a. Jean-Louis Vannier, "Au Fond de la Question avec Celine," *Au Pilori*, August 21, 1941.

270 **"With gold one buys":** Courtine a.k.a. Jean-Louis Vannier, "Ce Qui a Failli Arriver," *Au Pilori*.

271 **"In the blackest hovel":** Courtine a.k.a. Jean-Louis Vannier, "Les Rothschilds, Une Dynastie Néfaste," *Au Pilori*, January 6, 1944.

271 **"hook nosed bankers":** Courtine, "Le Cercle François-Villon," *Au Pilori*, February 14, 1941

271 **"liquidation":** Courtine, "La Maçonnerie Contre La France: Il Faut Anéantir la F.M.," *Au Pilori*, July 23, 1942.

271 **"hunt down":** Courtine a.k.a. Jean-Louis Vannier, "La Tradition Maçonique," *Au Pilori*, July 16, 1942.

271 **"armbands of infamy":** Courtine, "La Maçonnerie Contre La France: Il Faut Anéantir la F.M.," *Au Pilori*, July 23, 1942.

271 **"There is a Jew":** Courtine a.k.a. Jean-Louis Vannier, "Au Fond de la Question avec Celine," *Au Pilori*, August 21, 1941.

271 **"It is up to us":** Courtine, "Monsieur Benjamin et Son Tambour," *Au Pilori*, November 5, 1942.

271 **"French honor":** Courtine, "Si Nous Parlions de L'Académie," *Au Pilori*, November 19, 1942.

272 **"These are the true colors":** Courtine, "Plaidoyer Pour les Assassins," *Au Pilori*, January 28, 1943.

272 **"depraved Moroccan Jews":** Courtine a.k.a. Jean-Louis Vannier, "Querelles dans les Loges Marocaines," *Au Pilori*, December 4, 1941.

272 **"*HEC leads to everything*":** Courtine a.k.a. Jean-Louis Vannier, "Patrons Gaullist, Patrons de Combat!" *Au Pilori*, May 20, 1943.

273 **"To the Germans: you forgot the children":** author interview with Pierre Assouline, 2022.

CHAPTER 18: DISNEY WORLD

276 **"If you have any kind of problem":** author interview with Yanou Collart, 2018.

276 **"You need to talk to Paul Bocuse":** author interview with Collart, 2018.

278 **"The Three Musketeers":** Denise Vergé interview, Chatenier, *Mémoires de Chefs*, 288.

279 **"Having three of the greatest French chefs" and subsequent quotes in this section:** Bryan Miller, "With a Gallic Touch: 3 French Chefs at Epcot," *New York Times*, January 6, 1988.

279 **"We killed Cinderella" and subsequent quotes in this section:** Olivier Schmitt, "Qui a Tué Cendrillon?" *Le Monde*, October 30, 1982.

281 **"baroque, unusual, sublime" and subsequent quotes in this section:** Michel Guérard, *Mémoire de la Cuisine Française*, 167.

283 **"in search of harmony":** Pierre Troisgros, *Itinéraire d'un Cuisinier Gâté*, 58.

283 **"Very discreet":** author interview with Pierre Troisgros, 2018.

284 **"un saumon qui amait trop l'oseille":** Pierre Troisgros, *Itinéraire d'un Cuisinier Gâté*, 86.

284 **"Who cooks at your restaurant":** Colman Andrews, "A Chef Is More Than a Cook," *Los Angeles Times*, March 22, 1987.

285 **"ethereal food":** Robert Belleret, *Paul Bocuse, L'Épopée d'un Chef*, 142.

286 **"We understand perfectly":** Christian Millau, "Le Demi-Point Qui Agite les Toques," *Le Nouveau Guide Gault-Millau*, January 1985.

287 **"I have more respect for Mickey Mouse":** "Hostile Makeover," *Time*, December 12, 1988.

288 **"I'm not stopping anyone else":** "Bocuserie," *Le Monde*, February 7, 1987.

289 **"Otherwise, I would break his face!":** Raphaëlle Bacqué, "Le Jour Où: Les Lecteurs du 'Monde' Découvrent qu'ils Lisaient La Reynière," *Le Monde*, July 29, 2014.

290 **"If you invite Courtine" and subsequent quotes in this section:** author interview with Assouline, 2022.

291 **"The Jewish peril":** Courtine a.k.a. Jean-Louis Vannier, "Le Juif et la France," *Au Pilori*, September 11, 1941.

291 **"Leaving your kitchen":** Courtine, "La Cuisine Française Victime Les Chefs?" *Le Monde,* November 28, 1987.

292 **"the best female chef" and subsequent quotes in this section:** "La Cuisine du Nouveau ou du Rechauffé?" *Apostrophes,* December 10, 1982.

295 **"Gars Paul":** "Triomphe de l'ARC," *Le Monde,* February 11, 1989.

EPILOGUE

297 **"Chefs are crying in their kitchens":** Emmanuel Macron, Twitter post and official statement, January 20, 2018.

297 **"tireless self-promoter":** William Grimes, "Paul Bocuse, Celebrated French Chef, Dies at 91," *New York Times,* January 20, 2018.

298 **"Paul, we won't be sad":** Pierre Troisgros at Paul Bocuse's funeral, televised by BMF Lyon, January 20, 2018.

301 **"From the most execrable of politics":** Jean Planchais, "Robert Courtine, Deux Noms, Deux Vies," *Le Monde,* April 18, 1998.

Index

About the Author

LUKE BARR is the author of *Ritz & Escoffier* and the *New York Times* bestselling *Provence, 1970.* He lives in New York City with his wife and their two daughters.